PRAEGER LIBRARY OF U.S. GOVERNMENT
DEPARTMENTS AND AGENCIES

The Foreign Service
of the United States

PRAEGER LIBRARY OF U.S. GOVERNMENT DEPARTMENTS
AND AGENCIES

Consulting Editors

ERNEST S. GRIFFITH

Former University Professor and Dean Emeritus, School of International Service, American University; former Director, Legislative Reference Service, Library of Congress; and author of *The American System of Government* and *The Modern Government in Action*

HUGH LANGDON ELSBREE

Former Chairman, Department of Political Science, Dartmouth College; former Managing Editor, *American Political Science Review;* former Director, Legislative Reference Service, Library of Congress.

The
Foreign Service
of the
United States

W. Wendell Blancké
Foreword by Loy W. Henderson

FREDERICK A. PRAEGER, *Publishers*
New York · Washington · London

FREDERICK A. PRAEGER, *Publishers*
111 Fourth Avenue, New York, N.Y. 10003, U.S.A.
5, Cromwell Place, London S.W.7, England

Published in the United States of America in 1969
by Frederick A. Praeger, Inc., Publishers

© 1969 by W. Wendell Blancké

Library of Congress Catalog Card Number: 71–81191

This book is No. 18 in the series
Praeger Library of U.S. Government Departments and Agencies

Printed in the United States of America

To
FRANCES

Foreword

by LOY W. HENDERSON

Career Ambassador of the United States, Retired

From 1922, when I took my oath of office as a Vice Consul of Career and set out for Dublin, my first post, until my retirement in 1961, I naturally took a deep interest in the development of the Foreign Service of the United States. Since my retirement, this interest has not slackened.

It continues to be my firm belief that the President and the Secretary of State must have at their disposal a strong Foreign Service attuned to the needs of the times and prepared to assist wholeheartedly in the conduct of our foreign affairs. Fortunately, as the result of years of training, Foreign Service officers are adept at meeting new and delicate situations with both courage and resourcefulness. Beyond that, the Foreign Service as an institution is the repository of a vast store of experience on which the President and the Secretary can draw at will.

During my early years in the Service, the American people as a whole were hoping that our country would be able to remain aloof from the storms then threatening the peace of Europe and Asia. Only after the United States had become involved in World War II did it become clear to everyone that the destiny of our country was inextricably bound up with the destiny of the rest of the world and that events taking place in distant areas could eventually affect our own peace and security.

Since World War II, the Foreign Service has been constantly adjusting itself to the demands of a world subject not only to the clashes of ideologies, the upsurge of new types of nationalism, and the growth of interdependence but also to the challenges of the atomic, space, and computer age. The Foreign Service of today, with its manifold and diversified responsibilities and functions, is a quite different institution from the Foreign Service of the 1920's and 1930's. Nevertheless, in spite of a certain amount of restlessness and discontent presently found among some officers (much of it based on an urge further to strengthen the effectiveness of the Service), the hallmarks of the FSO of today—loyalty to government and to country and a keen spirit of public service—are identical with those that characterized the members of the Service I entered in the early 1920's.

Many useful books and articles have been written, and will continue to be written, about our foreign policy and the role of our Foreign Service in conducting it. An informative and readable history of the Service, with the same title as this book, but unfortunately already out of print, was published by the Department of State itself in 1961. Memoirs excepted, however, there have been few books—and none in recent years—written from the point of view of the "line officer" and dealing primarily with the Foreign Service at work. This is the approach of the present volume, although the author has not neglected the origins, development, and structure of the Service—or the problems that face it today and tomorrow.

Ambassador Blancké's book should serve as a useful reference work for those students of international relations who would supplement their reading on high-level policy and organizational matters with an amiable, workaday account of the role and status of the Foreign Service. I hope, also, that it will contribute to a deeper understanding and appreciation of the Service on the part of the American public—and, especially, on the part of young Americans who may be contemplating a foreign affairs career in the service of their country.

Preface

Although many books have been written about the diplomatic and consular services, relatively few Americans are familiar with the Foreign Service of the United States. Some still confuse it with the Foreign Legion; others think of it simply as "the State Department." It is my hope that the present volume will help clarify what our Foreign Service is and does.

The writing was finished before the elections of November, 1968. However, knowledge of the election results would nowise have affected what I have had to say about career problems present and future. Although every new administration exercises its right to make personnel and organizational changes in the executive departments and agencies, the career services remain in place and the problems of substance do not change, *ipso facto,* with the changing of the guard.

Some may find the book overly preoccupied with the day-to-day business of embassies and consulates, too little with central problems of policy and organization. They may be right. Nonetheless, I have preferred to focus primarily on people and operations. High policy apart, there is in my view nothing more vital to the success of our Foreign Service than the morale and performance of its career people abroad—those who take in stride a life that may be humdrum at one post, exciting at another.

I should like to take this opportunity to acknowledge with gratitude the friendly and unstinting cooperation I have had from my colleagues of the Foreign Service and the Department of State at every level, from the underground depths of the mail-and-pouch room to the rarified reaches of the seventh floor. All have been most kind and helpful, and I hope the book will please them.

W. WENDELL BLANCKÉ

Washington, D.C.
January, 1969

Contents

List of Tables

A section of photographs follows page 82.

The Foreign Service
of the United States

I

"Ambassadors, Other Public Ministers and Consuls"

The Foreign Service of the United States has had a long and varied history. Not until passage of the Rogers Act in 1924 did it assume its present formal title, but the United States has had a foreign service since 1781, when the Continental Congress created the Department of Foreign Affairs. And even earlier, the colonies seeking independence were well represented by their own diplomatic agents abroad.

Foreign Service people today perforce become accustomed to being erroneously referred to as "State Department types." They never like it. The Service is under the authority and direction of the Secretary of State, as is the Department itself, and its operations entail an interwoven relationship with the Department. However, the Foreign Service of the United States has managed through successive tinkerings and reorganizations to maintain its separate identity. Abroad, at least, it is an independent arm of the U.S. Government.

THE PRECURSORS

The life of an American diplomat in the days of the Revolution was never easy and, at times, not even safe. In monarchist Europe, he was suspect; in the eyes of British law, he was simply a rebel—and subject to seizure. Yet his mission was vital to the American cause, for the colonies could not hope to win independence without substantial military and financial aid from abroad.

3

Britannia ruled the waves, but the ocean had to be crossed. The armed sloop *Reprisal,* in which Benjamin Franklin traveled to France in late 1776, more than once cleared for action at sight of a suspicious sail. John Jay and John Adams traveled under equally hazardous conditions, and Henry Laurens, commissioned as minister to the Netherlands, was captured at sea by a British cruiser and sat out the war in the Tower of London—after his captors had added insult to injury by grappling up some of the most compromising of the confidential papers he had hastily weighted with shot and thrown overboard.

The King's navy covered the high seas; the King's cloak-and-dagger men, the continent. In France, despite official sympathy for the American cause, Silas Deane was badgered by British efforts to have him seized and delivered into their custody. In 1777, Arthur Lee, staying at a Berlin hostelry, met a pleasant stranger whom he took to be a casual traveler but who was, in fact, the British minister to Prussia, Hugh Elliot. While Elliot kept Lee in play for hours with convivial conversation, agents removed and copied Lee's confidential papers.

On the continent, in general, the Revolutionary representatives were tolerated but, for the most part, pointedly ignored. To the European ruling classes, these American diplomats were potential subversives, or at best uncouth colonials. Jay and William Carmichael were permitted to reside in Spain, but only as private individuals. Francis Dana cooled his heels for two years in St. Petersburg and had only one informal interview with the Foreign Minister to show for it. Ralph Izard never even got to the Grand Duchy of Tuscany, being dissuaded from the trip by the Tuscan minister at Paris who assured him it would be futile.

Yet, despite British chivvying, and rebuffs and frustrations at the hands of the governments they were striving to influence, the pioneer diplomats persevered. John Jay eventually won limited financial support from a grudging Spain prodded by France, while the untiring efforts of John Adams, who replaced the imprisoned Laurens in the Netherlands, bore fruit in 1782, when he succeeded in obtaining recognition as minister plenipotentiary. This recognition enabled him to negotiate first a much needed loan from Dutch bankers and then, later in the same year, a treaty of amity and commerce modeled on the Franco-American pact of 1778. (The French pact, along with a secret treaty of alliance, had marked the watershed of wartime American diplomacy—securing, at a critical hour, the all-but-indispensable support of France, then still the predominant power on the continent.)

But the crowning achievement of American diplomacy in the days of the Revolution was, without question, the able conduct of the favorable and definitive peace negotiations with Great Britain by the distinguished trio of Franklin, Jay, and Adams (joined at the end by Laurens, who had been exchanged in 1781 for General Lord Cornwallis). Of all the treaties Great Britain ever made, this is generally regarded as the one by which it gave the most and took the least. It seems fair to say that the first American diplomats, in their field, contributed no less essentially to the establishment of the United States as a nation than did the Revolutionary armies themselves.

The Continental Congress and Foreign Affairs

Prior to the adoption of the Constitution, the Continental Congress was vested with executive as well as legislative powers, and the conduct of foreign relations remained its responsibility throughout the period of its existence, 1774–89. The first Congress (autumn of 1774) was a consultative rather than a governing body; nonetheless, it undertook negotiations with the British Government, dispatching a petition to the King through the agents of the colonies then represented in London.* When it became apparent that the petition was not

* William Bollan, Arthur Lee, and Benjamin Franklin representing Massachusetts Bay; Thomas Life, Connecticut; Charles Garth, South Carolina; Edmund Burke, New York. Franklin also represented Pennsylvania and New Jersey.

going to succeed, the Second Continental Congress (April, 1775, on) began to look into the possibilities of outside aid and support in the event of a resort to arms.

Congress exercised its control sometimes directly and sometimes through committees. For the conduct of foreign relations, it named, on November 29, 1775, a five-man Committee of Correspondence headed by Benjamin Franklin, "for the sole purpose of corresponding with our friends in Great Britain, Ireland, and other parts of the world." The committee itself soon changed its name to the Committee of Secret Correspondence and entered into communication with various persons on the continent, with a view to assessing European sentiment toward the colonies and obtaining any other information that might be of use to the cause. It designated as its secret agents abroad Arthur Lee, then in London; Charles W. F. Dumas, a Swiss residing in The Hague who was dedicated to the American idea; and Silas Deane, who was sent to Paris. Deane's early diplomatic activity was limited largely to an initial sounding-out of the French Foreign Minister as to French reaction in the event that the colonies should be "forced to form themselves into an independent state," but he made a major contribution in getting munitions and supplies rolling soon after his arrival in mid-1776. After the Declaration of Independence and the appointment of a joint commission to the Court of France (Franklin, Lee, Deane), the Committee of Secret Correspondence acted as communications channel between the commissioners and their government.

By resolution of April 17, 1777, Congress changed the name of the group to the Committee for Foreign Affairs and provided it with a secretary, the Revolutionary pamphleteer Thomas Paine. It became progressively evident, however, that the committee system was neither efficient nor effective. There was no permanent chairman, and membership changed with the fluctuations in the membership of Congress, which made for a lack of continuity in policy and for a diversity of instructions to the agents abroad. In May, 1780, Congress finally named a committee to study the establishment of a permanent foreign affairs office, and, on January 10, 1781, it created the Department of Foreign Affairs.

Having taken this important step, Congress chose one of its members for the post of Secretary—Robert R. Livingston of New York, who had been on the Committee for Foreign Affairs—and he took the oath of office on October 20. His staff comprised two under secretaries, a translator of French, and a clerk, and he set up shop in a small house in downtown Philadelphia. Although Congress never gave him a very free hand, he managed to play a fairly substantial role in policy-shaping —and he corresponded extensively with his representatives abroad, sending them essential information and guidance and enjoining them to report to him regularly and in detail.

Livingston's successor was John Jay, who assumed charge in December, 1784. The seat of government was then in New York City, and Jay established his office first in Fraunces Tavern, at Pearl and Broad streets, and later on lower Broadway. He served ably and effectively, though he too had his difficulties with Congress over the extent of his powers, and, after his appointment as first Chief Justice, he continued to perform the essential tasks of the office until Jefferson was ready to take over. Jay thus bridged the gap between the old organization and the new. Under the Constitution, by act of September 15, 1789, the Department of Foreign Affairs was reorganized and expanded to become the Department of State. Its principal officer was designated Secretary of State, and he was to conduct the business of the Department in such manner as the President of the United States should "from time to time order or instruct." On March 22, 1790, after four years' service as minister to France, Thomas Jefferson entered on his duties as the first American Secretary of State.

The Constitution established a legal basis for a foreign service through the power it conferred on the President to nominate and, by and with the advice and consent of the Senate, to appoint "Ambassadors, other public Ministers and Consuls"

(Art. II, Sec. 2). It did not deal at length with the administration of foreign affairs, and its few relevant provisions gave no clear indication of the division of powers and responsibilities between the executive and legislative branches. It was only through developing experience in the handling of foreign affairs by successive administrations that the primary role of the President came to be established. The role of Congress also developed in its own way, deriving from that body's constitutional prerogative of declaring war and appropriating funds and, especially, from the powers of the Senate to advise on, and consent to, the ratification of treaties and Presidential appointments.

HIGH CALIBER OF EARLY REPRESENTATION

Benjamin Franklin is generally considered the father of the U.S. Foreign Service. He served as colony agent in England for some fifteen years prior to 1775, acted as agent of the First Continental Congress in London in 1774, and in 1776 was first to be named of the original trio of full-fledged diplomatic representatives of his government to France. When he presented his letters of credence to Louis XVI on March 23, 1779, he became America's first minister plenipotentiary. The esteem in which the French held Franklin is well known (his portrait was everywhere, on *objets d'art* from snuffboxes to chamberpots), and, although the French are said to have looked upon him as the personification of a noble but unsophisticated new world, he was an experienced and skillful diplomat who knew full well how to turn his popularity to the advantage of his mission.

A good example of Franklin's diplomatic skill is his note of apology to the French Foreign Minister the Comte de Vergennes when the latter had politely but firmly protested the conduct of the American commissioners in concluding preliminary peace negotiations with Britain without informing France (as Congress had instructed them to do). In his note, Franklin admitted that he and his colleagues had perhaps been lacking in propriety, but he assured Vergennes it had not been for want of respect for the honored and beloved King of France. He expressed the earnest hope that this single indiscretion would not ruin the great work now so nearly completed and then added an adroit suggestion: *"The English, I just now learn, flatter themselves they have already divided us.* I hope this little misunderstanding will therefore be kept a secret, and that they will find themselves totally mistaken."* With his bland apology, Franklin coupled a request for an additional French loan, to which Vergennes acceded.

Franklin, however, was but *primus inter pares* in the distinguished galaxy of what has been called the Golden Age of American diplomacy. In the beginning years, when the United States was striving to establish and consolidate its real and complete independence, the business of foreign affairs required the nation's best talent—and the best men were ready and willing to serve. Although not career diplomats in the modern sense, they were generally well versed in the theory and practice of government, and their preindependence training entitled them to be called professionals. They had handled the vexatious problems of the colonial struggle for land, trade, and political rights, they were experienced in travel and life abroad, and they were men of wide-ranging minds and catholic interests and tastes.

Every President between George Washington and Andrew Jackson had diplomatic experience: Thomas Jefferson, James Monroe, John Adams, and John Quincy Adams all served in diplomatic posts abroad and all but the older Adams as Secretary of State. James Madison, although he did not represent his country abroad, was Secretary of State for eight years and was thoroughly briefed on foreign problems. Washington himself was alive to the importance of foreign relations, and on taking office read through and made notes on the entire diplomatic correspondence (then only a few volumes). Many other citizens of demonstrated capacity and outstanding attainment

* Emphasis in original.

served their country abroad during the early years of the Republic—among them, to name a few, Albert Gallatin, Gouverneur Morris, Thomas Pinckney, William Pinkney, Robert Livingston, and the noted New England poet Joel Barlow.

The magnitude of the fiscal resources allocated to diplomatic activity further betokens the importance assigned to it by the early American leadership. Although the first "foreign fund" of 1790 authorized only up to $40,000 in expenditures, the level was revised drastically upward following the nation's proclamation of neutrality in 1793. At a time when the federal budget totaled less than 10 million dollars, Congress appropriated 1 million to defray the expenses of "intercourse between the United States and foreign nations." In 1806, when the United States was caught in the economic vise of Napoleon Bonaparte's decrees and Britain's orders in council, Congress voted a foreign affairs appropriation of 2 million dollars—over 20 per cent of the whole authorized budget. Such an amount could not have been approved had not the American citizenry been alertly and even passionately interested in foreign affairs. It is true that the right to vote was then still considerably limited by property and tax-paying qualifications, but the franchise was considerably broader than it had been under the old colonial charters, and public opinion was an important factor in shaping foreign policy. The citizenry demanded that its champions in the arenas of the world be of the best, and it was willing to give those who were chosen the means with which to operate.

George Washington was keenly aware that the Declaration of 1776 and the Treaty of 1783 had not made the young nation fully independent. Britain did not live up to the terms of the treaty for some time, other standpat powers looked askance at the new upstart republic, and France at first tended to regard the United States as a sort of satellite. Washington did not live to see his country fully independent, but by 1835 Alexis de Tocqueville could write:

The policy of the Americans in relation to the whole world is exceedingly simple; and it may almost be said that nobody stands in need of them, nor do they stand in need of anybody. Their independence is never threatened. . . . nothing is to be feared from the pressure of external dangers.

The Nineteenth-Century Service

For the best part of the nineteenth century, the dominant issues in American life were domestic rather than foreign, although foreign trade did become an important factor in commercial circles. Seldom were the ablest talents required for external affairs, and it was only during times of crisis such as the Mexican War, the dispute with Britain over Oregon, and the Civil War (when prevention of foreign intervention and the forestalling of aid to the Confederacy became crucial) that diplomacy was called upon to play a prominent role. In the absence of external threat, the prevailing attitude toward the outside world was one of indifference. Meantime, the spoils system initiated by President Jackson took a firm hold on the distribution of federal offices, and it was not long before diplomatic and consular appointments came to be governed almost exclusively by domestic and partisan political considerations. By the late 1850's, Consul Nathaniel Hawthorne, himself a beneficiary of the system, was led to write, "It is not too much to say, (of course, allowing for a brilliant exception here and there,) that an American never is thoroughly qualified for a foreign post, nor has time to make himself so, before the revolution of the political wheel discards him from his office."

American diplomatic and consular representation abroad continued to grow during the three decades preceding the Civil War. The number of diplomatic posts more than doubled, from fifteen in 1830 to thirty-three in 1860, while the separate consular service—reflecting the foreign trade boom of the times—exactly doubled from 141 to 282 posts during the same period. When Americans went abroad to establish themselves in business in places where there was no U.S. consulate, they usually sought and often brought pressure to bear for an appointment as consul—pressure the incumbent administration found it difficult to resist, since the businessmen generally had powerful political connections. Not only did such an appointment confer tactical commercial advantages, and rank and standing in the community, but the consul pocketed his fees and exacted his tribute from shipping. High diplomatic posts, for their part, usually went to generous and politically powerful campaign contributors who, being already well heeled, felt the urge to enhance their prestige and, not always incidentally, to satisfy the social ambitions of their wives.

Proposals for Reform

Under the circumstances typical of the nineteenth century, consular representatives of integrity and ability, such as Nathaniel Hawthorne at Liverpool, were a rare exception. Rapaciousness and fraudulent practice on the part of consular officialdom came to be taken almost for granted.* In the diplomatic field, there were able and distinguished men who rendered outstanding service—notably in the key posts of London and Paris—but it became a fact of spoils-system life that many American political appointees to diplomatic posts did not compare in knowledge and competence, and certainly not in experience, with the professional diplomats of the European powers.

In the 1830's, the subject of reform began to run like a perennial thread through the history of the foreign service. By far the most significant of the early reform proposals were those of Secretary of State Edward Livingston, who in 1833

---

* It must be said in defense of the consuls that their life was not simply one of easy pickings. Not only were they expected to succor errant countrymen and distressed seamen—the latter on an authorized "20 cents per diem, Federal money"—but they were obliged to put up a big front for visiting firemen from the States, who considered the mere fact of their being abroad to entitle them to "the treatment." It is not surprising that many consuls sought to extract all the advantage they could.

set two comprehensive reports before President Jackson, one on the diplomatic and one on the consular service. These cogent documents went at some length into existing conditions, analyzing their defects and shortcomings and recommending measures for improvement: primarily for (1) increasing the compensation of diplomats to relieve them of reliance on private incomes and (2) prohibiting consuls' engaging in private business, paying them suitable salaries, and fixing by law the fees they might charge.

The cause of reform in the national interest had little chance against the cause of self-interest, and the politicians managed to block congressional action for more than twenty years. Nonetheless, Livingston's initiative set the ball rolling, and in 1838 and 1844 subsequent proposals were made, both in and out of Congress, for reform in the consular service. Neither got very far, but in 1846 enough steam had built up to impel the appointment of a House committee to inquire into the situation. The committee found the service very imperfect indeed, and "by no means adequate to the present extended commerce of the United States." This report led in due course to revival of the Livingston recommendations and the successive adoption by Congress of the acts of March 1, 1855, and August 18, 1856, "To Remodel the Diplomatic and Consular Systems of the United States." The Act of 1855 ran into trouble because its wording raised a question of conflict with the Constitutional prerogatives of the President, and was repealed the following year. The Act of 1856 fixed salaries for ambassadors, ministers, and chargés—skipping over any question of grades or posts—and generally cleaned up the bases of the consular system, placing compensation on a salary basis, prohibiting those earning over $1,500 from engaging in private business, and establishing a tariff of consular fees while rendering the consuls accountable for what they collected. It also made a start toward the merit principle through provision for a corps of "consular pupils," to be appointed on the basis of qualifications and fitness for office.

Post–Civil War Changes

The Act of 1856 was potentially a basic charter for a career foreign service, but it could only be given effect through follow-up legislation, executive order, and active administration within the Department of State itself. These developments were not forthcoming. First came the Civil War, then postwar reconstruction and industrial development—and, again, American absorption in domestic affairs. The spoils system continued to hold sway. Because of loopholes in the consular fee schedule, fiscal irregularity did not noticeably abate, while the actual number of officials with permanent tenure under the 1856 "consular pupils" provision never rose above thirteen.

American representation abroad continued to expand, but at a considerably less rapid rate than in the period 1830–60. A noteworthy exception to the general slowdown was the expansion in consular agencies, offices run by private citizens to whom the consul delegated the handling of consular affairs in ports where there was no established consulate. These rose from 198 in 1860 to 437 in 1890; a fee-splitting arrangement between consul and consular agent made proliferation profitable. Attempts toward reform and a merit system continued to be made periodically. The movement for reform of the domestic spoils system was gaining strength throughout the country, and in 1883 its proponents pushed through the Civil Service (Pendleton) Act, which established the principle of selection by competitive examination. This Act did not apply to foreign service appointments, however, since these were made by the President with consent of the Senate.

Toward the end of the century, President Grover Cleveland, who had defined public office as a public trust, tried without success to get consular reform during his first term of office, and returned to the charge after his reelection. When Congress failed to respond to his attempt to get action through legislation, in 1895, he issued an executive order that at least made a start on consular reform by requiring oral and written entrance examinations. (The system was soon rendered meaningless through progressively lowered standards and laxer examination procedures.)

Meanwhile, in 1893, Congress, in its diplomatic and consular appropriations act, approved for the first time the appointment of full ambassadors in the words: "Whenever the President shall be advised that any foreign government is represented, or is about to be represented, in the United States by an ambassador . . . he is authorized, in his discretion, to direct that the representative of the United States shall bear the same designation."

This legislation was indeed a landmark in American diplomacy. Although the Constitution had authorized the appointment of "Ambassadors, other public Ministers and Consuls," the United States had never made any appointment higher than that of minister. Ambassadorial rank was considered too exalted for the representatives of a democracy and smacked, moreover, of monarchy, titles, and la-di-da. As a result, for more than a century U.S. envoys had chafed at being accorded a lower precedence than the representatives of considerably lesser nations who bore the senior title, and become inured to being shunted into antechambers while minor ambassadors were ushered in to the foreign minister ahead of them. Following the action of Congress, President Cleveland appointed ambassadors to Great Britain, France, Germany, and Italy, all in 1893; in 1898, the minister to Russia was also raised to ambassadorial rank. The first American to carry the title of Ambassador Extraordinary and Plenipotentiary was Thomas F. Bayard of Delaware, Secretary of State in the first Cleveland administration, who was appointed to Great Britain.

EARLY TWENTIETH-CENTURY REFORMS

When Theodore Roosevelt was elected President, he lost little time in attacking the spoils system, which he detested, and reiterated in successive annual messages his conviction that foreign service appointments must be based on merit rather than on partisan considerations. By 1906, Congress finally fell in line, and on April 5 of that year provided for a thorough reorganization of the consular service. Posts were classified and graded; positions paying $1,000 or more were required to be filled by American citizens who were required not to engage in private business; inspection was provided for, and a clear-cut system of accountability for fees introduced.

The Act of April 5 did not itself prescribe a merit system, but it made the application of such a system possible. In June, 1906, therefore, Roosevelt issued an executive order that, in effect, established a consular merit system by bringing appointments and promotions under the Civil Service Act of 1883. In explaining his action, the President said:

> The spoils system of making appointments to and removals from office is so wholly and unmixedly evil; is so emphatically un-American and undemocratic and is so potent a force for degradation in our public life, that it is difficult to believe that any intelligent man of ordinary decency who has looked into the subject can be its advocate. As a matter of fact, the arguments in favor of the "merit system" and against the "spoils system" are not only convincing, but they are absolutely unanswerable.

Consular reform paved the way for diplomatic reform, and in 1909 President William H. Taft, also by executive order, put all offices below the rank of minister on the same merit basis by giving them, also, Civil Service status. The order further directed the Secretary of State to report to the President from time to time the names of those higher-grade diplomatic secretaries who had demonstrated special capacity for chief-of-mission rank. A board of examiners was prescribed, as were qualifying examinations for appointment, and the efficiency report system was introduced. More than 100 years after the founding of the Republic, a foreign service based on merit began to appear possible.

There was still no statutory recognition of the merit principle, however, and the regulations were considered overly inflexible in that both grade and compensation were determined by post of assignment rather than by ability and performance. These shortcomings the Congress rectified by its Act of February 5, 1915, which gave statutory confirmation to the merit principle, established a new personnel classification system for both services, and introduced greater flexibility in manpower deployment by providing for the commissioning of officers to grades rather than to posts.

THE SERVICE BETWEEN THE WORLD WARS

The United States came out of World War I a dominant world power. Despite the country's rejection of the League of Nations and unwillingness to get involved politically in postwar Europe, American public and private resources were employed on a large scale for reconstruction, new overseas investments, and the promotion of exports. Before the war, the American diplomatic and consular services had done what they could to promote and protect U.S. interests abroad, but there were relatively few occasions when official assistance was invoked by American businessmen. This situation changed drastically in the postwar period when economic activity, especially in Europe, became subject to a high degree of government control, and the service was called upon to do many things it had never done before on behalf of American commercial and economic interests. Consular work also gained in volume and diversity with the growth of U.S. foreign trade investment, the expansion of American shipping interests as a result of wartime construction, and the increased travel of Americans abroad.

Moreover, despite the progress achieved under Roosevelt and Taft and the statutory confirmation of the merit principle in 1915, serious defects remained in the service. Appointment to the highest diplomatic posts still took wealth and political influence, while at the same time the turnover due to the fortunes of politics replaced chiefs of mission who had gained some experience with others who had none. The barrier against interchange between diplomatic and consular services made for personal as well as personnel problems. Some dedicated career men did develop in the younger generation, but the diplomatic service at all levels continued to be the almost exclusive preserve of the well-heeled and well-connected. The diplomats looked down on the consuls, and even though consular salaries were higher than those paid the diplomats, the money was not enough to lure able and competent men from the attractions of private enterprise.

The prevailing trend toward isolationism did not lessen the need for a sweeping reconstruction of the foreign relations machinery. Aside from the complexity of the issues affecting American interests abroad, the United States had become involved, however reluctantly, in a wide range of international problems.

The Rogers Act of 1924

Reform found a champion in Representative John Jacob Rogers of Massachusetts. He had visited Europe in 1919 to look into the possibilities for an independent corps of commercial attachés; while there he had become convinced that that issue was unimportant compared with the problem of existing relations between the diplomatic and consular services, and that an effectively unified service might obviate the necessity for attachés. A Republican who commanded bipartisan support, Rogers became keenly interested in reorganizing and improving U.S. representation abroad, and in 1919 pushed his first efforts toward that end with a bill that made little headway in Congress.

He was soon in contact with ranking State Department officers, and in 1920 Secretary of State Robert Lansing wrote him that the machinery of government for dealing with foreign relations was in need of "complete repair and reorganization." The Secretary went on to point out that broad remedial and constructive legislation was not only desirable but imperative, noting in particular the need for higher diplomatic salaries and for an amalgamation of the diplomatic and consular services. After much consultation with the Department, Rogers in 1922 introduced his definitive bill to reorganize the services, take them once and for all out of politics, and establish a permanent career service. After a period of legislative backing and filling, the bill became law on May 24, 1924.

The Rogers Act combined the diplomatic and consular services into the unified Foreign Service of the United States, with its permanent officers below the rank of minister designated Foreign Service officers (FSO's) subject to diplomatic or consular assignment interchangeably. It provided for appointment by open, competitive examination with promotion strictly on a merit basis, established a new salary and retirement scale, and gave authority for a system of representation (entertainment) allowances—thus putting the Service for the first time on a secure professional basis.

It is generally recognized that the Act, through its interchangeability provisions, was among other things aimed at the snobbery that had developed in the so-called white-spats brigade. No longer could a wealthy and well-connected young man be assured of spending his whole career in the plusher spots of Europe; there was no guarantee that he might not at any time be pulled out of the Paris Embassy for a stretch in Puerto de la Muerte, to cope with ships' papers and cargo manifests (not to mention drunken sailors) in a tropical and disease-ridden climate.

Changes During the 1930's

Although the Rogers Act, in formally establishing the Service, also did much to improve quality and morale, certain administrative inequalities remained. Principally, it soon became apparent that the "diplomatic branch" was exerting an inordinate amount of influence on the personnel board, and far more ex-diplomatic than ex-consular officers were making the promotion lists. This came to the attention of the Senate Foreign Relations Committee, and a series of proposals to rectify personnel and other inequities culminated in the Moses-Linthicum Act of February 23, 1931. The Board of Foreign Service Personnel was reorganized and the classification system modified; at the same time salaries were increased, and special living allowances and annual leave authorized. A noteworthy provision was that an officer on duty in the Division of Foreign Service Personnel was rendered ineligible for appointment as minister or ambassador for three years after his tour of duty in personnel—this to prevent the senior placement officers from taking unfair advantage in lining up their own assignments.

The initial success of the Rogers Act in raising morale and efficiency had been gradually dissipated through the Department's inability, at a time when economy in government was being stressed, to obtain sufficient appropriations for effective administration. Because of lack of funds, promotions lagged—not only in the officer corps but in the clerical staff—and morale was low.

The Moses-Linthicum Act remedied much of the problem on paper, but its improvements were not destined to become immediately effective because of the Great Depression and the resulting curtailment of government expenditures. The Foreign Service was hard hit. Promotions were suspended, salaries were cut, and various allowances either abolished or cut. On top of all this came depreciation of the dollar in 1933, followed by revaluation in 1934—a particularly rude blow to those living abroad and dependent on exchange rates. Congress finally took remedial action through the so-called Exchange Bill of 1934, and take-home pay was returned to more or less the former gold-standard level. Congress also restored allowances and salary cuts, so that by 1935 the Moses-Linthicum structure was virtually regained. The Service, however, was undermanned because no examinations had been held since 1932. These were resumed in 1935, and the FSO corps gradually increased to 723 in March of 1939—still below the level of mid-1932 (762).

Until 1924, the pre-Rogers Act diplomatic and consular services had been the only U.S. organizations of their kind. Under the unified concept of the Rogers Act, the Foreign Service continued to represent the interests abroad of all federal departments and agencies. Then, in 1927, Herbert Hoover, as Secretary of Commerce, had persuaded Congress to authorize a separate foreign commerce service; the 1924–29 boom in American exports had got to be rather too much for the regular Foreign Service to handle to Commerce's satisfaction. The new Commerce service comprised a corps of commercial attachés and trade commissioners, to operate under the general supervision of the Foreign Service posts and devote their efforts to the promotion of American exports. Next, in 1930, the Department of Agriculture had also succeeded in gaining congressional authorization for its own foreign service —on a somewhat more modest scale, in the form of a small but able group of agricultural specialists attached to posts abroad. Finally, the Bureau of Mines of the Department of the Interior was authorized in 1935 to place its own representatives in foreign countries, and sent a few minerals specialists abroad. These three separate foreign services reported directly to their own departments, making for duplication of effort, waste of public funds, and frequent jurisdictional disputes, and weakening their effectiveness abroad. A multiplicity of officials claiming to speak for the U.S. Government sometimes amused foreign officialdom but more often confused and annoyed it.

Repeated efforts toward adequate coordination came to naught, and by the late 1930's it was clear that remedial action was imperative. In 1939, President Roosevelt proposed to Congress the consolidation of the foreign operations of Commerce and Agriculture with the State Department's Foreign Service, and the proposal—known as Reorganization Plan II —received congressional approval and went into effect as of July 1, 1939. (The few Bureau of Mines specialists returned to the fold later, in 1943.) The reconsolidation added to the regular Foreign Service 105 commercial and nine agricultural attachés, and the Service was given sole responsibility for commercial and agricultural reporting and trade promotion. Much duplication of effort was eliminated, and the Rogers Act principle of a unified U.S. effort abroad reestablished.*

Although the Roosevelt Administration brought major changes in ambassadorial and ministerial appointments, a substantial share went to career men, with five out of fifteen ambassadorial and sixteen out of thirty-four ministerial posts going to the Foreign Service—a considerable morale-booster in itself. Roosevelt's political appointments, moreover, went generally to men of high caliber. Despite its money troubles, the Service performed effectively in dealing with the problems and situations of the pre-World War II period, keeping Washington well informed of the progress of the brewing storm and its implications for the American interest. In China, Ethiopia, and Spain—the then combat areas of the world—U.S. representatives responded well to the challenges that faced them. What the Service did not do, as will be seen below, was to make adequate preparation for the problems that war was bound to thrust upon it—and when war did come it had nothing like the numbers or the specialized know-how needed to handle a new and vastly changed situation.

WORLD WAR II

During World War II, the regular Foreign Service performed efficiently, and at times heroically, under fire. As the Germans advanced across Europe, the ordeal that began at Warsaw was repeated at many posts, and many are the Foreign Service stories of bombing attacks, destruction of American property, and narrow escapes, even before the United States entered the war. Nonetheless, the great expansion of

* The Foreign Agricultural Service was reinstated in 1954, but as a special measure. Other federal departments and agencies, notably Labor and Treasury, were and are represented abroad by attachés either from their own or Foreign Service ranks, but without the basis of an authorized foreign service. All are dealt with in later chapters.

U.S. foreign activities soon outstripped the capacity of the Service to keep pace. Emergency agencies and later the short-lived Foreign Service Auxiliary had to be established to deal with the mass of new war-related activity, and the regular establishment had to cope with the increase in its own normal work load while acting, insofar as possible, as foreign policy guide and coordinator to the new agencies.

In times of emergency, there is always the question whether problems are better met by expanding existing agencies or creating new ones. President Roosevelt chose the latter course, both during the Depression and during World War II. He believed that the fresh approach, with new blood, was a better way to handle unusual stresses and strains and strange new problems than by giving them to those traditionally devoted to "normal" ways of doing things.

Principal among the separate wartime entities given more or less independent overseas functions were the Economic Defense Board (later Board of Economic Warfare), the Lend-Lease Administration, the Coordinator of Inter-American Affairs, the Office of War Information, and the Office of Strategic Services. It is estimated that approximately 90 per cent of the expansion in civilian officer personnel sent out for foreign duty between July, 1939, and June, 1944, took place outside the Foreign Service. As was to be expected, serious problems of jurisdiction, administration, and policy coordination arose.

Meanwhile, by the spring of 1941, it was recognized that something had to be done about the greatly expanded work load of the Foreign Service itself, and the Foreign Service Auxiliary was created for the duration of the emergency. The Auxiliary was made up of two general groups, specialists and junior officers. Although the Service already had a number of its own commercial and agricultural specialists, the majority of wartime specialists were recruited through the Auxiliary. A number were in such fields as labor, civil aviation, press and information, and culture, but the largest group were those designated as economic analysts to handle the intelligence work connected with economic warfare. Junior officers of the Auxiliary were in the main younger men comparable to peacetime candidates for the regular Foreign Service, and were usually commissioned as vice consuls. (All recruitment to the regular officer corps via examination had been suspended for the duration.) By January, 1946, the Auxiliary outnumbered the career corps. It more than served its purpose, and, by the time it expired, on November 13, 1946, a number of its members had become interested in continuing their careers abroad; many entered the Foreign Service as soon as the opportunity was offered, by taking an examination of one kind or another.

REORGANIZATION: THE FOREIGN SERVICE ACT OF 1946

Planning for a reorganized postwar Foreign Service began before the end of hostilities. With the Auxiliary destined to be terminated, manpower problems loomed. The magnitude of wartime destruction and dislocation made it clear that world recovery—both economic and political—would involve the United States even more than it had after World War I. There would be new duties and tasks related to the administration of occupied areas, relief, rehabilitation, and refugees. At the same time, it was evident that some of the activities of the special wartime agencies should be carried on, notably in the fields of economics, intelligence, information, and culture.

As an emergency measure to help meet immediate personnel needs, Congress authorized appointment of not more than 250 additional career officers in a period of two years through the Foreign Service Manpower Act of July 3, 1946. Eligibility was based on American citizenship (at least fifteen years), age, previous military or civilian wartime service, and the passing of such examinations as the Secretary of State might prescribe.

Meanwhile, the regular Foreign Service examinations were resumed for the first time since 1941—first through in-service written and oral examinations (the writtens in March and

September of 1945), then through three similar examinations open to members of the armed services and veterans in late 1945 and in 1946. In September, 1947, the giving of regular, periodic career examinations was resumed.

The Manpower Act was a stopgap only. For some two years much thought and energy had been devoted—by members of Congress, many State Department and Foreign Service officers, and representatives of other interested agencies—to a thorough overhauling of the legislative bases of the Service. A new Foreign Service bill was finally presented to Congress, and approved on August 13. Three months later, in November, the Foreign Service Act of August 13, 1946, became effective. As amended, it constitutes the organic law of the Service today.

The Act revised and codified all previous legislation and introduced important and detailed innovations with respect to working conditions and the recruitment, classification, training, and utilization of personnel. Many deficiencies in organization and administration had been brought to light during the war and needed correction. In particular, the Act created the position of Director General of the Foreign Service, the Board of the Foreign Service, the Board of Examiners for the Foreign Service, and the Foreign Service Institute (a school for training). It significantly improved salaries, allowances, and retirement provisions, and reclassified all employees into the structure that, with relatively minor modifications, is in effect today. (See Chapter II.) The Act also introduced considerable flexibility in temporary assignment elsewhere—to other agencies of the government, to international organizations, to international conferences in various fields, and for special instruction or training with public or private institutions, associations, or firms. A noteworthy innovation—and often a contentious one—was that which introduced a modified version of the U.S. Navy's "promotion-up or selection-out"—the objective being to provide for more rapid advancement of the more able by the separation of those less able.

HOOVER, WRISTON, AND THE AMENDMENTS OF 1954–60

The world of foreign affairs was more complex than the planners during World War II had estimated, and before long new situations arose that, again, could only be dealt with on an emergency basis. Critics asserted that the 1946 legislation had not gone far enough, and numerous commissions and committees, public and private, got into the act.

In 1947, the Commission on Organization of the Executive Branch of the Government—called the Hoover Commission because it was chaired by former President Herbert Hoover—reopened the whole question of overseas representation. Primarily, it addressed itself to the organizational relationship between the Department of State and the Foreign Service. The Hoover Commission reported to Congress in 1949. A principal (and controversial) recommendation was that personnel of the Department and the Foreign Service, above certain levels, should be amalgamated in a short period of years into a single foreign affairs service, to serve both overseas and at home. The report pointed out that the split arrangement made for jealousies and inequalities between the Department (Civil Service) and the Foreign Service, and required two administrations for what was in effect one problem. It further noted that the Foreign Service officers, because of long duty abroad, lost touch with home (Thomas Jefferson had made the same complaint on the basis of his own experience) while departmental officers had too little contact with or understanding of other nations and the problems of those who worked directly with them.

The Hoover Commission's recommendations for internal reorganization of the Department were in the main carried out by the end of 1949; principally affecting the Foreign Service was a provision for returning the quasi-autonomous power of its Director General to the Secretary of State. The question of an integrated foreign affairs service, however, ran into resistance on both sides. The Foreign Service officers did not wish to give up their exclusive status, nor serve overmuch time in Washington, while many Civil Service officers had no wish to go overseas for protracted periods or be subjected to the more exacting Foreign Service promotion system.

Very little use had been made of the lateral-entry provision of 1946, and, after an advisory committee on personnel (the Rowe Committee, named for its chairman, James H. Rowe, Jr.) had studied the problem, lateral entry was liberalized in 1951—paving the way for partial integration. By the spring of 1954, however, only twenty-five new Foreign Service officers had been appointed through this route, although hundreds had been examined and many had passed examination.

Such meager results led Secretary of State John Foster Dulles in 1954 to appoint a "Public Committee on Personnel," headed by Brown University President Henry M. Wriston, to examine the problem once more and make recommendations for improvement consistent with the vastly increased responsibilities of the foreign affairs establishment. The chief recommendation of the Wriston report was to integrate the personnel of the Department of State and of the Foreign Service, where their official functions converged, into a single administrative system. Wriston, however, went beyond earlier committees by insisting on the urgency of completing such integration within a two-year period. Since it was evident from past experience that only through Draconian measures could results be achieved, Secretary Dulles approved the recommendations and directed that they be implemented.

Once that decision had been made, a vigorous program of integration was undertaken, based on the Act of 1946 amended, adjusted, and interpreted as the situation required. "Wriston-ization" proceeded apace in the period 1954–56, and by 1957 the Foreign Service Officer Corps had tripled in size. A total of 3,689 positions—1,450 in the Department and 2,239 overseas—were designated "Foreign Service officer positions." (Those not so designated abroad were and are considered "support" or staff corps positions.) Under the 1954–57 program, 1,525 persons were integrated, from the Department, Staff Corps, and other agencies, to build the total strength to an officer corps of 3,436 obligated to serve both at home and abroad. This change was not effected without unhappiness on both sides. Eventually, some 300 departmental positions in certain categories were redesignated as non-Foreign Service, so that the incumbents need not serve overseas. Conversely, a number of other positions, including many newly created, were designated as Foreign Service. The net result was a slight increase in favor of the latter. By 1960, the "Wristonees" had been largely absorbed and accepted. The emphasis today, as it was in 1946, is on an elite corps recruited at the bottom through examination and supplemented by lateral entry of specialists at the middle- and senior-grade levels.

By its amendments of 1954–55, 1956, and 1960, Congress effected various changes in the Act of 1946 recognized to be necessary and desirable. The 1954 Act was simply a one-paragraph amendment authorizing 500 additional Foreign Service officers at other than minimum salaries in the various classes. The Act of 1955 not only provided for a further considerable increase in officer positions but also added a number of new Service benefits: hardship-post differentials, a home-service-transfer allowance, an education allowance, retirement credit for military service, and medical examinations for dependents. It also liberalized appointments to the Foreign Service Reserve (see Chapter II) and the rules for assignment of Foreign Service personnel to other agencies.

The amendments of July 28, 1956, considerably improved salaries, retirement benefits and allowances, liberalized the provisions for hospitalization benefits, and facilitated the establishment of recreational facilities at posts abroad. They also expanded the class structure of the Service, from six to eight FSO classes below the supergrades of career minister and career ambassador (the latter established in August, 1955). Finally, the legislation broadened the lateral-entry provisions of the Act of 1946 by increasing the number of officers who could be integrated from other government agencies and by granting authority to integrate, without numerical limitation, Foreign Service Reserve officers considered qualified for permanent status.

By its amendments of September 8, 1960, Congress wrote into law a significant statement of policy on language and area qualifications—requiring, to the maximum extent practicable, a useful knowledge of the language, history, culture, and institutions of the country of service, and affirming that achievement of the objectives of the Act of 1946 demanded that an increasing number of Foreign Service officers "acquire functional and geographic area specializations and . . . pursue such specializations for a substantial part of their careers." (This requirement has been the chief basis for current emphasis on specialization, particularly in what are called the hard-language areas.) The Act of 1960 further provided for the appointment of a limited number of new officers directly to Class 7 rather than to bottom Class 8, and added various liberalizing provisions to the retirement and disability system.

As of Today

Legislatively speaking, since 1960 there have been no major adjustments to the Act of 1946, although there have been relatively small perfecting amendments—some as a result of the recommendations of the Committee on Foreign Affairs Personnel (the Herter Committee, named for its chairman, former Secretary of State Christian A. Herter) whose report, *Personnel for the New Diplomacy,* was published in December, 1962.

The most recent changes of a "perfecting" nature, of localized but critical import, are the so-called Vietnam amendments, which were signed into law on December 23, 1967. These amendments (1) make additional provision for "visitation travel" by families separated by evacuation from hazardous posts, and for compassionate travel of dependent family members in cases of serious injury or illness; (2) amend the leave regulations to provide that no charge shall be made for leave when an employee is injured or seriously ill as the result of enemy action; and (3) extend continuing medical treatment for illness or injury incurred as a result of service abroad—not only to an employee in the event he is separated from the Service (e.g., mandatory retirement) but also to his dependents if he dies or is separated. Although it was the Vietnam situation that called forth these amendments, their provisions apply equally to personnel in other, similar situations.

Statutory considerations apart, it might be noted that in recent years the office of the Director General of the Foreign Service—whose powers were curtailed in 1949 because the Hoover Commission considered that the Act of 1946 put him, in effect, outside the authority of the Secretary of State—has in recent years again come to play a key role (*de facto,* not *de jure*) in the foreign affairs establishment. Indeed, the Director General's office, under dynamic and dedicated leadership, has become a focal point for the current ferment—particularly among junior officers—about what the role and structure of the Foreign Service should be and how it can be further improved.

II

Role, Structure,
and Organization

In the American system, the President has basic responsibility for the formulation and direction of foreign policy, subject to the pertinent powers reserved to Congress, and the Secretary of State is the President's chief adviser and primary agent in that field. For the information and counsel essential to his task, and for the execution of foreign policy and the day-to-day conduct of foreign affairs, the Secretary looks to a domestic staff in the Department of State and to an overseas staff consisting principally of the Foreign Service. The latter body has been described as the eyes, the ears, and the mouth of the Department of State, but actually it is set up as a key overseas arm of the government as a whole. Through it, American policy is given substance and made manifest throughout the world.

The Foreign Service is not in itself a policy-making body—Washington determines that—but is rather the instrument that executes agreed-upon policies abroad. Nonetheless, the Service cannot help but influence the shaping of policy to some extent, since Washington must depend on reports from the field for the background and bases of many of its judgments and decisions. Needless to say, it is important, therefore, that reporting by Foreign Service officers be accurate, their analyses well-founded, and their representations to foreign powers ably and unequivocally presented. Careless or self-servingly slanted accounts can do great harm.

The Service may be and sometimes is bypassed by higher

authority. Especially in these days of rapid travel and almost instant communications, it is not unusual for the President or the Secretary to send a special emissary to deliver personal messages or handle tricky, one-shot negotiations. They may even take on the job of personal contact themselves. Moreover, foreign policy decisions are not infrequently announced through direct press and radio releases without advance notice to the interested missions abroad. These missions may have contributed to the decisions, and anticipated what will be decided, but as Foreign Service posts they are primarily servicing bodies and not in the line of decision-making command.

The Foreign Service Act of 1946, as amended, directs the Secretary of State, except where authority is inherent in or vested in the President, to "administer, coordinate and direct the Foreign Service of the United States and the personnel of the State Department." It further authorizes the Secretary to designate positions in or under the Department as "Foreign Service Officer positions to be occupied by officers and employees of the Service."

Until passage of the Act of 1946, assignment of an FSO to the Department meant resignation from the Foreign Service and appointment to a departmental position. With the transfer requirement removed, and with the ever-growing trend toward amalgamation of foreign affairs personnel, a great measure of the Service's institutional apartness has gone. However, it is still distinct from the Civil Service. Whether on duty in the United States or abroad, Foreign Service personnel serve under their own system—selecting, assessing, and promoting from within on the basis of standards more rigorous than those of the Civil Service, to which departmental personnel belong. (In the Civil Service, it might be noted in passing, rank and advancement attach to the job; in the Foreign Service, to the man.)

STRUCTURE OF THE SERVICE

In 1968, over 11,000 American Foreign Service employees —some 3,900 in the United States and some 7,100 abroad—

staffed 261 overseas posts, 117 diplomatic and 135 consular, plus 9 special missions (to the United Nations, the Organization of American States, the North Atlantic Treaty Organization, and so on).* The American members of the Service fall into three categories: Foreign Service officers (FSO's), Foreign Service Reserve officers (FSR's), and Foreign Service staff officers and employees (FSSO's and FSS's). Not included in the total of 261 regular posts are 15 consular agencies, 9 of whose part-time incumbents are U.S. citizens. (See Table I.)

TABLE I

SUMMARY BREAKDOWN OF AMERICAN FOREIGN SERVICE PERSONNEL
January 1, 1968

Category and Class	Totals	Serving in U.S.	Serving Outside U.S.	Male	Female
Chiefs of Mission					
Career Ambassador	5	—	5	5	—
Career Minister	28	—	28	28	—
FSO-1	41	—	41	39	2
FSO-2	1	—	1	1	—
Non-Career	32	—	32	31	1
Total	107	—	107	104	3
Non-Chiefs of Mission					
Career Ambassador	2[a]	2	—	2[a]	—
Career Minister	25[a]	21	4	25[a]	—
FSO-1	278[a]	152	126[a]	274	4[a]
FSO-2	450[a]	208	242[a]	437	13
FSO-3	651	273	378	619	32
FSO-4	643	273	370	586	57
FSO-5	528	214	314	502	26
FSO-6	422	148	274	399	23
FSO-7	255	60	195	231	24
FSO-8	109	14	95	96	13
Total	3,363	1,365	1,998	3,171	192
FSR-1	126	102	24	123	3
FSR-2	245	179	66	238	7

* Statistics in this chapter are as of January 1, 1968, unless otherwise noted. This was shortly before President Johnson's "balance of payments" cutback in overseas personnel, which brought more people back for home service. Table I gives official figures for the stated date.

TABLE I (*Cont.*)

Category and Class	Totals	Serving in U.S.	Serving Outside U.S.	Male	Female
FSR-3	363	219	144	332	31
FSR-4	336	148	188	291	45
FSR-5	240	121	119	203	37
FSR-6	158	74	84	129	29
FSR-7	202	140	62	177	25
FSR-8	59	43	16	52	7
Total	1,729	1,026	703	1,545	184
FSS-1	110	57	53	102	8
FSS-2	265	107	158	230	35
FSS-3	316	90	226	249	67
FSS-4	418	127	291	242	176
FSS-5	541	140	401	255	286
FSS-6	1,079	182	897	603	476
FSS-7	971	255	716	525	446
FSS-8	1,009	161	848	482	527
FSS-9	775	210	565	239	536
FSS-10	311	185	126	55	256
Total	5,795	1,514	4,281	2,982	2,813
American Consular Agents	9	—	9	9	—
Unclassified	1	—	1	1	—
Grand Totals	11,004	3,905	7,099	7,812	3,192

[a] Does not include FSO chiefs of mission counted above. Table includes all Foreign Service Americans in the United States and overseas, excepting 24 resident staff employees.

(Source: Department of State-Summary of Employment)

Finally, there is the numerically largest group of 12,900—the aliens known as Foreign Service Local Employees (FSLE's)—who support the American staff at Foreign Service posts abroad.

Foreign Service Officers

The FSO corps, numbering 3,438 (including 75 FSO chiefs of diplomatic mission), constitutes the career professional group, which is the operational core of the Service. Of this total, 194 are women.

Foreign Service officers are divided into eight numbered

classes, with Class 8 at the bottom, plus two supergrades of career minister (53 officers) and career ambassador (7 officers). They are appointed by the President, by and with the advice and consent of the Senate, after examination. Upon appointment, a new FSO normally receives a commission from the President as a Foreign Service officer of the United States and another commission as a consular officer and secretary in the diplomatic service of the United States. An officer assigned to an embassy will use his diplomatic title (e.g., third secretary of embassy); the same officer assigned to a consulate* will use his consular title (consul or vice consul). If assigned to the Department or to special duty, he will use his title of Foreign Service Officer. Outside of regular "line-officer" service in an embassy or consulate, or in the Department of State, FSO's may be detailed for duty with international organizations, commissions, or bodies or assigned for varying periods of time to universities, foundations, Congress, the White House, or to other federal agencies† as a means of broadening their background and deepening their understanding of domestic problems. A few draw duty at one of the State Department's passport offices outside Washington, others at reception centers for cultural-exchange travel in major U.S. ports of entry. At the same time, there are always a number of officers in training programs, either at the Department's Foreign Service Institute or elsewhere.

Officers initially appointed to one of the "entrance classes"

---

* The term "consulate" is used throughout this book to denote any regular consular post outside the host-country capital, whether consulate general or consulate. Consular agencies are flagged as such.

† In 1968, as the balance-of-payments problem began to bring more officers out of dollar-eating posts, "other-agency detail" was accounting for some 10 per cent of officer strength. Although by far the largest such element was not located in Washington, being detailed to the Agency for International Development in Vietnam, there were officers working on reimbursable detail, not only in such major departments as Defense and Commerce but also in Housing and Urban Development, Office of Employment Opportunity, Export-Import Bank, and others. Some officers, notably a fair percentage of those in the Pentagon, were assigned on an exchange basis with their counterparts working in State.

(FSO-8 or FSO-7) are in probationary status until they receive their first promotion and have passed a prescribed language examination. Supervisory officers are encouraged to give them rotation through as many types of work as feasible during their first tour of duty; after that they are normally assigned to one job per tour. (See Appendix I for the hypothetical pattern of a Foreign Service career.)

Foreign Service Reserve Officers

The Foreign Service Reserve was created by the Act of 1946, primarily for the temporary recruitment of specialists with needed skills. Until August, 1968, Reserve officers (FSR's) were recruited to serve up to two consecutive five-year periods, renewable for two more such periods following at least a year's break in service after the first two.

On August 20, 1968, when the President signed into law the act providing the United States Information Agency with a career officer corps, an amendment was added authorizing the Department of State and the USIA to grant "unlimited tenure" (i.e., career status) to selected FSR's under specified conditions. This amendment caused quite a stir in career ranks (its implications are touched upon in Chapter X). Briefly stated, within three to five years an FSR may receive appointment as an FSO, FSS, or FSR with unlimited tenure (FSRU)— or, if not so appointed within five years, must be terminated. (An officer from another government agency assigned to State as an FSR with reemployment rights to his agency may, however, be extended an additional five years, for a total of ten.) It was stressed that implementation of the amendment would in no wise be made a crash program, and that all interested-party groups would be consulted in the course of a thorough-going inventory of positions and requirements. With this in view, extensive implementation was not believed imminent.

The Foreign Service Reserve Corps, with 1,729 officers, has been used (and at times misused) for various types of recruitment, but its principal utility has been as a means of obtaining the services of needed specialists—for example, science attachés, minerals experts from the Department of the Interior or elsewhere, intelligence specialists, commercial, labor, and financial attachés from outside Foreign Service ranks. Previous government service is not a requisite, although most FSR's have in fact come from within government. Some reserve officers whose specialties are in continuing demand have already been taken into the Foreign Service officer corps. A note- worthy example is the present (1969) medical director of the Department of State and the Foreign Service, who served as an FSR regional medical officer at Baghdad and Manila, then as assistant medical director for U.S. programs and clinical activities, during which time he effected "lateral entry," then had a tour as FSO regional medical officer at Bangkok.

Reserve corps classes correspond to those of the Foreign Service officer corps. Appointments are made by the Secretary of State rather than by the President, but aside from that (and their hitherto temporary status) FSR's serve under much the same conditions as FSO's. As specialists they usually carry the title of attaché, which does not require a Presidential commission, but they may be granted regular diplomatic or consular titles if their situation calls for it.

Foreign Service Staff Corps

This is intended basically as a clerical, technical, and housekeeping category, and comprises two groups: Foreign Service staff officers (FSSO's—2,729 persons) and Foreign Service staff employees (FSS's—3,066 persons). Grades FSS-1 through FSS-6 carry officer status; grades FSS-7 through FSS-10 do not.*

The staff corps supplies many of the services, especially

---

* Foreign Service usage may confuse the uninitiated: isn't everyone on the staff, and isn't everyone an employee? Yes, but the word "clerk," formerly used for those were not officers, has come to be considered de- meaning, and the term "noncareer vice consul" for non-commissioned officers has fallen out of use with the vast expansion in variety of such officers' activities. Thus, the Foreign Service Act of 1946, as amended, provides for ten classes of "Foreign Service staff officers and employees."

those of a technical nature, necessary to the operation of a post abroad. In the main, FSSO's are career specialists in the administrative and consular fields and may be granted diplomatic or consular titles if their work calls for it. The FSSO roster also includes, *inter alios,* legal specialists, foreign building specialists, radio and communications technicians, and procurement and supply specialists.

Foreign Service staff employees (FSS's) are found chiefly in secretarial or clerical work (e.g., typists, code clerks) although the category also embraces many traveling couriers and some junior technicians and other specialists.

Under the Wriston program, in 1954, 802 of the then 1,180 staff officers were integrated into the Foreign Service officer corps. The objective was to fill as many as possible of the officer positions both in the Department and the Foreign Service with FSO's, effecting corresponding reductions in Civil Service personnel. This step has proved to be a mixed blessing. Although a number of the staff people made good—two, in fact, made deputy under secretary—the integration caused unhappiness among many who had no desire to compete for promotion with "examination-entry" officers better equipped for the functions of diplomacy in general. At the same time, some FSO's well trained for diplomatic assignments found themselves in routine administrative jobs at posts where there was no need for them to be so employed.

Wristonization was admittedly a serious venture, and the virtuous old saw about omelets and eggs was cold comfort to the broken eggs. Hence, in the early 1960's, a number of wrongly-Wristonized FSO's (many of them women) were discreetly permitted to return to staff officer status on advantageous terms. A career as an FSSO can now offer much to the technician whose goals are relatively modest (he can rise to the equivalent of the FSO-3 level) and who prefers an atmosphere somewhat less competitive than that of the Foreign Service officer corps.

Staff corps personnel are appointed by the Department of

State on the basis of their qualifications for clerical or specific officer positions. Most of the secretarial and clerical positions, and a goodly number of the administrative jobs (e.g., budget and fiscal, personnel) are filled by women—many of them impelled by an urge to "join the Service and see the world." Qualified staff members may transfer to the Foreign Service officer corps through successful competition in the regular FSO examinations.

Consular Agents

In the early days of the republic, when a consular district included more than one seaport regularly visited by American ships, consuls were authorized to appoint consular agents in other ports than their own—with preference given to American citizens when other qualifications were equal. As noted in Chapter I, the number of consular agencies rose from 198 in 1860 to 437 in 1890. From then on the number dwindled. By 1960, there were only twenty-five, and by mid-1968 only fifteen, with several incumbencies unfilled. The Act of 1946 includes provision for the employment of consular agents but says nothing of their duties. The consular agent of today is an American or foreign businessman, usually resident in a busy port town (e.g., Valparaíso, Chile) where it is impracticable to establish a regular consulate. His principal duties concern shipping and the certification of invoices, plus aid and comfort to regular consular officers visiting his bailiwick, and he keeps the fees he collects.

Foreign Service Local Employees

In earlier days, aliens could be employed as clerks by principal consular officers but could not legally serve at diplomatic missions except as interpreters, or in custodial or other menial jobs. By World War II, however, they were holding down positions of relative responsibility in many diplomatic as well as consular posts. The Act of 1946 makes provision for the employment of aliens, whose compensation "shall be based upon prevailing wage rates and compensation practices for corresponding types of positions in the locality, to the extent consistent with the public interest." (Sec. 444)

The FSLE's, generally known as "local employees" or just "locals," fill a wide variety of jobs: at the bottom as janitors, chauffeurs, and messengers; at the middle level as clerks, accountants, and translators; at the top as "assistants" (political, economic, commercial, labor, and so on). Aside from those in the more menial positions, most of whom speak little or no English, the principal utility of the local employee—aside from getting out the paper work—lies in his language abilities and his knowledge of host-country customs, conditions, and people.

It is a truism to say that no post could operate without locals.* But their value is perhaps not sufficiently recognized outside the Service, or even, at times, in it. In a visa section dealing with the public on a large scale, it is the locals who receive the daily crush of applicants and process them right up to the decision-making interview with an American officer. Many of these employees are women, often well-bred girls whose parents would not permit them to work "in commerce" —but their jobs are by no means "social" and they put in long, hard hours of devoted service. Some take and pass the Department's correspondence courses in visa and citizenship work, and a few marry Foreign Service men and become American citizens.

Types of local employees may range from old-timers who started as messenger boys back in the days of Cordell Hull to bright young men who are putting in eight or more hours a day as commercial assistants while working nights for a Master's degree in economics. Not only are they valuable for their

* Even the small stay-behind American group that kept the consulate at Hanoi open for sixteen months after Dien Bien Phu (1954–55) employed one white-collar local, one French-to-Vietnamese interpreter, and a small custodial staff (gardener, chauffeur, messenger). It was recognized that these employees must report to the North Vietnamese authorities on what went on at the consulate, and they were told to "feel free."

local connections and know-how but, especially at smaller posts, they provide the important ingredient of continuity in the work of an office. Since Bureau-of-the-Budget policy seldom permits an overlap between an officer and his successor, the locals in a section with only one American must often break in the new boss, and, more often than not, an interim incumbent from another section before he arrives.

Locals are not employed in jobs that affect the security of the United States, of course, and they are not allowed access to "classified" material (i.e., documents stamped with a classification, from "Limited Official Use" up to "Top Secret").

Salaries vary widely according to countries and standards of living, but FSLE's are generally quite well paid by host-country criteria. They have a retirement system and, in many countries, some form of medical coverage. Needless to say, however, their lot is not always enviable, especially in countries unfriendly to the United States. (One elderly political assistant in Baghdad, for example, was detained and interrogated at length by the political police; he was finally released and allowed to return to work, but by then his health was broken and he retired soon thereafter.)

The U.S. Government has done much in recent years to improve the lot of the FSLE, but progress has been slow and hard won, not only because of inertia on the American side but also, in some cases, because of uncooperativeness on the part of host governments. Benefits apart, it behooves the Foreign Service to ensure the maintenance of a warm personal relationship with its locals. They are a loyal and indispensable group and deserve well of their employers.

CLASSES, TITLES, AND POSITIONS

An officer, be he FSO, FSR, or in certain cases FSSO, holds both a rank, which is his class in the Service, and a title, which is determined by his assignment as well as by his rank and which establishes his status at a post. Diplomatic titles regularly used are those of ambassador, minister, counselor, first, second, or third secretary of embassy, attaché, and assistant attaché. Consular titles are three: consul general, consul, and vice consul.

"Chief of mission" is the title of an officer in charge of an embassy or other diplomatic mission. Since there are no more American legations, and relatively few U.S. missions to international organizations, the term "chief of mission" as used in these pages will be synonymous with "ambassador" unless it is specified otherwise.

"Principal officer," by definition of the Foreign Service Act of 1946, means the officer in charge of an embassy, legation, or other diplomatic mission or of a consulate general, consulate, or vice consulate. (Vice consulates, like legations, no longer exist, but they did when the Act was passed.) In present-day Service parlance, a principal officer is the head of a consulate or consulate general, but it suits the uses of this book to follow the definition of the Act. "Principal officer" may mean chief of diplomatic mission or chief of consular post (or both) unless the context restricts it to the latter.

"Chargé d'affaires ad interim"* is the title assigned an officer temporarily in charge of a diplomatic post in the absence of the chief of mission. This is almost always the Number Two, the senior counselor of embassy now known as the deputy chief of mission (DCM). At larger posts, the DCM may have the personal rank of minister. Until recently, a middle-grade officer might serve as DCM (and chargé), but the rank of counselor was restricted to Class 3 and above. In mid-1968, it was announced that, when assigned as second-ranking officer at a diplomatic mission, an officer of any class might henceforth be designated as counselor.

By current custom, the title of "attaché" (or "assistant attaché") is usually given an officer performing a specialized function (e.g., labor attaché, financial attaché). Officers of

---

* Permanent chargés d'affaires are still maintained by some small countries wishing to avoid the expense and trappings of maintaining a minister or ambassador.

the armed services detailed directly to diplomatic missions, as distinct from the military aid and assistance groups (MAAG's), are assigned as army, naval, or air attachés—with the senior among them known as the defense attaché.

In addition to rank and title, an officer holds a position, i.e., the job he fills at the post. The following table is illustrative of class-title-position combinations that might be held by three different officers on duty at an embassy:

Class	Title	Position
FSO-1	Counselor of Embassy	Deputy Chief of Mission
FSO-3	First Secretary of Embassy	Chief of Political Section
FSO-7	Third Secretary of Embassy	Economic Officer (Member of Economic Section)

A comparable table for a consular post might be:

Class	Title	Position
FSO-1	Consul General	Principal Officer
FSO-4	Consul	Commercial Officer
FSO-6	Vice Consul	Visa Officer

In current practice, officers of classes 7 and 8 are third secretaries of embassy; of classes 6 through 4, second secretaries; of Class 3 and above, first secretaries. At consulates, classes 8 through 6 are vice consuls, those above 6 are consuls (only one is *the* Consul: the principal officer). The above equivalents are automatic, although there may be exceptions. The senior titles of counselor of embassy and consul general are not automatic, being granted on the basis of position only; these are usually held by officers of Class 1 or Class 2, although Class 3 or lower is possible at smaller posts. At a consulate general, which is a larger and more important consulate, there is only one consul general, the principal officer. At a diplomatic mission, there may be several counselors of embassy.

As mentioned earlier, every Foreign Service officer holds both a diplomatic and a consular commission, but he uses only the title appropriate to his given assignment. In a typical career, assuming a reasonably regular rate of promotion, an officer entering at the bottom might serve successively as a vice consul, a third secretary, a second secretary, a Foreign Service officer (Department), a consul, a first secretary, a consul general, a counselor of embassy (DCM), a Foreign Service officer (inspector), and an ambassador.*

When an officer is assigned to a diplomatic position, the post simply notifies his appointment to the foreign ministry. If he is assigned to a consulate, or to a consular job in an embassy, his commission is submitted to the ministry and the latter grants its license to practice, or exequatur ("he may perform"). Many countries dispense with this formality nowadays (some of the recently independent nations appear never to have heard of it) while others grant only one "umbrella" exequatur to the principal officer for all his staff. The United States, surprisingly, has held to the conservative line so far; the Department still hands out handsomely engrossed exequaturs to all practicing consular officers, vice consuls included.

Conditions of Employment and Career Backgrounds

Appendix II, "The Foreign Service as a Career," goes into such matters as entrance and eligibility requirements for the Foreign Service in general, the cycle of qualification for appointment as a Foreign Service officer, and information on recruitment to the Foreign Service Reserve and to the staff corps. It also touches on salaries, allowances, and other benefits. Synoptically put, candidates for admission at the junior FSO level (ages twenty-one to thirty-one) must pass a written

---

* Many an ambassador, of course, does not go this route. It is the President's privilege to make political appointments to important diplomatic jobs from the ranks of distinguished men in business, the academic world, and public life.

and an oral examination. Success in both tests, plus accepta-
bility on physical and security grounds, makes them eligible
for appointment as an FSO-8. Successful candidates who are
at least twenty-three years old and who demonstrate special
qualifications may be appointed directly to Class 7.* Also, a
continuing program for lateral entry into the FSO corps under
certain prescribed conditions envisages the recruitment of
small numbers at the middle and senior levels and is aimed at
obtaining people whose general qualifications or specialized
skills the Service can put to good use.

An idea still persists that the Foreign Service is the almost
exclusive preserve of effete Easterners, hence unrepresentative
of the American people as a whole. Although once largely
justified, the assumption is no longer true. The East and West
Coast states make the best regional showing, but all sectors
seem to be reflected in reasonably close ratio to population—
and every one of the fifty states is represented in the Foreign
Service officer corps.

Only raw data are available on the backgrounds of the full
corps, but the Board of Examiners has kept fairly close tabs
on the three groups of officers appointed yearly via examination to entrance classes 7 and 8 from the period beginning
July 1, 1965, and ending June 30, 1968 (in bureaucratic terms,
fiscal years 1966, 1967, 1968). The regional origins of these
520 officers were as follows:

Region	Number Appointed	Per Cent
Middle Atlantic	141	27.3
Pacific	87	16.7
East North Central	71	13.7
South Atlantic	57	11.0
New England	36	6.8

* In the light of Congress's order for an arbitrary employment rollback
as part of the price of its surtax bill, no written examinations were given
in the fall of 1968. They are expected to resume in 1969. Meanwhile, plans
are to catch up on the waiting list of those passed, through admission of
several groups of new officers.

Region	Number Appointed	Per Cent
West North Central	35	6.7
District of Columbia and Maryland	29	5.6
Mountain	24	4.6
West South Central	20	3.8
East South Central	12	2.3
Hawaii	6	1.1
Alaska	1	0.2
Canada	1	0.2
Totals	520	100.0

These statistics, it might be noted, are based on legal residence at the time of appointment, not necessarily birthplace. The five leading states were: New York, 102; California, 71; Virginia, 28; Pennsylvania, 21; Ohio, 20. During the period tabulated, there were no appointees from Maine or West Virginia in the East nor from South Dakota or Wyoming in the West.

Companion to the place-of-origin misunderstanding is the even more widely held idea that the Foreign Service is a sort of Ivy League club, that too many of its officers are graduates of too few, too select schools in the East—hence, again, unrepresentative of the United States. Table II (again based on the 520 examination-entry officers) does give the edge to some (not all) of the Ivy League schools, but the true touchstone appears to be academic excellence rather than Eastern exclusiveness. A lesser but related factor may be that of foreign languages, which few Middle- and Far-Western schools require. This shortcoming is taken care of to some extent by the current practice of not requiring a language at the time of examination, but language study still contributes—if only by way of orientation—to a candidacy for the diplomatic service.

In Table II-c (graduate schools), the traditional giants hold their own but share star billing with other, clearly Foreign Service–oriented institutions—not only the Johns Hopkins School of Advanced International Studies and the Fletcher School of Law and Diplomacy but also such schools as Washington's American University (School of International Service) and George Washington University (School of International Affairs). American University, with fourteen graduate students, scored only two on the undergraduate list—not enough to qualify for Table II-a. It might further be noted that, in addition to the London School of Economics and the University of Paris, Cambridge produced one and Oxford two graduate appointees. (The writer was tempted to lump them as Oxbridge and qualify the resulting three entrants.)

Languages or academic standing and orientation apart, however, the Foreign Service is open (within prescribed age limits) to all citizens without regard to race, religion, sex, or economic circumstances. Of the 520 examination-entry appointees, one even made it without a college education. This candidate was admittedly an exception among officers starting at the bottom via examination, but there are still many FSO's —principally those who came in through Wristonization— who have not had a higher education. John E. Harr's 1962 studies show that some 14 per cent of the then officer corps had either not gone to college at all or had gone but failed to earn a degree.

The 520 appointees under discussion came from 205 different schools, and over half of them (289) entered with a master's degree or better, from 116 different graduate schools. Tables II-b and II-d show the leading undergraduate and graduate major subjects studied. As is the case with the officer corps as a whole,* history, political science, international relations and economics lead the field—although economics cedes place to law at the graduate level. While one commonly

* Harr's statistical data show four leading Service-wide majors: for undergraduates—history, 705; political science, 571; international relations, 543; economics, 383; for graduates—international relations, 291; history, 186; political science, 155; economics, 119. In the undergraduate category, each of these fields had more than 10 per cent of the total, and no other fields as much as 5 per cent. Harr notes that the State Department, unlike most institutions, treats political science and international relations as two separate fields. If the two were considered one, political science would far outdistance history as the major Foreign Service discipline (as in fact it does in Table II, though not by far).

TABLE II

ACADEMIC BACKGROUNDS OF FSO's APPOINTED TO

Three-year period, July 1, 1965–June 30, 1968; Total number of

II-a: UNDERGRADUATE SCHOOLS

52 schools attended by 3 or more appointees
(university unless marked (C) for college)

Harvard	24	George Washington	5	Cincinnati	3
Georgetown	23	St. Louis	5	Johns Hopkins	3
Yale	23	Minnesota	5	Lawrence (C)	3
California		Tufts	5	Lehigh	3
(Berkeley)	21	Denver	4	MIT	3
Dartmouth (C)	13	Kansas	4	Michigan State	3
Stanford	11	Manhattan (C)	4	North Carolina	3
Brown	10	Michigan	4	Occidental (C)	3
CCNY	9	Queen's (C)	4	Oregon	3
Cornell	9	Smith (C)	4	Rice	3
Columbia	8	Southern		St. John's	
Hamilton (C)	8	Methodist	4	Annapolis (C)	3
Princeton	8	Syracuse	4	Swarthmore (C)	3
Northwestern	7	Virginia	4	Florida	3
Wisconsin	7	William &		Pennsylvania	3
Williams (C)	7	Mary (C)	4	Texas	3
UCLA	6	Baylor	3	U. of Washington	
Washington	6	Bryn Mawr (C)	3	(St. Louis)	3
Colgate	5	Carleton (C)	3	Wayne State	3

Total of 205 schools attended by 519 appointees
(One appointee with no college education)

II-b: UNDERGRADUATE MAJORS

Subjects studied by three or more students

Political Science/Government	163	Business Administration	9
History	151	Social Sciences	8
International Relations	50	Engineering	6
Economics	37	Latin American Studies	4
English/English Literature	31	American Studies	3
Natural Sciences & Mathematics	24	Anthropology	3
Foreign Langnuages	17	International Trade	3
Philosophy	10	Journalism	3
		Psychology	3

Students offering two majors, 21

ENTRANCE CLASSES 7 AND 8 VIA EXAMINATION

officers appointed, 520; Average age on entry, 25.1

II-c: GRADUATE SCHOOLS

37 schools attended by three or more appointees

Johns Hopkins SAIS	32	Indiana	5
Columbia	31	Michigan	5
Harvard	17	CCNY	4
Fletcher	15	Cornell	4
American	14	Hawaii	4
California	14	London School of Economics	4
Georgetown	13	Texas	4
George Washington	10	Vanderbilt	4
Syracuse	10	Chicago	3
Virginia	10	Duke	3
Pennsylvania	9	Florida	3
Princeton	9	North Carolina	3
Yale	9	Oregon	3
Stanford	7	University of Paris	3
Wisconsin	7	San Francisco State	3
Maryland	6	Washington	3
Minnesota	6	Wayne State	3
New York University	6	Western Reserve	3
Pittsburgh	6		

Total graduate schools attended, per man-year, 411
(79 per cent of undergraduate strength)
Number of different graduate schools represented, 116 (20 of these abroad)

Appointees entering with graduate degree:

M.A. or equivalent, 250; L.L.B., 34; Ph.D., 5

II-d: GRADUATE MAJORS

Subjects studied by three or more students

International Relations[a]	100	Asian Area Studies	6
Political Science/Government	67	Education	6
History	59	International Trade & Business	6
Law	43	Natural Sciences & Mathematics	6
Economics	33	Public Administration	4
Business Administration	12	Social Sciences	4
Arab Language & Area Studies	9	Theology	4
English/English Literature	7	Anthropology	3
Languages (European)	7	Agricultural Economics	3
Russian Language & Area Studies	7	Latin American Studies	3

[a] Includes, in graduate and undergraduate studies: foreign affairs/policy; international relations/affairs/studies/politics; diplomatic history, diplomacy and world affairs.

hears that "a liberal arts background" is the best preparation for a career in diplomacy, our tables suggest that this might be modified to read "a diplomatic arts background."

Women in the Foreign Service

In 1947, there were five women Foreign Service officers—approximately ½ of 1 per cent of the corps. By the late 1950's and early 1960's, following Wristonization, the number had risen to over 300, but the level began to decline thereafter—largely, it is assumed, because a number of Wristonees opted to return to FSSO status, since there has been no appreciable change during these years in the intake at junior levels. At the beginning of 1968, the count was 194, slightly less than 6 per cent of FSO strength. (See Table I, which also shows: FSR, 184, or almost 6 per cent; FSSO, 1048, or almost 40 per cent; and, in the clerical ranks, FSS-7 through 10, a total of 1,765 women to 1,301 men.) Today's "ladies' list" shows about the same middle-aged spread as the men's, with the greatest number of officers in classes 3 and 4. Above Class 3, the ladies slim down considerably.

In mid-1968, two women career officers were on duty as chiefs of diplomatic mission: Miss Margaret Joy Tibbetts and Miss Carol C. Laise (the latter having made headlines in 1967 by marrying another ambassador, widower Ellsworth Bunker, with both continuing at their separate posts in Nepal and Vietnam). Miss Frances E. Willis, the first woman FSO to be appointed chief of mission, was named ambassador to Switzerland in 1953, to Norway in 1957, and to Ceylon in 1962. She was promoted to the rank of career minister in 1955 and to career ambassador in 1962. She was the first and only woman to reach either rank until 1968, when Miss Laise was promoted to career minister.

Although the Foreign Service officer corps is open to both sexes, there have always been certain inevitable reservations (frequently denied) about women officers. The major difficulty, of course, is the possibility of marriage, which poses problems in freedom of assignment, if nothing else. Most women FSO's recognize the difficulties and resign upon marrying. There have been noteworthy exceptions, however, in addition to Miss Laise, including one lady careerist married to a free-lance writer who can work where he chooses, another to a retired British officer who follows whither she goes.

But marriage is not the only source of problems for female officers. There are still areas of the world where custom and convention do not permit of women in responsible public positions—although this attitude appears to be losing strength. The problem overlaps with another: the general question of what positions a woman officer can or cannot usefully fill. Can she act as economic chief in a Latin American country and hold her own with male business leaders who have Latin ideas? Can she visit a pest-infested jail to cope with a drunken compatriot, surrounded by leering inmates, not to say police? In the writer's experience, the answer is that often as not she can —but that few male supervisors are willing to risk giving her a try. The result is that, by and large (with the outstanding exceptions noted, and a few others) the tendency is to assign the women to larger embassies and consulates—the "respectable" posts. This luck does not endear the ladies to their male colleagues who draw such garden spots as Upper Tarzania or Outer Neurasia.

One place where women are always more than welcome is in the FSS ranks—secretarial and clerical, and so on, in any country. There they are in chronic short supply. Many such jobs are filled by college graduates interested in seeing a bit of the world, for pay. Some do just that: take on one or two tours of duty and then settle down to life at home. Others get "hooked" and make a career of it. Not a few make a career of it in a different way. Bachelor officers (this writer among them) often marry American girls they meet in the Foreign Service milieu, who—aside from having other attractions— have proved they can take the rigors of Foreign Service life.

Minority Groups

The Foreign Service, made up in the main of reasonably enlightened and internationally minded people, has traditionally been hospitable to minority groups within its ranks. Among Negroes, especially, there have been some highly felicitous non-career chief-of-mission appointments and many officers on temporary appointments in specialized jobs. Until recently, however, the forbidding reputation of the Foreign Service examinations, and the preparation required therefor, has daunted all but a few of the hardiest from trying for an FSO appointment from scratch. (An outstanding example of the hardy few is the Honorable Clifton R. Wharton, who entered the State Department as a law clerk in 1924, became an FSO in 1925, and rose to the rank of career minister in 1959. He was appointed American minister to Romania in 1958 and ambassador to Norway in 1961—the first Negro ambassador to any European country.)

A strong step toward opening the career to minority talents was taken in 1963 when the four-year Foreign Affairs Scholars Program, funded primarily by a grant from the Ford Foundation, was set up to give students from minority backgrounds (Negroes, Orientals, Spanish-Americans, American Indians) the opportunity to become acquainted with the foreign affairs field by serving as summer interns with the State Department, the Agency for International Development, and the U.S. Information Agency. The program also provided various kinds of special training for the summer interns, as well as one-year fellowships for graduate study in international affairs. Although fewer of the participants took and passed the Foreign Service written and oral examinations than had been hoped for, the program was considered a success in that it did make many minority-group students aware of the opportunities available in the field of foreign affairs.*

* As of mid-1968, 17 foreign affairs scholars had passed the Foreign Service written examinations; of these, 2 withdrew before the oral, 1 failed

A newly established venture, the Foreign Service Reserve–Junior Officer Program, is taking advantage of this awakened interest and carrying on the work. The new program enables qualified minority-group youth to join the Service as junior Reserve officers via oral examination only. (See Appendix II for entrance and eligibility requirements and procedures.) Although only a limited number of positions are available under this program, it is expected to contribute considerably toward making the Service more representative. It also enables the Department to carry on a year-round recruiting program in minority communities and encourage young people to seek foreign affairs careers.

The record meanwhile has improved perceptibly over that of earlier days. As of mid-1968, there were twenty-six Negro Foreign Service officers, of whom thirteen had entered via the regular examination cycle.

TRAINING AND CAREER DEVELOPMENT

The Foreign Service Act of 1946 recognized the need for regular in-service training in its Title VII, which authorized establishment of the Foreign Service Institute "to furnish training and instruction to officers and employees of the Service and of the Department, and to other officers and employees of the Government for whom training and instruction in the field of foreign relations is necessary." Title VII further authorized appropriate orientation and language training to family members of officers and employees about to go on foreign assignment. The Foreign Service Institute (FSI) was established in 1947—with a school of foreign affairs and a school of languages—and is now the focal point of foreign affairs training for the Service and for other foreign-affairs–oriented agencies.

it, 2 had not yet taken it, 6 had been appointed to the Service, and 6 were attending graduate or professional schools. Most of the remaining 137 participants were still in undergraduate, graduate, or professional schools, 34 were working for various government agencies (including military service) and 8 were teaching.

Congress has from time to time toyed with the idea of a national foreign service academy (on the lines of the army, naval, and air academies) for training prospective foreign affairs personnel at the undergraduate level. Opposition to such an academy, in the Service and out of it (so far successful) has been based on two principal arguments: (1) that appropriately qualified officers are now being recruited from the universities and colleges and (2) that it would be a costly, impractical, and incomplete duplication of what the academic world has to offer. (It might be added that there is no desire to cast FSO's in a mold, as the military is sometimes accused of wishing to do.)

The FSI does not attempt to compete with the universities but draws heavily on them for graduate-level instruction in those disciplines pertinent to the needs of the Service. In addition, the Institute brings in university professors and other experts to assist in developing as well as to participate in certain programs. Some Foreign Service personnel also attend programs offered by the military service schools and other government agencies. The FSI has full-time programs, part-time programs (usually before and after office hours), and correspondence and extension programs.

Full-time training varies in length from two years, in the case of a few esoteric languages, to one-week special courses. Detail to short-term training is arranged among the regional and functional bureaus, personnel officers, and the FSI; long-term assignments are made by the central personnel system in conjunction with the bureaus. An officer's completion of a long-term assignment in either a language or a function becomes a major consideration in determining subsequent assignments, for he then has a specialty.

Officers compete with one another for full-time training assignments on the basis of what FSI enumerates as "performance, potential, motivation, experience, and previous academic background." Those training programs devised to broaden an individual and help develop his capacity are considered "career training"; those that prepare him to perform specific types of duties are regarded as "vocational training." Career training programs are offered only to those who show potential for rising to top-level responsibilities in the Service.

A few programs combine career and vocational training. Advanced university training in a particular geographic area is directly and vocationally relevant to an immediately following assignment dealing with the affairs of that region—and since the trainee will also spend much of his career in the area, such a program could also be called career training.

As officers reach the threshold of the senior level (Class 3) they may aspire to selection for an academic year at one of the senior military service colleges* or in a prestigious university program. Two other senior programs, equally prestigious, are the Senior Seminar on Foreign Policy and the Senior Fellows Program, both limited to classes 1 and 2, and also for an academic year. The senior seminar is directed toward an examination of the U.S. domestic scene and its effect on foreign policy; "senior fellows" are assigned to engage in independent research, lecture on- and off-campus, and counsel students interested in a career in foreign affairs.

President Lyndon B. Johnson's 1968 decision to reduce the number of official personnel abroad was seen as giving the Service a substantial opportunity to move toward the training goals it had never been able to achieve in the past because of relative scarcities in personnel and fiscal resources. As of mid-1968, the new central personnel system was doing very well in getting a goodly number of balance-of-payments returnees into training which they should have had before but for which they "couldn't be spared." At that time, 229 officers were in ad-

* National War College and Industrial College of the Armed Forces, both at Washington, D.C.; Army War College, Carlisle, Pennsylvania; Naval War College, Newport, Rhode Island; Air War College, Montgomery, Alabama. One officer per year is also sent to the OAS-run Interamerican Defense College at Washington, D.C., the Imperial Defence College at London, and the Canadian Defence College at Kingston, Ontario, while one officer attends each of two half-year sessions at the NATO Defense College at Rome.

vanced, long-term training* representing 6.6 per cent of the
FSO strength of Table I (3,438). (In 1962, the Herter Committee had noted a then comparable count of 5 per cent and
recommended 10 per cent.) If the increases proposed for
1968–69 are fully realized, there will be some 8 per cent of
the FSO corps in long-term training by mid-1969.

Specialized advanced work apart, there is a continuing,
large-scale turnover in the general career training given FSO's
at various stages of their service. There is a basic eight-week
course at the outset, a two-week management seminar to prepare returning young officers for the ways of Washington bureaucracy, and a mid-career "cluster" (one to two weeks) in
which middle-grade officers assigned to the Department
receive "core" courses—in management, Communism, economics—as well as courses on labor, science, the computer
and foreign affairs, and the like.

Newly appointed staff officers attend the basic eight-week
course at the FSI and receive language and area training appropriate to their first assignment. Specialized functional training in consular or administrative work is provided as necessary,
and they are eligible for certain of the FSO mid-career cluster
courses. Reserve officers may receive functional and language
training appropriate to their assignment but are not normally
considered for long-term training.

Language and Functional Training

In Chapter I, it was noted that Congress, in its 1960
amendments to the Foreign Service Act, inserted a statement
of policy to the effect that Foreign Service officers should,
wherever feasible, have a useful knowledge of both the language and the culture of the countries of their service. The

* This figure included 95 in hard-language training at the FSI or overseas
—Beirut, Tangier, Taichung, Yokohama, Tel Aviv, Garmisch (Slavic); 46
in economics (42 at the FSI, 4 in universities); 36 in advanced area or
functional training or research at universities; one in "industry training"
(petroleum); 42 in the various senior service colleges and the senior seminar; 9 senior fellows.

statement also encouraged functional and geographic area specialization by an increasing number of officers "for a substantial part of their careers."

Training on these lines is directed toward assisting selected officers to achieve proficient specialization in a function important to the Service and/or in a certain geographical area of the world. Class 5 is considered the ideal level at which to begin such specialization, though officers of classes 6 and 4 are often chosen (and even an occasional FSO-3).

There are many forms of functional training offered by the FSI—many of them for a full academic year, others for four or five months. To list some high points briefly, these include: administrative and management training; Armed Forces Staff College (politico-military affairs); economic/commercial training; advanced university economics; labor; systems-analysis—and, as interesting recent additions, courses in petroleum and in scientific matters. There is a full roster of long-term geographical area training, plus a short, three-week area studies course.

The FSI's language program is guided by Section 578 of the Foreign Service Act, which directs that certain positions overseas shall be filled by officers having a useful knowledge of the language of the country. All FSO's are expected to acquire an S-3/R-3 proficiency in at least two foreign languages during their career.* No junior FSO may receive more than one promotion until he has received a tested rating of at least S-3/R-3 in a "world language" (French, Spanish, German, Italian, Portuguese) or S-2/R-2 in a "hard language." Junior FSO's and FSSO's who do not have this proficiency are given sixteen weeks' full-time language training prior to proceeding to their first post (this in addition to the eight-week basic course for all new officers) and are expected to continue lan-

---

* FSI-testing grades those it examines on a scale rising from S-0/R-0, no practical speaking or reading proficiency, to S-5/R-5, native or bilingual speaking and reading proficiency. S-3/R-3 denotes minimum professional proficiency, or "useful," in both speaking and reading. One may, of course, be rated S-3/R-4, or any appropriate S/R combination.

guage study at the post for an hour a day until they have reached the required proficiency.

Hard-language training ("hard" for difficult) is given to certain officers who have superior language aptitude, are above average in performance and are, preferably, under age 35 and in classes 7, 6, or 5. It is considered that adequate return on the training investment has been received only after at least two tours in the language area. Regular training varies from twenty-four weeks in Swahili and Indonesian to two years in Chinese, Japanese, and Arabic. Selected junior officers may take introductory hard-language work for six months in a special program, and those who do well are considered for long-term training. (Training "starts" are geared directly to anticipated openings where the language is spoken.)

The Service's preoccupation with the language problem is well-founded, in the writer's opinion, for two principal reasons. Firstly, the post–World War II expansion—what with specialists, Wristonees and others, many of them past the age of easy learning—has pressed the Great American Monoglot into service abroad. Secondly, the teaching of languages gets less and less attention in the average American school, so that many junior officers must depend on in-service training (often over a period of several years) to remove their language condition.

These two factors should be borne in mind when reading Table III, which is based on FSI statistics. While the showing is far from discreditable, the grand total of 4,722 useful-level languages for 3,438 officers (with hard languages down to the passing level of S/R-2 included) is a far cry from the desired two languages per officer. A September, 1967, inventory of the corps showed 735 officers proficient in two languages, 238 in three, and 64 in four or more.

Wives and other adult dependents are given the opportunity for orientation and language training appropriate to their assignment. A two-week program is designed to give them understanding of the wife's role overseas, an insight into foreign

TABLE III

WORLD LANGUAGE COMPETENCE
(By rating S-3+/R-3+, or better,[a] as of January, 1968)

Officer Class	Number in Class	French	German	Spanish	Italian	Portuguese	Aggregate Skills
CA	7	6	1	1	2	—	10
CM	53	33	13	13	10	5	74
O–1	319	140	64	81	18	18	321
O–2	451	171	121	113	46	19	470
O–3	651	270	158	170	68	33	699
O–4	643	217	129	183	74	37	640
O–5	528	197	125	171	36	30	559
O–6	422	142	70	123	31	18	384
O–7	255	65	26	54	6	5	156
O–8	109	17	8	9	1	2	37
	3,438	1,258	715	918	292	167	3,350

*HARD-LANGUAGE COMPETENCE, AGGREGATE OF ALL CLASSES**

	S/R-3+	S/R-2		S/R-3+	S/R-2
Afrikaans	3	9	Korean	8	8
Amharic	2	1	Lao	4	4
Arabic	107	62	Nepali	6	1
Bengali	—	2	Persian	22	24
Bulgarian	9	7	Polish	46	12
Burmese	8	5	Romanian	17	7
Chinese	75	39	Russian	126	76
Czech	13	14	Serbo-Croatian	63	21
Finnish	18	8	Swahili	12	19
Greek	52	35	Tamil	3	2
Hebrew	7	10	Thai	21	22
Hindi	18	24	Turkish	25	20
Hungarian	21	4	Urdu	19	19
Indonesian	37	24	Vietnamese	27	21
Japanese	61	42			

TOTALS: S/R-3+—830; S/R-2—542; ALL—1,372

[a] Higher of tested or self-appraised skills.

cultures, and perspectives for interpreting the United States to people of other countries. Additionally, the opportunity to learn techniques for teaching English to non-English speakers is provided.

Adult dependents are encouraged to study the language of the country of assignment. Posts are authorized to provide a minimum of 100 hours' training in the post language program, with training beyond that authorized where there is a specific need.

Career Development

The Secretary's 1954 (Wriston) Public Committee on Personnel recommended the establishment of a career management program for the Foreign Service. Such a program was launched in 1956 with the setting up of a career development and counseling staff as an advisory arm of the deputy assistant secretary for personnel; its general objective was to meet present and future staffing needs through evaluation of officers' skills, abilities, personal qualities, and development potential, and by periodic advance planning of their assignments and training.

To start, a Service-wide questionnaire went out surveying the self-appraised skills, interests, hopes, and fears of the officer corps. A second element in the program was a periodic inventory of data received, to be evaluated by a panel of senior officers and kept current for manpower-planning needs. A third element was the preparation of career plans for individual officers, not only suggesting the nature and locus of the officer's next assignment but projecting the direction in which he should move (including training) over a six-year period. These career plans were destined for the assignment panels, where it was expected that they would be taken seriously into account in the assignment process.

Judgments as to what degree of success the career development counseling exercise has had vary according to source and viewpoint. Most counselors maintain that not nearly enough attention is paid their recommendations; most placement officers maintain the opposite—that too often the career development staff is the tail wagging the dog. In the writer's experience, the hard-headed haggling of the placement officer usually wins out. It is he, the "flesh-peddler," who must match up available bodies with available slots—and in this harsh day-to-day struggle it is inevitable that more often than not the optimum must be sacrificed in favor of the bird-in-hand.

As will be seen in Chapter III, the whole personnel empire —recruitment, training, placement, counseling, evaluation, discipline, and retirement—has recently been placed in the office of the Director General of the Foreign Service, under the deputy assistant secretary for personnel. That key officer is now primarily responsible for the long-needed integration and unification of what have in effect been separate and often warring personnel kingdoms.

Specialist Versus Generalist

A major element in the career-planning exercise has been that of specialization—in function or in area. Many see the problem of "specialist versus generalist" as dichotomic, and a question often asked is: does the specialist suffer vis-à-vis the generalist in terms of promotion? There is no simple yes or no. The excellent research done by John E. Harr on the anatomy of the Service indicates that area specialization, at least in the hard-language areas, pays off very well in terms of both job-assignment and promotion. His data on functional specialization do not answer the advancement question so clearly, since his largest group (administrative specialists) is made up chiefly of staff corps Wristonees whose educational level is markedly lower than that of the examination-entry officers. His second largest group is that of consular specialists, many of whom have also been Wristonized from the staff corps. On this basis, the functional specialists do not do as well as the generalists. On the other hand, the more formally trained functionalists—administrative and management specialists as well as those in economics, labor, politicomilitary affairs, and the like—appear to hold their own easily with respect to promotion, although it should be noted that they tend to become more and more generalists as they rise in the profession.

When all is said and done, no officer can expect to reach

the highest levels of the Service unless he has something more than either deep specialized experience or broad generalized experience. In his 1963 testimony before the Senate (Jackson) Subcommittee on National Security and Staffing Operations, Ambassador Samuel D. Berger's comments on the "specialist versus generalist" question have so exactly reflected the writer's views that he takes the liberty of quoting the opening passage here:

> This subject has been endlessly debated, but I have long felt that the argument was more theoretical than real. The great need in overseas work is for more people of the highest quality to fill senior officer positions: Deputy Chief of Mission, Political and Economic Counselors, Consul General, and special assistant on aid matters. There are certain requirements at the senior level: great energy; passionate interest in the work; mature judgment in foreign affairs that comes only with long and varied experience in the Foreign Service; the capacity to lead and inspire staff; insistence on precision in all parts of the work; a liking for working in foreign countries with all its interest as well as disadvantages; a capacity to adjust to change; and a capacity to win the respect, and, hopefully, the affection of his colleagues and the people of the countries in which he serves. These do not exhaust the list of requirements, but they are among the main ones. Officers who do not possess these qualities should be kept from appointment to senior positions, or weeded out, if they occupy them, in order to make room for top-flight officers.
>
> It is not whether a man is a generalist or specialist that brings him to the top, but whether he has capacity, breadth, interest and initiative—what we call "flair."*

Promotion

The Foreign Service being a competitive career, promotion from class to class depends upon an officer's performance in comparison with that of all other officers in the same class.

---

* Ambassador Berger himself entered the Service as a labor specialist, during World War II.

The principal instrument used in evaluation is the "efficiency report," prepared by the officer's immediate supervisor and reviewed by an officer higher up. These appraisals are prepared annually unless an officer changes jobs or supervisors, in which case there may be two or more during a given year. Other vehicles of evaluation are the efficiency reports by Foreign Service inspectors, "end-user" reports from Washington or elsewhere, and a variety of other documents—pro or con— which are considered appropriate for inclusion in an officer's personnel file. The main elements of an efficiency report consist of information relating to character, ability, conduct, industry and work-quality, experience, dependability, and general usefulness—plus comment on spouse and family when married.

The policy on how much of an efficiency report may or must be shown to the rated officer changes from time to time. As of mid-1968, the report was prepared in two parts, the "Performance Rating Report" and the "Development Appraisal Report"; the first was shown, the second was not (except under unusual circumstances), but the officer might read it on his return to Washington. In any case, whether there is complete or partial disclosure it is the bounden duty of the rating officer to call attention to any weaknesses well in advance of rating time, to give the rated officer a chance to correct them before the report is written.*

Every fall, all FSO dossiers (except those of probationers) are carefully studied and compared by "selection boards" —one board per class†—each composed of senior FSO's, a public member, and representatives of Commerce, Labor, USIA, and AID (although not always all four of these). Precepts governing the work of the selection boards are designed to ensure that due regard is given to specialization in the middle

* In June, 1968, it was reported that the American Civil Liberties Union was calling for an end to "secret evaluation reports on Foreign Service personnel overseas."

† As of early 1969, there was discussion of revamping the selection board structure for classes below FSO-3.

grades, with proportionately greater emphasis on executive ability at the senior level. The precepts are designed also to permit younger officers of exceptional ability to be promoted at relatively frequent intervals.

The final product of the selection boards, usually put together after six to eight weeks of reading, discussion, and deliberation, is a list for each class called a rank-order register —all names in descending order of merit as adjudged—and as many are promoted from the top of the list down as the year's appropriations and vacancies permit. Besides promotion from class to class, officers whose performance has been judged satisfactory receive annual "in-class" salary increases ranging from over $200 in Class 8 to over $1,000 in Class 1 (though the latter class is limited to two such raises). Additional in-class increases may be granted as a reward for specially meritorious service.

FSR's are rated on the same forms as FSO's, and their files are reviewed by the same boards. The forms on junior FSO's in probationary status are prepared at least twice a year. Staff Corps people are judged for promotion by different sets of selection boards, which meet annually.

"Selection-out"

The expression "selection-out" is not, as some seem to think, an adaptation from the sayings of Samuel Goldwyn; it was taken from the U.S. Navy's "promotion-up or selection-out" by the framers of the Foreign Service Act of 1946. Although the term is a euphemism for being dropped from the Service, it connotes not a discharge "for cause" but rather elimination in what is a continuingly competitive career.

The basis of selection-out is twofold. Firstly, an officer may not remain overlong in one class, i.e., be passed over for promotion too many times. The maximum permissible period in class, established by the Secretary of State, has been changed from time to time since 1946. In 1968, it ranged from four years for junior officers to twelve for those in Class 1. Secondly, an officer may be selected out if an official finding is made that his performance level has consistently not been up to that of his class, that is, when several successive selection boards rank him in the bottom 3 per cent. A decision was reached in 1968 that, for the foreseeable future, the primary channel for separation would be that of time in class rather than that of substandard performance. At the same time, mitigating provisions were set up for those just a bit short of full retirement on the basis of 50 years' age and 20 years' service (see below, under "Retirement").

Procedures are carried out as equitably as possible. Each finding that an officer is in the "selection-out zone" for substandard performance is subject first to consideration by an administrative review panel, then, if upheld, by a panel of three senior officers chaired by the deputy under secretary of State for administration.

Both the promotion system and its concomitant selection-out process have been criticized, principally because of the subjectivity inherent in the efficiency rating procedure. An oft-heard complaint is that the same officer may receive high ratings from one supervisor and low from the next. Such a thing does happen from time to time, and the reasons are sometimes petty and personal. Nonetheless, the norms and procedures have been conscientiously laid down, most efficiency reports are conscientiously prepared with a view to fair appraisal, and higher review is equally painstaking. The selection boards for their part soon learn to "rate the rating officer" as well as the ratee—i.e., take into account not only what is said but who has said it, and under what circumstances. Finally, when all is said and done, in any rank-order register there has to be a top and there has to be a bottom. (Board member A: "Well, I don't think Conifer is all that bad!" Board member B: "O.K., who you gonna put in his place?") Members of selection boards spend many a sleepless night during the final weeks of their duty.

The competitive selection-out principle applied until recently only to FSO's. Now, however, FSR's with unlimited tenure (FSRU's) are included under the legislation of August 20, 1968. Other employees may be removed by the Secretary if they perform their duties in an unsatisfactory manner or are found guilty of misconduct or malfeasance in office.

Retirement

Under Title VIII of the Act of 1946, as amended, Foreign Service officers have been provided with an equitable and generous retirement and disability system (now also to be extended to FSRU's). Other employees participate in the regular U.S. Civil Service retirement system. The basic features of the FSO plan follow:

1. Benefits are paid from a fund supported by contributions from both the government and the officer. The latter's contribution (compulsory) is 6½ per cent of his salary, deducted automatically each pay day. These deductions earn 4 per cent interest compounded annually.

2. Retirement is compulsory at age 60 for all but those who attain the rank of career minister or career ambassador; they retire at 65. If the Secretary determines it to be in the public interest, he may extend an officer's service for a period not to exceed 5 years; he may also recall any retired officer for temporary duty. An officer with 20 years' service who has reached age 50 may retire voluntarily with the approval of the Secretary.

3. An officer retiring under any of the above conditions is entitled to a lifetime annuity equal to 2 per cent of his average salary for his highest-paid five consecutive years of service, multiplied by the number of years of service—not to exceed 35 years.* (Rule of thumb: 30 years' service yields 60 per cent of salary; 25 years', 50 per cent; and so forth.)

Upon retirement, an officer may elect to receive either his full annuity or a reduced amount with arrangement for a survivorship annuity (up to 50 per cent of the full amount) to

* Legislation is pending to raise the limit to 40 years.

be paid his wife if he predeceases her. There are equitable provisions for dependent children, as well as for officers who die with less than 20 years' service. In case of retirement for disability (if not brought on by "vicious habits, intemperance, or willful misconduct") the annuity is free of federal income tax, and that of an officer with at least 5 years' service is computed as if he had served for 20, provided the additional credit does not put him over the amount he would have got had he served till mandatory retirement. An officer of class 1, 2, or 3 who is selected out receives an annuity based on his length of service. Others receive a bonus on the same basis—and, if they have at least 5 years' service credit, may opt either to have their retirement deductions returned with interest or to receive a deferred annuity at age 60.

Generally speaking, the Foreign Service officer corps has good reason to be grateful to those who framed the Act of 1946, and to the Congress which made it law, for an attractive and advantageous retirement system. A fair number of officers take advantage of the fifty years' age–twenty years' service provision; these are usually people who feel it unlikely they will reach the top and prefer to start a second career at an advantageous age. Most officers, other things being equal, serve right through to mandatory retirement. After that, some continue on the payroll as part-time consultants, some take jobs in the academic or business world, some vegetate—and some write books about the Foreign Service.

III

The Foreign Service at Home

Order.
[No. 21.]

It is hereby ordered that there shall be established in the Department of State a Division of Near Eastern Affairs, which shall have charge of correspondence, diplomatic and consular, on matters other than those of an administrative character in relation to Germany, Austria–Hungary, Russia, Roumania, Servia, Bulgaria, Montenegro, Turkey, Greece, Italy, Abyssinia, Persia, Egypt, and colonies belonging to countries of this series. Mr. Evan E. Young, formerly Consul at Saloniki, is hereby designated as Chief of the Division of Near Eastern Affairs.

All correspondence in relation to the countries named, except routine correspondence relating to deaths, marriages, citizenship, passports, sanitary reports, invoices, applications for Section 6 certificates, bills of health, and similar subjects, will be sent by the Index Bureau direct to the Division of Near Eastern Affairs, subject to such special instructions as the Secretary or Assistant Secretary may issue from time to time.

The Chief Clerk of the Department will provide room for the new Division and will assign such clerks as the work of the Division may require.

P C KNOX

Department of State
Washington, December 13, 1909

The above order, signed by President Taft's Secretary of State Philander C. Knox, marked the beginnings of one of the Department's present five regional bureaus, the Bureau of

Near Eastern and South Asian Affairs (NEA). Although it has lost Germany, Austria-Hungary, Italy, "Abyssinia," and the Balkans, NEA's domain today stretches from Egypt to India and includes nations whose names were unknown in 1909.* The first chief of the Division of Near Eastern Affairs started out with a staff of two clerks. The present chief, an assistant secretary of State, is supported by three deputy assistant secretaries and ten country directors in a total staff of nearly 150.

The Top Management

The Department's top management echelon comprises the Secretary of State, the under secretary of State who is his deputy, a second under secretary for political affairs, and deputy under secretaries for political affairs and administration. These are the "Big Five," with across-the-board responsibilities; directly under them in the hierarchy come the assistant secretaries.

Although there are assistant secretaries at the head of economic, cultural, public, and international organization affairs and congressional relations—as well as various other senior chiefs of comparable rank but without the title—it is the five "regional" assistant secretaries† and their ranking subordinates who are, in effect, the line officers of the Foreign Service within the State Department. They deal directly with the posts abroad and with the foreign embassies in Washington, and their offices are staffed—save a few brilliant exceptions—with officers experienced in the areas they represent. The primacy

* The full list and their State Department designations are as follows: Lebanon, Jordan, Syrian Arab Republic, Iraq (ARN); Saudi Arabia, Kuwait, Yemen, Aden (ARP); Cyprus (CYP); Greece (GRK); Israel & Arab-Israel Affairs (IAI); India, Ceylon, Nepal, Maldive Islands (INC); Iran (IRN); Pakistan, Afghanistan (PAF); Turkey (TUR); United Arab Republic (UAR). As of mid-1968, the Syria, Iraq and Yemen missions were closed, while in the UAR an eleven-man mission was functioning as the U.S. interests section of the Spanish Embassy in Cairo.

† For the following: Africa (AF); Inter-American Affairs (ARA); East Asia and Pacific (EA); Europe, including the Soviet Union, (EUR); Near East and South Asia (NEA).

of the regional (or geographical) assistant secretaries in operational Foreign Service business is generally recognized within the Department; President John F. Kennedy in 1961 declared that these regional assistant secretaries were more important officers of the government than most members of the Cabinet.

Each assistant secretary has under him several deputy assistant secretaries. Division of responsibilities may vary according to area or function. In NEA, to take a representative geographical bureau, the three main areas of the region—South Asia, the Arab world, and the Greece-Turkey-Iran grouping —are each the primary responsibility of a deputy assistant secretary well-versed in his area's affairs.

An ambassador is the personal representative of the President to the chief of state of his accreditation, but he seldom deals directly with the President. He normally works within the framework of the State Department, receiving his instructions from the Secretary of State acting for the President—or, as is more usual in actual practice, from an assistant secretary of State acting for the Secretary. In day-to-day dealings, it is the assistant secretary who acts as an ambassador's opposite number. This relationship may be delegated when appropriate to a deputy assistant secretary, and not infrequently—as will be seen below—to the country director, a senior officer specifically charged with the affairs of the country in question.

THE COUNTRY DIRECTORATE, NEW VERSION OF THE "DESK"

Taking Turkey as a typical NEA country, let us consider how the Foreign Service Officer serving in the State Department as Country Director for Turkey would figure in negotiations over a P.L.–480 program,* in which several agencies of the U.S. Government are actively interested parties. The prime

* Public Law 480 describes the manner in which U.S. surpluses of certain agricultural products may be disposed of in countries where those items are scarce and paid for in part with local currencies, the local currency amounts to be used in turn for U.S. programs within the countries in question.

mover would be the Department of Agriculture, supplier of the surplus products. The executor of the program is the Agency for International Development, which handles the procedural end of the transaction. Since balance of payments is a problem, the Treasury Department has an important interest in the form of payment. But because the program primarily concerns foreign relations it is the Department of State (and the U.S. Embassy in the recipient country), which plays the supervisory role. Within the Department, the Bureau of Economic Affairs has a recognized interest, because of the United States's general worldwide trading obligations under such agreements as the General Agreement on Tariffs and Trade, (GATT), but the role of coordinator and catalyst in the operation falls to the assistant secretary of State for NEA and the American Ambassador in Ankara. Within NEA, the key man is the Country Director for Turkey, an officer who has no specific interest in the products or the financing involved but who does have a full-time, abiding interest in everything connected with "his" country—policies or politics, relations or operations.

In the current organizational pattern of the State Department, a country director is an FSO-1 (or sometimes O-2) and an authentic language-and-area specialist, with long and active experience in his area. Working under him are one or two officers, generally FSO-3's, also both experienced in the area. Although not equal in rank, these officers form a sort of troika; the major fields of responsibility are divided rather than echeloned, with due regard for flexible interchangeability. Together with their clerical support, they are the country directorate, a new and more senior version of the classical "country desk."

"Desk officer" is a longstanding (and still often used) term for the man who works full-time on a given country—or, in some cases, a related cluster of countries. Until mid-1966, the country desk officer* was usually an FSO-4 or O-5 (there were some O-3's and a few O-6's) and he worked under an office

* Proper title: Officer in Charge of "X" Affairs, generally called the OIC.

director responsible for a group of area countries, who in turn reported to the regional assistant secretary and his several deputies. Two decades ago, when there were still less than sixty nations in the United Nations, this system worked well enough. As the number of countries multiplied and then finally doubled, the desk officer felt the effects of inflation and his authority became more and more diluted. In normal times, he had too little rank or standing to advocate his causes effectively; in times of crisis, he was superseded.

In testimony before the Senate (Jackson) Subcommittee on National Security and Staffing Operations, Secretary of State Dean Rusk in 1963 was already proposing an upgrading in the standing and experience of the desk officer—the man who had the opportunity, in the Secretary's words, "to brood twenty-four hours a day on the problems of a particular country." He also suggested that one way to cut down the problem of layering (i.e., too many levels of clearance) would be to upgrade the level of the country desk officer, in order to place a high degree of competence and experience at a point where it was most critical. At a later time, in a statement to the Department and the Foreign Service, Secretary Rusk said:

> I particularly hope that the new and increased responsibilities given to the geographic Assistant Secretaries and the gradual establishment of the new positions of "Country Directors" will enable us better to serve both the President and our missions abroad. I look to the Country Directors to assume full responsibility, under their Assistant Secretaries, for all the activities in the country or countries assigned to them, and to be the single focal points in Washington to serve our Ambassadors. In a sense, we are applying the valuable experience that has been gained in the operations of Country Teams abroad to operations here in Washington.

The country directorate system was put into operation on July 1, 1966, with the vertical layer of office director eliminated and with the country director responsible to his regional assistant secretary of State and, under him, the deputy assistant secretary responsible for his area. The new system has its disadvantages, to be sure. The Secretary's desire, expressed before the Jackson Subcommittee—to move toward a situation of far more chiefs and far fewer Indians at policy levels—was all very well, but even policy levels need a few Indians for leg work. Not only must senior- and middle-grade officers do a good bit of this, but the junior group misses a chance to gain valuable on-the-job experience in a headquarters policy-making operation. However, the country directors have at least the authority and prestige of the former office directors, and—more importantly—there is greater senior expertise focused on a given bailiwick. (One country director relates that when he was a deputy office director responsible for four countries, the economic man knew more economics, the petroleum man knew more petroleum, and the desk officer knew more "country." Now, at least, he is Number One on "country.")

In the current NEA set-up, there are ten country directorates, each comprising a team working full-time on one country or group of countries (with the strength of the team scaled to the size of the group). Above the ten directors are three deputy assistant secretaries, for a total of thirteen high-ranking officers under the assistant secretary—all well briefed on each other's problems and working as an integrated whole. These thirteen equate in rank and experience to eight under the former system: two deputy assistant secretaries, three office directors, and three deputy office directors. There is thus now more than half again as much senior fire-power focused on the NEA area and its problems.

Internal and Interagency Coordination

As with Big Business, so with Big Government. If two executives from different offices get together, there is a discussion or exchange of views. If three or more do the same, the chances are it will be called a meeting. In government, the so-called staff meeting has become a way of life. Unless overdone, it represents the best way yet devised for coordination and teamwork, to ensure that representatives of offices with interests in the same area or the same projects (even though these interests may be conflicting) are kept informed of what their colleagues are doing and thinking.

The country director for Turkey, whom we are taking as typical of his kind, participates in four types of periodic staff meetings regularly scheduled. First is a brief, thrice-weekly, early-morning meeting of all NEA country directors or their representatives with the assistant secretary and/or his deputies; rarely does more than one or two of these four show up at the same time, but the meeting will certainly be attended by that one who is scheduled to attend an immediately ensuing thrice-weekly meeting at the next higher level—that of the under secretary of State. Secondly, the country director will join with his colleagues for Greece, Cyprus, and Iran to meet once a week with the deputy assistant secretary charged with that area of NEA. Third is the weekly interagency staff meeting, designed to keep the representatives of interested agencies informed of what is going on—and to hear from them in turn. This relatively large meeting is attended by the ten country directorates plus NEA's regional office director; by representatives of the Department's intelligence, science, legal, cultural, AID, and international organizations offices; and by representatives of agencies from without the Department. The assemblage is called for Friday in the late morning, thus giving officers with problems a regular occasion to buttonhole opposite numbers and/or lunch together after the session. Finally, biweekly in principle but not necessarily that regularly, the country director convenes what he calls a "little country-team meeting," including representatives of more or less the same elements working on Turkey at the Washington end as would make up the U.S. Ambassador's country team meeting abroad.

In relations with other offices and agencies, the level-of-contact equation is variable: a country director may deal, on the one hand, with people of considerably lesser rank than his and, on the other hand, with officers more senior. The equation depends in part on the *modus operandi* of the other agency, in part on the importance of the country director's enterprise to the other agency. In any case, there is no stratified caste system, and an officer is generally free to use the channel most suited to his needs—higher or lower as the case may be.

The Country Director and the Ambassador

The desideratum voiced several years ago by both Secretary Rusk and the Jackson Subcommittee—that a desk officer should be comparable in competence to the Ambassador he deals with in the field—has not quite been realized by the establishment of the country director system. As mentioned above, the Ambassador generally equates himself with his assistant secretary for operational purposes. Nonetheless, the country director has something more than a subordinate's relationship to his Ambassador, whom he almost invariably knows personally and whom he may often call by his first name under appropriately discreet circumstances. Much business between embassies and their respective country desks is transacted via the so-called official-informal letter, which permits more forthrightness than the wide distribution of regular channels for tricky problems or sensitive issues. A country director may and often does correspond with his Ambassador but his more usual channel is the deputy chief of mission (DCM), or—when the occasion calls for it—one of the counselors of embassy or the principal officer at a consulate.

In any well-coordinated desk operation, as in any mission abroad, there is flexibility insofar as channels are concerned. In many instances, the director's subordinates carry on correspondence at their own or higher levels—with their chief's knowledge, of course—and often, when they need more weight behind them, draft correspondence for the director's signature.

Relations with the Foreign Embassy

The level of departmental contact with a foreign embassy in Washington depends on circumstances, situations, and the relative importance—self-assigned or otherwise—of the foreign ambassador in question. Most mission chiefs who represent well-established countries prefer to deal with an assistant secretary or his deputy on matters that to them are of primary importance, if only for the sake of their credibility and stature back home. ("I saw Assistant Secretary of State Farthingale today and discreetly but firmly urged upon him the courses of action proposed in the Ministry's X-123 of April 1 last.") A number of ambassadors maintain relations at the country-director level wherever appropriate, reserving the assistant secretary or above for bigger moments,* but most country directors do their day-to-day business at the counselor-of-embassy, or second, level. When a country director has a problem recognized as one he should discuss with the chief of mission himself, he usually does so informally—possibly over tea, coffee, or drinks—in order to avoid the trappings (and possible news-attention) of a formally scheduled appointment.

OTHER ELEMENTS OF THE BUREAU

This chapter has dealt at some length with the assistant secretary–country director chain of command because, at present, this is the working line-officer structure and focal point for the day-to-day conduct of foreign relations with specific countries and areas. However, each geographic bureau, needless to say, contains other elements that are part of the Foreign Service at home.

A major component of the regional bureau, which in the case of our example, the NEA, might be called its eleventh "substantive" element (along with the ten directorates) is its

* Foreign ambassadors are of course entitled to deal with the Secretary of State, as American ambassadors deal with foreign ministers abroad. The Washington pace being what it is, however, it would be quite impractical for even the most prestigious chief of mission to insist on dealing solely with the Secretary (let alone the President, to whom he is personally accredited). Contrast this situation to that in many new mini-republics, where the American Ambassador may see the head of state as often as he does the foreign minister (in at least a few cases, it might be noted, because the former does not trust the latter).

Office of Regional Affairs.* As its name indicates, this office covers the NEA spectrum, principally in a coordinating and advisory role and as liaison with other departments and agencies on bureau-wide questions. The regional affairs roster includes, in addition to the director, a senior regional adviser, a political-economic adviser, a political-military adviser (army colonel on exchange), a labor and social affairs adviser, and a multilateral organizations adviser. The director is an FSO-1 who doubles in brass as the assistant secretary's executive officer and coordinator for interdepartmental business and also provides staff support in such area-wide activities as collating data for congressional presentations.

The bureau's "executive director," an FSO-1 or O-2 who has had experience as a counselor of embassy for administration, heads up NEA's considerable administrative empire: clerical, budget and fiscal, post management, personnel, foreign buildings, communications, and the like. He must not only keep the bureau's house in order but must supervise and look to the staffing, housekeeping, and general welfare of its many embassies and consulates.

The bureau also has its own public affairs adviser, a senior USIA officer (FSR-2) on detail, assisted by an FSO-3 Near East specialist recently returned from the area. Finally, it goes without saying, there are the several staff and special assistants and others who form the immediate entourage of the assistant secretary. Like its counterparts for other world areas, the Bureau of Near Eastern and South Asian Affairs is a highly professional group; almost without exception, its substantive officers, and not a few of its supporting staff, have had

* The term "substantive" as used in present-day Service parlance (and, perforce, in this book) has nothing to do with any of the several meanings listed in Webster's International, second or third editions. It generally connotes such activities as reporting, negotiation, policy-planning, and the like, but basically almost all work in the Service today is considered either substantive or administrative. Economic reporting is substantive; the economics of providing the reporter his salary, office, desk, paper, and so on, are administrative.

experience in one or more of the bureau's three regions—and a fair number of them have the right to be called experts.

THE OFFICE OF THE DIRECTOR GENERAL

If the geographical bureaus are Washington's focal points for the day-to-day conduct of foreign relations at home and abroad, the office of the Director General of the Foreign Service might be called the operations center for intra-Service relationships, institutions, and principles. In Chapter I, we noted that this office—after having been divested of certain quasi-autonomous powers in 1949—has in recent years again come to play a key role in the foreign affairs establishment.

The Director General has little authority *de jure*. The powers vested in the Secretary of State are delegated to the under secretary and, through him, to the deputy under secretary for administration. These officers retain suzerain rights, which they may exercise at any time. In practice, however, it is the Director General's office that plays the major operational role in Foreign Service recruitment, training, placement, counseling, evaluation, discipline, and retirement. It thus also plays a major policy-planning role in the entire field of personnel. In this capacity, the office works closely with the deputy under secretary for administration (as it does in other aspects of Service policy and operations) while at the same time it lends an attentive ear to the American Foreign Service Association, voice of the unofficial Service.

The Director General's primary responsibility for such operations, under the deputy under secretary for administration, was established by an instruction dated November 17, 1967, the introduction to which reads as follows:

> To strengthen the direction and management of personnel operations, the Office of Personnel is established within the Office of the Director General. As the head of this Office, the Deputy Assistant Secretary for Personnel will have direct responsibility for all phases of personnel management. He will be primarily responsible for implementing career management

principles for all categories of Foreign Service and Civil Service personnel.

The Office of Personnel (DG/PER) will serve as the focal point for liaison with the regional and functional bureaus on personnel management activities.

The office now has responsibility for direction and supervision of the following activities: *Presidential appointments* (ambassadorial and other appointments as the President's special representative); *community advisory services* (speaking engagements and trailer trips for FSO's on home leave); *special assignments* (assignment of senior officers to key positions other than Presidential appointments); *officer assignment and career management* (everything to do with officer placement, training and development, including junior officers); *staff support assignment and career management* (as above, for staff and local employees); *board of examiners* (junior-officer written and oral examinations; lateral entry); *employment* (recruitment of all non-FSO personnel); *medical* (care of both Department and Foreign Service personnel); *professional placement* (assisting departing employees to find other jobs); *personnel services* (personnel transactions, travel documentation, files, reports and statistics, position information, leave and retirement, administrative support of the Office of Personnel, and handling of the several awards programs).

A number of lesser kingdoms have thus been brought under one empire, and the Director General's deputy has become, in effect, the personnel chief of the Foreign Service and of the Civil Service element within the Department. He is the focal point of current aspirations toward an integrated, unified personnel management system, carefully developed and conscientiously carried out to increase efficiency and fortify morale both at home and abroad.

OTHER DEPARTMENTAL ASSIGNMENTS

The regional bureaus and the office of the Director General, along with the Foreign Service Institute (which is discussed in detail in Chapter II), might be called the principal nuclei of the Foreign Service presence in Washington. Besides these, in addition to persons on detail to other agencies or occupied elsewhere in the United States, there are Foreign Service people in some numbers scattered throughout the functional bureaus of the Department: economic affairs, education and cultural affairs, public affairs, intelligence and research, international organization affairs, international scientific and technological affairs, congressional relations, and security and consular affairs—as well as in the upper reaches of the "seventh floor," hallowed domain of the Secretary of State, his high command, and his hard-worked entourage.

Two other major Foreign Service groups are based in Washington, and hence their activities belong in this chapter on the Service at home, although their work is carried out for the most part abroad. These are the Foreign Service inspectors and the U.S. diplomatic couriers.

"The Inspectors Are Coming!"

Dear Mr. Ambassador:

An inspection of the Embassy at Neumania has been scheduled for April 1 to May 13, 1968. Foreign Service Inspectors John Doe and Richard Roe have been assigned to conduct this inspection.

Inspections are carried out for the Secretary of State and his principal assistants pursuant to Section 681 of the Foreign Service Act of 1946. The Foreign Service inspectors have been directed by the Secretary to assess how all United States programs and activities are coordinated and directed toward the achievement of United States policy objectives. It is not a primary purpose of the inspection process to find fault or criticize but to help solve problems and improve operations. You will find the inspectors ready and eager to be of all possible assistance to you and your staff.

Occasionally, airline schedules or other factors require a few days deviation from the established schedule. The inspectors will send you advance notification of their exact travel plans, whether wives are accompanying, and the types of accommodations desired.

. . . I hope you will write if there is any aspect of the inspection process which is not clear to you or on which you need additional information.

Sincerely yours,
NORRIS H. CENSOR
Inspector General

Such a letter as this heralds one of those climactic periods through which every Foreign Service post must pass from time to time, for its own good. Every officer knows that today's inspectors are not bogeymen, and that they may in fact help him in his career—but everyone reacts by scurrying about with cries of "The inspectors are coming!" and everyone heaves a sigh when the visitors have gone. A post preparing for inspection is never a post at ease. Principal officers may be heard to mutter, with the general confession: "We have left undone those things which we ought to have done, and we have done those things which we ought not to have done; and there is no health in us."

Yet few Foreign Service officers would do away with the rigorous but beneficial exercise of inspection, if only because it periodically obliges them to sweep the dust from under the rugs and burrow to the bottom of their in-boxes. The Service cherishes its right to select, promote, and assess from within, and inspection is an integral part of that system. One occasionally hears criticism of the procedure as a sort of self-whitewashing rite, but there is no sound basis for such charges. On the contrary, Foreign Service officers serving as inspectors know far better what to look for, and how to recognize what they find, than any lay "efficiency expert" could—and this without arousing the resentment that an outsider does.*

Officials charged with inspection missions were sent abroad

---

* There is, of course, a distinction between operational inspections by laymen and a Service-wide study from the outside such as that done by the Herter Committee, whose conclusions were welcomed.

on an *ad hoc* basis in the nineteenth century to look into suspected irregularities or abuses. (Even today, the idea persists in some quarters that inspectors are sent out only when malfeasance is suspected, and an inspector sometimes has to assure local community leaders, American and foreign, that the mere fact of his being there does not mean Ambassador White or Consul General Black is in trouble.) Not until 1906 was the framework of a permanent inspectorate set up by the Consular Reorganization Act, which established the post of consul general at large and charged its occupant with checking into the operations of consular officers abroad, supplying them with authoritative guidance, and determining their fitness for their duties. Then, the Rogers Act of 1924 created the new post of Foreign Service inspector, with authority to inspect not only consular but diplomatic offices (which had previously been subject to inspection only by special arrangement), and, finally, the Foreign Service Act of 1946 set up the inspection corps as it is today, "to inspect in a substantially uniform manner and at least every two years the work of the diplomatic and consular establishments of the United States."

The Act of 1946 further empowered the Secretary, if he had reason to suspect improper conduct, to authorize an inspector to suspend any officer or employee of the Service excepting a chief of mission—and even, if necessary, to administer a consular post in place of the principal officer for up to ninety days. Such drastic steps have seldom been taken, but inspectors are sometimes asked to look into and report separately on special problems in the areas they cover (with disciplinary action by Washington a possible result).

Although they spend most of their time on the road, the inspectors are Washington based and considered part of the home complement. Their chief, an FSO of career minister rank, carries the title of Inspector General of the Foreign Service. They are an élite corps, picked not only for their knowledge of the workings of the Service but also for what a distinguished ex-inspector of H.M. Foreign Service has called "the milk of human kindness." They must further have strong

The Treaty of Paris, crowning achievement of American Revolutionary diplomacy: Above, the American signers of the preliminary articles of peace, as painted by Benjamin West. Left to right are Jay, Adams, Franklin, Laurens, and William Temple Franklin, who, as secretary to the American commissioners, attested their signatures. Presumably, the blank space on the canvas was reserved for the British signers, whom West was unable to persuade to sit for the picture; at the right is the first page of the definitive treaty.

In 1968, Ambassador Ellsworth Bunker and members of the Embassy staff, the Marine Guard, and the U.S. Armed Forces conduct a grim inspection of the U.S. Embassy in Saigon after the Viet Cong's "Tet" attack of January 31.

DUTIES OF AN AMBASSADOR

In 1957, Ambassador Bunker presents a member of his staff to the King of Nepal.

The U.S. Embassy at Lomé, Togo.

This huge eagle stands atop the U.S. Embassy in London.

The U.S. Embassy in Paris.

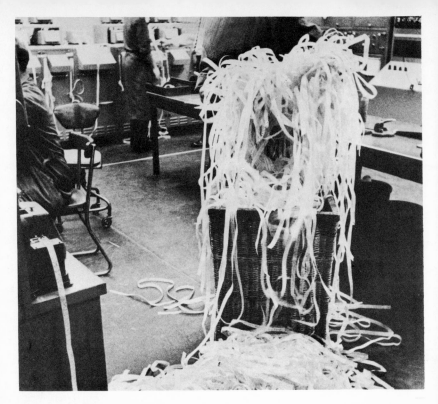

In Paris, the U.S. Embassy's wire room disposes of thirty-six hours' Teletype tape.

A U.S. diplomatic courier checks the visas he will need for one trip.

A U.S. diplomatic courier boards a plane with his pouch.

CONSULS AT WORK

A woman vice consul carries out the required inspection of the crew roster of an American ship.

A consul talks with an American merchant seaman, in jail after failing to join his ship when it left port.

An American naval petty officer brings his Japanese bride to the U.S. Embassy to register for a visa that will permit her to accompany him to the States.

In a nonimmigrant-visa waiting room, a consular officer interviews applicants and provides information.

The Honorable Warren R. Austin, while serving as representative to the United Nations, gives a press conference during his 1950 good-will mission to Cuba. An FSO press officer interprets.

An embassy officer discusses the problems and needs of a Latin American neighborhood with two savvy sources—the owner of a bar-restaurant and his son.

A diplomatic banquet is held at the Royal Palace in Brussels.

For the ceremony of presenting letters of credence, coaches are used to carry a new American ambassador and his entourage to Buckingham Palace.

While the wives of six American VIP's inspect an Indian village, a Foreign Service wife holds their umbrellas.

The American Consul at Kuching joins with the Governor of Sarawak and other Malayan dignitaries in a traditional local ceremony.

This marble tablet in the Diplomatic Lobby of the Department of State was erected by the American Foreign Service Association in memory of its honored dead. A matching tablet, facing it across the lobby, will provide continuing space for this roll of honor and will include the names of Ambassador John Gordon Mein and others who fell recently in the line of duty.

The Marine Guard at Frankfurt am Main lays the forty-nine–star flag to rest with full honors, before raising its fifty-star successor at the Consulate General's 1960 Fourth of July reception.

ERECTED BY MEMBERS OF THE AMERICAN FOREIGN
SERVICE ASSOCIATION IN HONOR OF DIPLOMATIC
AND CONSULAR OFFICERS OF THE UNITED STATES
WHO WHILE ON ACTIVE DUTY LOST THEIR LIVES
UNDER HEROIC OR TRAGIC CIRCUMSTANCES

WILLIAM PALFREY
LOST AT SEA 1780

JOEL BARLOW
EXPOSURE ZARNOWICE 1812

RICHARD C ANDERSON
CARTAGENA COLOMBIA 1826

NATHANIEL G INGRAHAM Jr
FEVER TAMPICO MEXICO 1824

CHARLES E FUDGER
HURRICANE ST THOMAS 1837

JAMES A HOLDEN
LOST AT SEA 1857

JOHN S MEIRCKEN
LOST AT SEA 1857

WILLIAM SHALER
CHOLERA HAVANA 1833

WILLIAM S SPARKS
CHOLERA VENICE 1849

THOMAS T TURNER
EPIDEMIC BAHIA 1849

THOMAS J MORGAN
YELLOW FEVER RIO DE JANEIRO 1850

HARDY M BURTON
YELLOW FEVER ST THOMAS 1852

GEORGE R DWYER
COAST FEVER MOZAMBIQUE 1854

BEVERLY L CLARKE
TROPICAL FEVER GUATEMALA 1860

ISAAC S McMICKEN
YELLOW FEVER ACAPULCO 1860

GEORGE TRUE
MALARIA TIENTSIN 1863

EDWARD W GARDNER
LOST AT SEA 1865

CHARLES O HANNAH
YELLOW FEVER DEMERARA 1866

ABRAHAM HANSON
AFRICAN FEVER
MONROVIA LIBERIA 1866

HIRAM R HAWKINS
EPIDEMIC TANGIER MOROCCO

ALLEN A HALL
EPIDEMIC LA PAZ BOLIVIA 1867

H E PECK
YELLOW FEVER HAITI 1867

JAMES WILSON
YELLOW FEVER VENEZUELA 1867

JAMES H McCOLLEY
YELLOW FEVER CALLAO 1869

WILLIAM STEDMAN
YELLOW FEVER
SANTIAGO CUBA 1869

CHARLES E PERRY
SHIPWRECK COLOMBIA 1872

THOMAS BIDDLE
EPIDEMIC GUAYAQUIL 1875

JOHN E FLINT
DROWNED SAVING LIFE
LA UNION EL SALVADOR 1875

PHILIP CLAYTON
YELLOW FEVER CALLAO 1877

HENRY H GARNET
AFRICAN FEVER
MONROVIA LIBERIA 1882

JESSE H MOORE
YELLOW FEVER CALLAO 1883

DAVID T BUNKER
YELLOW FEVER DEMERARA 1888

VICTOR F W STANWOOD
MURDERED MADAGASCAR 1888

WILLIAM D McCOY
FEVER MONROVIA LIBERIA 1893

JOHN R MEADE
YELLOW FEVER
SANTO DOMINGO 1894

ALEXANDER L POLLOCK
YELLOW FEVER SAN SALVADOR 1894

FREDERICK MUNCHMEYER
YELLOW FEVER SAN SALVADOR 1895

JOHN B GORMAN
MALIGNANT MALARIA
MATAMOROS MEXICO 1896

ALBERT S WILLIS
MALARIA HONOLULU 1897

ROUNSEVELLE WILDMAN
LOST AT SEA 1901

THOMAS T PRENTIS
VOLCANIC ERUPTION MARTINIQUE 1902

AMEDEE TESTART
VOLCANIC ERUPTION MARTINIQUE 1902

THOMAS NAST
YELLOW FEVER GUAYAQUIL 1902

WILLIAM F HAVEMEYER
CHOLERA BAGHDAD TURKEY 1904

PHILIP CARROLL
FEVER MANZANILLO MEXICO 1905

BENJAMIN H RIDGELY
EXHAUSTION MEXICO CITY 1908

ARTHUR A CHENEY
EARTHQUAKE MESSINA 1908

JOHN W GOURLEY
SMALLPOX
CHITRAL KASHMIR MEXICO 1911

THEODORE C HAMM
SMALLPOX DURANGO MEXICO 1914

ROBERT N McNEELY
LOST AT SEA 1915

CHARLES F McKIERNAN
SMALLPOX CHUNGKING CHINA 1916

CHARLES E BRISSEL
CHOLERA BAGHDAD 1916

ALFRED L M GOTTSCHALK
LOST AT SEA 1918

MADDIN SUMMERS
EXHAUSTION MOSCOW 1918

JOHN O CREAR
YELLOW FEVER VERA CRUZ 1918

LUTHER K ZABRISKIE
SMALLPOX
AGUAS CALIENTES MEXICO 1921

CARL R LOOP
SAVING LIFE CATANIA 1923

MAX D KIRJASSOFF
EARTHQUAKE YOKOHAMA 1923

PAUL E JENKS
EARTHQUAKE YOKOHAMA 1923

CLARENCE C WOOLARD
EPIDEMIC CAPE HAITIEN HAITI 1925

ROBERT W IMBRIE
MURDERED TEHERAN PERSIA 1924

WILLIAM T FRANCIS
YELLOW FEVER LIBERIA 1929

WILLIAM J JACKSON
DROWNED ATTEMPT TO SAVE LIFE
MATANZAS CUBA 1929

JOHN T WAINWRIGHT
DROWNED ATTEMPT TO SAVE LIFE
MATANZAS CUBA 1929

G RUSSELL TAGGART
HURRICANE
BELIZE BRITISH HONDURAS 1931

J THEODORE MARRINER
MURDERED BEIRUT SYRIA 1937

JOHN M SLAUGHTER
EARTHQUAKE CHATANGO 1939

THOMAS C WASSON
SHOT BY SNIPER JERUSALEM 1948

DOUGLAS S MACKIERNAN
KILLED IN GUNFIRE TIBET 1950

ROBERT LEE MIKELS
KIDNAPED AND KILLED BY REBELS
MELLAH SORAJA 1953

DAVID LEBRETON Jr
DROWNED SAVING LIVES
TOMO 1953

WILLIAM P BOTELER
KILLED BY GRENADE
NICOSIA CYPRUS 1956

ROBERT A McKINNON
TROPICAL DISEASE
OUAGADOUGOU 1961

BARBARA A ROBBINS
KILLED IN BOMBING OF EMBASSY
SAIGON 1965

JOSEPH W GRAINGER
MURDERED VIET-NAM 1965

JOSEPH R RUPLEY
KILLED BY GUNFIRE
CARACAS 1965

constitutions, since the life is one of constant travel, changing diet, and demanding deadlines.

An inspection team usually consists of two senior Foreign Service officers with broad experience in the substantive and administrative fields. Since 1965, teams occasionally carry "public members"—distinguished private citizens who participate in the inspection process and contribute to it. The substantive inspector, senior member of the team with the rank of career minister or FSO-1,* is in charge of the operation. At very large posts (e.g., London, Paris), two or more teams may be assigned to the job, with the senior-ranking officer in charge of the over-all operation. At small subordinate posts, the inspection is sometimes conducted by only one member of the team. Secretarial help is furnished by the post, usually a senior embassy employee who works with the team throughout the inspection and accompanies them to the consulates as well.

It is not always possible to adhere to the statutory requirement for inspection "at least every two years"; since 1946, the number of posts has doubled while the inspection teams remain at eight. Full-dress inspections are therefore supplemented by periodic visits from the Inspector General or his deputy, to ascertain whether new problems have arisen that might require another full inspection at an earlier date than would normally be the case.

Inspectors may take their wives along but must pay their fare. Some wives travel regularly, some part time, some not at all. Much depends on whether family stakes can be pulled up without undue financial or other inconvenience—and also, of course, on individual inclination.

Unlike certain inspectors of the past—notably one famous character who made a practice of showing up unannounced and taking careful note of how he was received as an unknown—the inspectors of today do not "jump" a post. Aside

---

* In mid-1968, there were six former ambassadors in a corps of sixteen traveling inspectors (eight teams); four inspectors held the rank of career minister, and the rest were FSO-1's or O-2's.

from announcing their coming well in advance, they send ahead instructions and a series of "check lists," which the post is to have answered by the time they arrive. These lists are so thorough that if the post does its job properly it should have completed what amounts to a self-inspection by the time the inspectors arrive to look things over (although the latter, of course, do not simply take the post's answers at face value).

It goes without saying that there is more to inspection than check lists, files, reports, and inventories. An experienced inspector can sense almost on arrival whether a post is running well or badly—and his final conclusions carry considerable weight. Aside from evaluating over-all post performance and examining the workings of each operation, the inspectors prepare individual efficiency reports on every Foreign Service employee at the post. These are based on job performance as observed but also, more importantly, on a confidential interview. Every employee has his day in court, and he will often tell an inspector things he would not dream of mentioning to his colleagues; even the best-adjusted of officers appreciate an avuncular ear sympathetic to a rehearsal of their hopes and fears. The inspectors also read the efficiency reports prepared by supervisors at the post, and submit comment if they find these overly strict or unduly favorable. (Many inequities have been righted through this procedure.)

Most inspectors further make a point of talking to the leading local employees, and they are always alive to anything they may discreetly pick up from American or foreign community leaders. Finally, of course, it is part of the job to size up wife and family, where applicable, and to evaluate the subject's fitness as a representative of his country abroad. On the subject of social activities, the Inspector General's "Instructions to Post" have this to say:

> The inspectors will welcome the opportunity to meet as many members of the staff and their families as possible and to visit their homes. They do not seek entertainment *per se,* nor do they wish to cause personnel at the post inconvenience or expense.

Nevertheless, the opportunity to meet informally with the personnel of the post and others is a necessary aid to the inspectors in their task of evaluating both the post and its personnel. Normally, hospitality extended should be simple and informal. However, if officers are planning functions for regular representational purposes during the inspection, it would be appropriate to include one or more inspectors on the guest list.

The wording is delicate but the meaning is clear: Sorry to be a bother, but we do have to see you in action with the Neumanians (or, if you are clerical and not on the Neumanian circuit, to see you in your habitat and how it is you live). Any knowledgeable couple, with inspection in the offing, will carefully plan a casual affair to be graced by their most prestigious Neumanian lions. This requires effort, to be sure, but the results are almost always a credit to the Service.

Few of the inspected stop to think of the cumulative strain on the jaded inspectors. One officer inspecting in the Near East attended three successive evening parties at which the drill was an exotic buffet served in a dim, candle-lit patio; he could never quite see what indigenous food he was eating, but he did know that two out of three times he got unmistakable indigestion. But, if the life of an inspector can be rough, its rewards are great, and the writer is proud to have served in the corps. The inspection procedure as a whole almost invariably adds up to a fair, competent, and thorough appraisal, dispassionate but sympathetic, of the post and its people. As one chief of mission told an inspector he had long known, on the day the latter paid his arrival call: "Well, John, I don't *think* there's anything radically wrong with us here, but if there is I'm sure you'll find it. All I ask is that you let me be the first to know."

The Swift Couriers

The scene is Windhoek, South West Africa, the date April 20, 1968. Following earlier rains, the skies have cleared and the stars are out on a clear but moonless night. A London-

bound Boeing 707 taxies out to the runway at 8:50 P.M., with 116 passengers and a crew of twelve. One passenger who has tarried too long over a last farewell drink watches unhappily as the big jet prepares to take off without him. At an altitude of some 600 feet, a port engine suddenly bursts into flame, the plane lurches, then shallow-dives to the ground at high speed, and explodes into four sections. The forward section breaks free, but the wings and the tourist section aft catch fire and the tourist passengers are doomed.

In the forward section, which has skidded and tumbled to a stop some 6,000 feet away, is Thomas W. Taylor, at age thirty-six a ten-year veteran of the U.S. Diplomatic Courier Service.

Taylor is in what he later describes as a hole, with another passenger, seats, and debris on top of him. He helps the other man to get off him, gropes through darkness and disarray while helping to free other passengers, then climbs through a hole in the fuselage and sets about dragging people outside— aided by two local farmers who have hurried to the scene in a four-wheel-drive Land Rover. A larger rescue group finally makes it over the difficult terrain and Taylor, dazed and walking minus a shoe over thorn-covered ground, searches the wreckage for his diplomatic pouch—without success—until a helicopter arrives to carry out the living.*

Not all U.S. diplomatic couriers have been as lucky as Tom Taylor. Since the expansion of the courier service with the nation's entry into World War II, five have died in the line of duty. The writer recalls sadly that at Brazzaville in 1963 he was one of the last to talk with young Joseph Capozzi just before he took off on an *Air Afrique* flight that crashed into Mount Cameroon and left no survivors (although Capozzi lived on for five days). All that was recovered of his mail was

---

* This account is condensed from a digest, prepared in the Washington Regional Diplomatic Courier Office, of newspaper accounts and statements of the surviving courier.

the metal hasp of a pouch and the charred remains of a few papers. Another courier, Frank Irwin, was aboard a Yugoslav Airlines Convair that crashed into a mountain while approaching Vienna on a foggy night; although he was badly injured, he retrieved his pouches and clung to them till he could hand them over to accredited American officials. Irwin, fortunately, survived. He is now a senior courier supervisor.

At the time of the accident described above, Taylor was one of twenty-eight "traveling couriers" working out of the Washington regional office, carrying classified correspondence to and from the posts on his route. He was on weekly Route 300A, which took him from Washington via New York to the west coast of Africa, with stops at Dakar, Monrovia, Accra, Lagos, and Kinshasha (formerly Léopoldville) before reaching the South African capital of Pretoria, whence he proceeded to Luanda, Angola, with a stopover at Windhoek. Had the mishap at Windhoek not occurred, Taylor would have continued to Luanda, then back to Pretoria. As it was, he spent five days in the local hospital and then returned to Washington, a somewhat banged-up out-patient. After a brief vacation, fortuitously planned beforehand, he was soon back on the road.

Taylor's pouch, a mailsack of heavy canvas,* was found the day after the crash at Windhoek by the police and handed over intact to an American consular officer from Capetown, who had flown to the scene to take charge of U.S. interests. He, in turn, handed it on to John Walck, a courier who, two days before Taylor's accident, had been in Freetown, scheduled to leave for Dakar to catch a flight to the United States later the same day. As luck would have it, this was the date of an army mutiny in Sierra Leone, and the Freetown airport was closed. Walck so notified Washington and was told to catch the next

* There would be more than one sack on a longer run; Taylor was on a side trip from Pretoria to Luanda and back. Each padlocked sack contains a number of smaller linen bags of various sizes and colors. The big sacks are handy as emergency containers, and when lying unused between runs are often put to quite unauthorized uses by embassy people.

Dakar-New York flight, on April 22. He was thus in Dakar, immobilized, at the time of the Windhoek crash, and so was ordered to proceed to Pretoria to carry on for Taylor. He finished Route 300A, making another side trip from Pretoria to Lourenço Marques and back, after which he retraced the west coast route up to Dakar—followed by an inland run through Bamako, Ouagadougou and Niamey, then back to Dakar again. After a final coastal side trip to Conakry, then Freetown via Bathurst and back to Dakar once more, he took off for the United States. Normal duration of trip: nineteen days. (This one took a little longer, with a slight hiatus in service.) Miles logged: 25,020.

It should be noted that a single courier does not cover this ground without interruption. Shortly after Windhoek, Taylor ordinarily would have passed his baton to another runner, taken a breather, then picked up the baton of still another runner. But at best, couriers keep to a grueling schedule. Routes cover the worldwide network of the Foreign Service, with 86 traveling couriers working out of 3 regional offices: Washington (28), Frankfurt am Main (42) and Manila (16); 10 of the 86 have supervisory duties and are on the road only part time. Over them is a headquarters detachment of 3 in Washington, all ex-travelers. Mid-1968 statistics show that the average courier covers 184,419 miles, or 7-plus times around the earth, per year. Those working out of Washington average an annual 284,101 miles; those out of Frankfurt, 127,393; those out of Manila, 230, 033. The idea that in a year every courier does the equivalent of a trip to the moon (mean distance: 238,857 miles) is therefore somewhat exaggerated; only one working out of secluded Washington averages that much.

Great nations of almost every age have had courier systems. Egypt used them extensively; in 1380 B.C., Amenhotep III, anxious to get an important but not urgent message through an encircling spy ring, is said to have shaved his courier's head, inscribed the message on his pate, then waited till the hair grew back before sending him forth. Britain's King's (or Queen's) Messengers are by far the oldest official courier service in existence today; their proud record dates from late medieval times and their prized silver greyhound badge from at least the seventeenth century.

The United States had no established courier service till 1918, when a system utilizing the armed services was installed —first to carry military mail, then the despatches of the American delegation to the Paris peace conference. When the conference ended, the service was disbanded, and U.S. diplomats had to revert to reliance on members of their own service, ship captains, and other trustworthy travelers. In 1934, at the London economic conference, President Roosevelt learned to his astonishment that the U.S. had no organized courier system, and ordered its immediate reestablishment.

Unlike their aged but agile British counterparts, American couriers are recruited young and unmarried and must agree to stay single for the first year after appointment. Entrance is between 21 and 31 years of age, with at least 2 years of college and with military obligations in order. The minimum tour of duty is 2 years. Most couriers carry on for about 5 years, although some serve longer; an exceptional record is that of John C. Grover, the "courier's courier" and past president of the U.S. Diplomatic Courier Association, who traveled for 20 years in spite of repeated offers of supervisory status. After their travels, some couriers go into the less mobile branches of the Foreign Service and others into the world of private enterprise. One thing they are unlikely to become is traveling salesmen.

Candidates for today's service should understand that the chances of their being offered a bribe are virtually nil, as are those for encounters with exotic princesses anxious to exchange favors for papers; also, that couriers are not permitted to carry arms. The job has quite enough to offer without the trappings of popular fiction. In a life where outlandish hours and crash landings are part of the day's work, and where every man realizes he is pushing the law of averages, there is high morale and *esprit de corps* and vacancies are few and far between.

It may be asked why, with today's rapid and relatively secure international communications, couriers are considered as necessary as they were in the days of the Pharaohs. Aside from the fact that Service regulations require safe-hand delivery of certain categories of sensitive material, many governments are still not gentlemen and still read each other's mail whenever they get the chance. The Foreign Service holds its diplomatic couriers in highest regard because of their outstanding record for dependable delivery of large volumes of classified mail under rugged circumstances, but also because, without them, the work of the Service—in Washington as well as abroad—would become immeasurably more complicated.

IV

"Reposing Special Trust and Confidence"

The President of the United States of America

To John Quincy Doe, of Kansas, Greeting:

Reposing special trust and confidence in your Integrity, Prudence and Ability, I have nominated and, by and with the advice and consent of the Senate, do appoint you a Foreign Service Officer of Class eight of the United States of America, and do authorize and empower you to do and perform all such matters and things as to the said office do appertain, and to hold and exercise the said office, during the pleasure of the President of the United States.

In testimony whereof, I have caused the Seal of the United States to be hereunto affixed.

S
E
A
L

Done at the City of Washington this first day of August, in the year of our Lord one thousand nine hundred and sixty-eight, and of the Independence of the United States of America the one hundred and ninety-third.

By the President:

_____

Secretary of State

It is with this heartening endorsement that the newly appointed FSO goes to his first post and, *mutatis mutandis,* the senior FSO to his last. Together with the commission as a For-

91

eign Service officer, which is his basic license to practice, the newcomer receives a second document—also signed and sealed by the President and countersigned by the Secretary—which is in fact two commissions in one: his appointment as a consular officer and as a secretary in the diplomatic service of the United States. Throughout his service, and depending on his assignment of the moment, the officer's status and title will stem from one of these three commissions.

Unless his first posting is in the United States or to a special mission or international body (in which case his title will be simply Foreign Service Officer) the new FSO will join the staff of a regular U.S. overseas establishment as a third secretary of embassy or, if assigned to a consular post, as a vice consul.

The American mission abroad has been called a house of many skills, and it may truly be said that, excepting in the mini-missions, there are numerous occupations and a variety of expertise assembled under an embassy's aegis. The purpose of this chapter is to examine the structure of an overseas mission and the role of the Foreign Service element in it. There are of course a number of non–Foreign Service elements as well, the representatives of affiliated agencies of the American foreign affairs community—and at not a few posts they are the tail that wags the dog. Their place in the scheme of things will be touched on as appropriate here, but the roles they play and the relationships they maintain with "the Embassy" will be gone into in more detail in a later chapter.

STRUCTURE OF AN EMBASSY

Let us begin with the composition of a typical mission. Table IV is based on the officer strength (all agencies) at a fair-sized embassy in Latin America where there is a representatively broad range of U.S. activities. In addition to the Embassy proper with its executive, political, economic, consular and administrative sections, the mission includes armed services attachés and representatives of the Foreign Agricultural Service of the Department of Agriculture, the United

TABLE IV

COMPOSITION OF A SAMPLE U.S. MISSION

Executive Section
Chief of Mission
Deputy Chief of Mission
Executive Assistant

Political Section
Counselor for Political Affairs
5 Political Officers[a]
Labor Attaché

Economic Section
Counselor for Economic Affairs
4 Economic Officers[a]
Commercial Attaché
2 Commercial Officers
Petroleum Attaché
Financial Attaché
Transportation & Communications
  Officer

Consular Section
Consul General
5 Consular Officers
Visa Assistant
Consular Assistant

Administrative Section
Counselor for Administration
Administrative Officer
General Services Officer
2 General Services Assistants[a]
Personnel Officer
Budget & Fiscal Officer
Disbursing Officer
Communications and Records
  Supervisor
Communications and Records Clerk
Telecommunications Specialist
Security Officer

Service Attachés
Defense Attaché (and Army
  Attaché)

Assistant Army Attaché
Naval Attaché
Assistant Naval Attaché
Air Attaché
Assistant Air Attaché

Foreign Agricultural Service (FAS)
Agricultural Attaché
Assistant Agricultural Attaché

*United States Information Service
  (USIS)*
Counselor for Public Affairs
Executive Officer
Information Officer
Assistant Information Officer
Assistant Information Officer
  (Labor)
Cultural Affairs Officer
3 Assistant Cultural Affairs Officers
Public Affairs Trainee
Director, Binational Center
Director of Courses, Binational
  Center

*Agency for International Develop-
  ment (AID)*
AID Representative
Controller
Program Officer
Programs Analysis Officer
Development Officer
Manpower Adviser
Agricultural Credit Adviser
Industrial Officer
Sociologist
Public Affairs Adviser
Chief Public Safety Adviser
Deputy Chief Public Safety Adviser
6 Public Safety Advisers
General Engineer
Auditor

TABLE IV (*Cont.*)

*Peace Corps*b	Chief, Joint Plans and Operations
Peace Corps Representative	3 Officer Advisers
Deputy Peace Corps Representative	Chief, Army Section
8 Associate Representatives	12 Officer Advisers
3 Physicians	Chief, Navy Section
	8 Officer Advisers
Military Assistance Advisory Group	Chief, Air Force Section
(*MAAG*)	6 Officer Advisersc
Commander of Group	Chief National Guard Adviser
Chief Administrative Officer	3 Officer Advisers

a Including 1 of 3 junior officers on rotational assignment. Consular section is also part of rotation when its turn comes. Note that USIS also has a junior officer trainee.

b Headquarters detachment: does not include "the troops"—325 Peace Corps volunteers scattered throughout the countryside.

c Including 2 on duty in a provincial capital.

States Information Service (USIS),* the Agency for International Development (AID), the Peace Corps, and the Defense Department's Military Assistance Advisory Group (MAAG). Table IV shows an officer strength of 133. The total American strength-on-board—including clerical and technical employees of the civilian agencies, enlisted office staff of the military, and the Marine security guard—is 223. More chiefs than Indians on the American side, but the local-employee complement redresses the balance.

The home and hub of the diplomatic mission is the chancery, which is the main locus of embassy business and is where the Ambassador and his central staff have offices. There may, of course, be annexes and outbuildings—especially to house a dog-wagging AID mission or a MAAG. In the prewar days of smaller staffs, it was not unusual for the chancery to form a part of the Ambassador's residence, with the chief of mission and often some of his officers living and working in different wings of the same large house. Today, the Ambassa-

* Abbreviated USIS abroad, this is the overseas arm of Washington's United States Information Agency (USIA). For a full account of both USIS and USIA activities, see *The United States Information Agency*, by John W. Henderson (Praeger, 1969).

dor's home is called "the Residence"; a visitor asking a cab driver for "the American Embassy" will normally be taken to the chancery.

Not shown on Table IV are two constituent consular posts outside the capital. In the country picked as an example each of these has three consular officers and a resident AID man. One of the consulates has two American USIS officers; the other has none, but has a USIS reading room and library staffed by local employees and supervised by a consular officer.

Our table begins modestly with a three-officer "executive section," which includes the chief of mission and his deputy. If, instead of a table, we had used one of those schematic charts beloved by bureaucrats, these two positions would be set in empyrean splendor in blocks one over the other at the top—with all the lesser blocks and blocs of blocks descending vertically or shooting off horizontally beneath them. Before we descend to these workaday levels, let us turn our eyes topside and look for a time at Number One and Number Two— the Ambassador and his deputy chief of mission, usually referred to as the DCM.

"MR. AMBASSADOR"

An ambassador's first order of business is to present his credentials to his host-country's head of state. The ceremony might proceed as follows:

A long limousine flanked by outriding motorcycle police and followed by other cars enters the gates of a palatial edifice and pulls up at the main entrance. An aide opens the car door and two figures in formal morning clothes descend.* One is the host-country chief of protocol; the other is the new American Ambassador, come to present his "letter of credence." The two pause while members of the Ambassador's entourage alight from the other cars and form behind him. These are his

---

* The traditional four-wheeled coach has all but vanished in favor of the limousine. Dress is still generally formal—tails or cutaway according to local ground rules—although some governments now ask for business suits. One small Asian nation considers "ice cream tux" (white dinner jacket) to be the dress for any formal occasion at any hour.

ranking embassy officers and his armed services attachés, the latter resplendent in dress uniform with what the French call *décorations pendantes*. The group passes an honor guard in review and proceeds sedately into the palace. In older, established countries they will most likely be received by the chief of state and his foreign minister (plus supernumeraries), but in more recently independent nations there may be quite a reception committee. (One African president was flanked not only by his whole cabinet and the president and vice president of the national assembly, but also by his three favorite American missionary couples.) The chief of protocol makes *pro forma* introductions, and the American Ambassador then makes a brief, conventional statement of the purpose of his visit, before handing the chief of state the letter of credence, signed by his President.

The model text follows:

Great and Good Friend:

I have made choice of Richard Pinckney Roe, a distinguished citizen of the United States, to represent the United States of America in the quality of Ambassador Extraordinary and Plenipotentiary to the Republic of Indépendance. He is well informed of the relative interests of the two countries and of the sincere desire of this Government to strengthen even further the friendship now existing between them. My knowledge of his high character and ability gives me entire confidence that he will constantly endeavor to advance the interests and prosperity of both Governments and so render himself acceptable to Your Excellency.

I therefore request Your Excellency to receive him favorably and to give full credence to what he shall say on the part of the United States and to the assurances which I have charged him to convey to you of the best wishes of this Government for the prosperity of the Republic of Indépendance.

May God have Your Excellency in His wise Keeping.

Your Good Friend,

———————————

(There is a somewhat less cordial version for less friendly countries.)

The chief of state takes the envelope politely and hands it to an aide (or to his foreign minister, who already has a copy), then the Ambassador proceeds (or not, if he deems it inappropriate) with what his instructions call "a brief address suitable to the occasion." What the occasion usually calls for is something in the local language that will be "good for relations" when reported in the press ("NEW U.S. ENVOY KEYNOTES FRIENDSHIP AND UNITY") without going beyond the amicable generalities that are expected at this stage. The chief of state has already seen the Ambassador's text and replies in kind—also with an eye to the evening editions. Then, after the Ambassador has presented his staff, the two principals sit down for a chat. Depending on local usage, there will be champagne, spirits, tea, or coffee—perhaps a choice. Before long, the host makes a discreet gesture and the Ambassador and his escort take their leave, reviewing the honor guard in reverse as they head for their cars.

When the chief of state is a sovereign, there will be a court chamberlain with the foreign minister and the affair will probably be held in the throne room. Royal ceremonies involve a set sequence of bows at proper intervals—the chamberlain briefs his charges on these—and, if tradition is strictly followed, an exit walking backwards. Nowadays, excepting in the most formal and traditional of courts, a few symbolic backward steps, plus a final bow at the exit, will generally suffice.

Although he may invite a few senior aides to call him by his given name in private, an American chief of diplomatic mission is always "Mr. Ambassador" before his staff and in public. In correspondence, he is "The Honorable." In most foreign societies, he is addressed as "Excellency"—an honorific the Department of State also uses in its treatment of chiefs of mission accredited to Washington.

These are some of the trappings of what the *Foreign Service Manual* calls "Protocol, Precedence, and Formalities."

Once an ambassador has presented his credentials—and has thus, diplomatically speaking, begun to exist—he sets out on a round of official calls on cabinet ministers, other local bigwigs, and his diplomatic colleagues.* Although the ceremony of "leaving cards" has not changed much, these calls are not as formal or as time-consuming as they once were—and more often than not they afford the new boy a convenient opportunity to size up and be sized up by those he will be dealing with for the next several years. Meanwhile, the Ambassador, having made the acquaintance of his own staff and got to know his key people fairly well, is free and ready to get down to business.

Many learned and informed studies have been done on the subject of an American ambassador's authority, or lack of it, and the commentators are by no means of one mind.† The writer does not wish to enter the debate, preferring to let his developing narrative show by example what an ambassador is and does, but the basic elements of the discussion might usefully be summarized here.

1. An ambassador's lines of communication run through the Department of State, and he normally receives his instructions through the Secretary of State or the appropriate regional assistant secretary. He is, nevertheless, the personal representative of the President to the chief of state to whom he is accredited, and is so identified in the President's letter of credence. His success in impressing the reality of that status on those he deals with in host-country circles will be the measure of his effectiveness.

2. In principle, a chief of mission, like the President he

* In this day and age, he will probably have met many of them informally —especially if there has been a delay in the accreditation ceremony. In earlier times, even up until World War II, a European mission chief who was a stickler for tradition would have had a fit-and-a-half if an unaccredited colleague so much as presumed to pass the time of day.

† A highly readable study of the ambassadorial role, succinct but many-sided, is "The Secretary of State and the Ambassador," a Jackson Subcommittee publication edited by the Senator. (Praeger, 1964).

serves, is chief executive of a large and complex establishment, the active interpreter of policy and director of programs abroad. Practice sometimes falls short of principle; he is, nonetheless, the President's man and the Number One official American in the country of his accreditation, not just a chairman of the board. The efforts of four successive Presidents (Truman through Johnson, and, most importantly, John F. Kennedy) have confirmed the primacy of the American Ambassador in his territory. His authority is not absolute—in cases of deep disagreement, other-agency heads may appeal to higher authority in Washington—but unless he and they are notified to the contrary they are bound to abide by his decisions.

3. Much has been said, not all of it new, to the general effect that the long-distance telephone, the transoceanic cable, and the jet airplane have reduced the role of today's ambassador to that of a glorified Western Union messenger.* Indeed, more than one mission chief has thought wistfully of Minister Adams in early nineteenth century St. Petersburg, affixing his John Q. to a meticulously indited despatch, then sitting back to wait months for a reply. It cannot be gainsaid that rapid communications and travel have reduced an ambassador's discretionary role in important ways, but it should be borne in mind that as the speed of communications increases, so does the pace of events. Moreover, what the United States does in the world today is far more important than it was fifty or even twenty-five years ago. The margins within which an American ambassador works—what with the new burdens imposed by

* In England, the Royal Commission of 1861, investigating H.M. Foreign Service, preoccupied itself with the influence of the telegraph on diplomacy. Were ambassadors really necessary when such rapid communications could be made with foreign powers? The considered answer was yes: there still had to be a man on the spot to talk and report. Secretary of State Charles Evans Hughes and the leading French diplomat Jean Jules Jusserand, among others, came emphatically to the same conclusion. It will be noted that they were addressing themselves to the question whether there should be ambassadors at all—a proposition unthinkable in today's world.

U.S. assumption of world leadership and the corresponding accretion of operating responsibilities—are in many ways wider than ever before.

The consensus seems to be that a chief of mission has the authority he needs but must be strong and able if he is to use it to full advantage. To be sure, he must refer many matters back to Washington, if only to make certain that his country operation is in step with worldwide U.S. policy and capabilities. But no amount of referral or consultation, or visitations from headquarters, can replace the exercise of independent judgment under field conditions. Secretary Rusk once said: "There is almost never a week that passes when we don't have instances of a judgment that had to be made on the spot by an Ambassador to deal with a situation before he could get Washington to comment or give him instructions."

So much for what might be called, in a nonpejorative sense, the high-level bureaucratic approach to the problem. The writer would add another, more personal, dimension. Whether or not an ambassador gains full credence as the President's *missus dominicus,* whether or not he can keep his other agencies in line, whether he be messenger boy or field commander, there is one basic quality he cannot do without—the outgoing personality of a natural-born communicator, both sender and receiver. The importance of this in dealings with host-country and other people outside the office is generally recognized. Its importance internally is not so generally recognized.

To a staff working and living away from home, the Ambassador stands in effect *in loco parentis;* he is head of the family, with all the responsibility that that entails. He may be a keen political analyst, a wily negotiator, a top-flight economist or a master manager, but if he cannot both give and command loyalty he can never be fully effective as chief of mission. To his staff, from counselor to code clerk, the knowledge that the boss will see to it that they get a "fair shake," that he is genuinely interested in their well-being and their problems, can make the difference between a good post and a bad one—wretched climate, unpredictable plumbing, unpleasant inhabitants, or other such considerations notwithstanding.

The good boss and his wife will make certain that everyone gets his due measure of social recognition (most importantly, invitations to the Big House and acceptance of invitations to the little ones) but excepting at the smallest missions they cannot be expected personally to keep abreast of all the goings-on below stairs—when young Branson's wife is going to have her baby, what is bothering the boys in the code room, who is homesick and who is lovesick, and so on. For this sort of thing, the Ambassador has a trusted source and central channel, his deputy chief of mission or DCM, who as "exec" must keep his finger on the pulse of the mission. Collecting and sifting scuttlebutt is but one of the many jobs of this key senior officer, to whose role we now turn our attention.

THE DCM

Until the post-World War II expansion, a diplomatic mission—embassy or legation—was headed by an ambassador or a minister.* Under him, was a counselor of embassy or legation, known as *the* counselor. With the growth of inflation, in rank as well as in numbers, it was not long before some of the largest posts had as many as half a dozen officers with the rank of counselor. Even when there were two or three, it became necessary to distinguish the senior counselor as such. At larger posts, he was given the personal rank of minister and styled minister-counselor—then, eventually, at superposts the "counselor" was dropped and he became "the minister." (By 1968, rank-inflation was reaching absurd proportions, with the personal rank of ambassador, instead of minister, extended to deputy representatives in the United Nations and

* Since November 1966, when Budapest and Sofia were raised to embassy status, there have been no American legations. It will be recalled that until 1893, when the first U.S. ambassadors were appointed, all regular American diplomatic missions were presided over by ministers (envoys extraordinary and plenipotentiary).

to two "deputy ambassadors" in Vietnam.) Concurrently with all this, use of the term "deputy chief of mission" spread throughout the Service, and today even most mini-missions have their DCM's.

The role of the DCM depends largely on the wishes of his chief: he is what the Ambassador makes him. Where there is a noncareer chief of mission without previous Foreign Service experience, it is customary to provide a veteran DCM of proven capability, one who can take all or any desired part of "running the shop" off the chief's shoulders and at the same time counsel him on the ways of the Service and of diplomacy in general. An experienced career chief of mission may by contrast choose to break in as DCM a promising "comer" whom he knows and trusts. But whether the Ambassador is career or noncareer, freshman or old hand, the DCM has a basic dual function, which, with very few exceptions, varies only in emphasis from post to post. On the one hand, he is the Ambassador's understudy and principal adviser; on the other, he is executive officer or chief of staff, responsible for the smooth and effective operation of the mission while leaving the Ambassador free for high-level contact work, travel, and special projects.

As understudy, it is the DCM who assumes charge when the Ambassador is away from the post, and this in itself sets him apart as something more than *primus inter pares* among the counselors. If the chief of mission leaves the country, the DCM becomes chargé d'affaires, ad interim ("Ambassador left for Islandia conference today. Have assumed charge. Doe"). This ascendancy will normally be for short periods, but it sometimes happens that there is a longish hiatus during a change in chiefs and a DCM may remain in charge for months. (In the writer's personal experience, the record is eight, but he is certain there will have been longer "interims.")

As executive officer, the DCM's role can vary considerably according to the nature of the post and the style of the chief of mission. Some ambassadors treat him as an almost inter-

changeable alter ego in sharing the burden of day-to-day operations. Others use him more as an office manager and "follow-
through" man on policy decisions. Still others put the accent
on coordination of mission-wide activities such as the country
team. In the writer's view, the mean pattern is probably best
reflected in a set of practical ground rules laid down by one
veteran chief of mission out of his own experience and quoted
in a State Department brochure:

> The DCM should . . . so allocate his time and attention as
> to enable him to supervise the activities of all elements of the
> Embassy and rely upon the heads of the individual elements
> and sections to direct the work of their subordinates. The
> proportion of the DCM's time and attention devoted to any
> field naturally varies according to the nature of the mission's
> work (i.e., in some countries U.S. policy objectives are more
> economic than political in nature, while in others the reverse is
> true) and with the ability of the heads of the several sections
> of the mission. As a general rule, I suggest that a DCM divide
> his time in roughly the following proportions: political (in-
> cluding military) 30 per cent, economic (including AID) 25
> per cent, administrative 25 per cent, USIS 15 per cent, and
> consular 5 per cent.

Whatever the mix and whatever the *modus operandi,* the
DCM must be recognized throughout the mission as enjoying
the Ambassador's full confidence and support, and there must
be a free and full exchange of information between the two.
But, no matter how much responsibility a chief may delegate
to his deputy, the ultimate responsibility is his own, and he
could not shake it if he wanted to.

On the subject of the DCM, one final consideration is pertinent: that of his own potential for chief-of-mission rank.
Present-day personnel policy virtually demands that any officer assigned as DCM be recognizedly of ambassadorial caliber
—not necessarily ready for his own mission as the immediate
next step, but certainly fit for duty in the foreseeable and not-
too-far future. In practice, many DCM's are "often a brides-

maid, never a bride," but they must be ready and able in the event a proposal comes.

The writer has done a small bit of informal digging on his own in this respect, checking the January, 1968, *Foreign Service List* against the 1967 *Biographic Register* of the foreign affairs community. The roughly accurate exercise showed that at the beginning of 1968 almost two-thirds of the FSO ambassadors in charge of missions had served at least once as DCM's. On a much smaller scale, the roster of senior officers inspected by the writer in 1964–65 included nine DCM's, of whom four were in Class 1—and two of the four had "made ambassador" by 1968.

The Rest of the Executive Section

Under the Ambassador and the DCM is the rest of the "executive section" of the Embassy. (It is called the executive section in the *Foreign Service List,* but the term is seldom used at the post.) Our Table IV shows one executive assistant, but at a superpost there might be two or even more, one of them possibly a junior officer on duty as staff aide. Small posts seldom need or can afford the full-time assignment of even a staff aide, let alone an executive assistant.

The executive or special assistant (or the senior of these if there are two or more) will generally be a middle-grade officer. Although his duties are what the Ambassador makes them, as with the DCM, the essence of his job is usually that of a two-headed but unsurly Cerberus. One head is a sheepdog riding herd on people and projects, worrying the former till they achieve the latter; the other head is a watchdog, guardian of the interests as well as the peace of mind of his chief. To succeed in this two-fold task, an officer must be both hard-working and level-headed, neither a petty tyrant arousing resentments nor an obsequious currier of favor and esteem. The job appears to be reserved by tacit agreement for officers looked upon as comers; no one is picked who is not likely to be "going places."

Completing the executive section is the clerical element, not included in Table IV: the secretaries of the Ambassador and the DCM (and, at larger posts, one or more lesser helpers). Needless to say, the Ambassador's secretary is top girl in the Embassy's clerical hierarchy; even at mini-posts she will be an FSS-6 or above, often with the title of secretarial assistant. The DCM's secretary occupies the same relative position as her boss—that of Number Two—and is a power in her own right.

Chiefs of mission have the unwritten privilege of choosing their secretaries. Not all exercise it, but many not only do so but take these trusted assistants with them from post to post. An ambassador's secretary must be well organized and technically competent—that is taken for granted—but she must also have the judgment and poise of maturity and be blessed with social grace. She is not hired as a social secretary, but in a diplomatic mission there is never a hard-and-fast line between social and business activity—and even on the strictly business side she must meet and take care of top-level officials of the host country and the ranking representatives of others, not only officially but sometimes socially.

These are the standard elements of an executive section. At some larger posts, it includes other officers, usually for reasons of hierarchical fitness not directly connected with their work. The science officer* is often one of these; another, occasionally, is the post's senior consular officer when he holds counselor rank and has supervisory responsibilities over the embassy consular section and the mission's constituent posts.

Having had a look at the "front office," let us turn our attention to the four units that carry the "Foreign Service" load of an embassy's work. Soon after a Foreign Service oral ex-

---

* In 1949, the Department instituted a science attaché program, assigning scientific specialists to six major embassies. The program was languishing by the mid-1950's, but Sputnik I revived interest and there are now science officers at a number of embassies. They are recruited as FSR's, usually of Class 1.

amination gets under way, the candidate may be asked to name the four basic activities of the Service. The answer is political, economic, consular, and administrative, and he is supposed to say yes when asked whether he would be willing to serve in any or all of these. This does not mean that every officer must engage in all four during his career—few do—but it does mean that he must be prepared to accept assignment to any of them. We now take up these four activities section by section.

THE POLITICAL SECTION

Table IV shows a total of seven officers in the political section of a fair-sized embassy: a chief with counselor rank, four regular political officers and a trainee, and a labor attaché. At a superpost, there might be a dozen or more officers, with possibly one or more of these working in some specialty, such as politico-military affairs. At a small mission (up to, say, ten Americans in all), the section would probably comprise one or two middle-grade or junior officers, with one of these handling labor work part time and with the DCM doubling in brass as section chief. The Ambassador and his deputy generally interest themselves more directly in the work of the political and economic sections than in the more routine activities, since there is usually a close tie-in with their own duties in reporting, negotiation, and representation.*

In recent years, the political officer has been the target of much criticism, particularly on the part of those who advocate what amounts to total specialization. These critics appear to look on the political officer as the latter-day manifestation of

---

* This seems a good time to take note of the basic, twofold meaning of the term "representation" in diplomatic usage: (1) informing foreign governments of official U.S. views and interests and striving to create a favorable climate for them, acting for the United States via formal and informal contacts with host-country officials, diplomatic colleagues, and influential private citizens, and (2) offering official or semiofficial hospitality (via a "representation allowance"), making speeches and other public appearances, and so on. In both contexts, the objects are to win friends and influence people.

the rich dilettante "gentlemen observer" of the bad old diplomatic service. One commentator has charged that despite new tendencies toward specialization, the political officer remains the Service's *beau idéal,* with the economic, commercial, and other officers forming a rather grubby supporting cast. There is just enough vestigial truth in such allegations to make them worthy of passing note, but the political officer of today is a far cry from his reputedly white-spatted forebear who spoke only to the foreign office, other diplomats, and a small élite of social leaders. Even in the period between world wars, an American diplomat could limit his professional role largely to observing and reporting—almost, one might say, as an informed but uninvolved bystander. The U.S. world role having become what it is today, however, no officer can maintain a posture of such passivity.

To be sure, accurate, perceptive, and timely reporting is as important as it ever was, if indeed not more so. The political officer is expected to develop a deep understanding of the political forces, power structure, and personalities of the host country, and he must understand and relate U.S. policies and interests to these factors. But the knowledge he acquires must be used for something more than spot and analytical reporting to Washington.

He must actively solicit and gain support for U.S. viewpoints and policies, not only within the government but among political, labor, industry, and other leaders—and among the rank-and-file, in the capital and out of it. At many posts, he may be called upon to negotiate officially (on treaties or agreements, for example) both as an aide to the chief of mission and, on lower-level projects, in his own right. The head of the section must serve as political adviser, not only to the Ambassador and the country team but throughout the mission —to ensure that all sections and agencies are informed of trends and conditions that might affect their activities. He and his officers must be prepared, on demand, to brief special visitors, such as congressmen and journalists. They must work with special target groups—political parties, youth, labor, the military, agrarian groups, and so on—and with the political opposition to the extent that the local situation permits it. They must be *en rapport* with the host-country press, and must contribute to and "vet" speeches and other public statements to be made by their colleagues—as well as doing some speaking themselves. The section is also responsible for obtaining clearances of visits by U.S. naval vessels, scientific expeditions, merchant marine training ships, and U.S. Government aircraft. Far from being routine, such clearances can become political hot potatoes in some areas—with the possibility of incidents and repercussions ever present.

What It Takes to Be a Political Officer

What kind of officer is needed for such work? Not a specialist, according to most experts—or at least they do not call him one. A political officer may have devoted a good bit of his schooling to history, political science, and allied disciplines, but he is seldom trained in specific techniques. The junior political officer will bring little more to his job than a presumably adequate academic and linguistic background, plus what bits and pieces he may have picked up in the initial orientation courses, but he will start forthwith in what used to be called the school of hard knocks: on-the-job training. He will get what guidance he needs, he will observe and learn—giving his calves a good daily workout in the process—and if he has what it takes, before too many posts he may call himself a seasoned political officer.

"What it takes" includes one all-important ingredient, that of political sense—what the Germans call *Fingerspitzengefühl*. When asked what he most looked for in new recruits for the career, Ambassador Loy W. Henderson (revered as "Mr. Foreign Service") replied, after a moment's thought, "Political sensitivity—without it, a Ph.D. is useless. With it, a high school student is invaluable." Such sensitivity is, of course, important to any aspect of diplomacy, but nowhere more so than in the work of a political officer. The benefit of hindsight is never his.* He has to report on history—to recognize and assess it, if possible outguess it—as it happens.

Another all-important ingredient (and, again, this goes for every aspect of diplomacy but particularly for the political) is that of courage—courage to report objectively and honestly even when the truth may be unpopular back home. "Timidity" is a term frequently heard for the failure to do so, but often as not it is more a matter of temptation—temptation to slur over the unpleasant points in making an official representation, to report one's own role in the best possible light, to tell Washington what it wants to hear. It can only be said that in diplomacy, as in other walks of life, honesty *is* the best policy. Dishonesty will catch up with one sooner or later—often far sooner than one may think.

Political reporting can become tedious and routine, but at times things happen so fast that it might seem easier to operate from inside a cyclotron. Still, a good political officer likes nothing better than a crisis—provided, of course, that the crisis does not move in to stay.

Take, for example, a revolution. Not the blood-red upheaval of a Russia or a China but a simple power play where the in's go out and the out's come in—often a "bloodless coup," which means that people get hurt, but not on purpose. First, there are the pre-rumors, then the rumors. Little men sidle in or out of chanceries or are met in odd places; big men talk discreetly out of the side of the mouth. Embassy officers compare notes with friendly diplomats and with each other, and the whole mission is on the alert for portents. Then comes the break. It may be an inside job—for example, a group of officers with selected troops surround the palace during the night, parley with the president over the phone or in person,

---

* Well, hardly ever. One officer, in interim charge at an outpost in crisis, used to report separately on about every possible contingency in the situation, then, when something did happen, would lead off his message with "As predicted in my X-123 . . . ," a reference to the appropriate contingency report.

lead him away peacefully or not, and announce on the morning newscasts that democratic government has returned to Siraqia. In such cases, the political section may look forward to an active couple of days trying to fit all the pieces into the jigsaw and keep Washington up to date. If it is an outside job, with the soldiery abroad and skirmishing, the jigsaw work goes on upstairs but the streets are a spot reporter's paradise. A junior leg man may cover himself with glory, sweat, and perhaps a bit of blood.

Then there are the political demonstrations not necessarily connected with *coups d'état*. Today they are often as not domestically motivated, and these make good reporting, but the pattern of xenophobia is still classic—with its torchlight parades, flag- and effigy-burnings, ink and stink bombs, broken glass, and bad oratory (not always directed at the United States, it might be noted). Chiefs of mission, security officers, and housekeepers worry about staff safety and property damage—and the U.S. posture—but not the political officer. Chances are he will be right out there observing and making mental notes. He may even be in the mob.

Another political section sport, somewhat more sedentary but always absorbing, is election-guessing—not only who will win, but by what margin. Will the Christian Social Democrats gain on the Democratic Christian Socialists? Will the party in power have to coalesce to continue? Where there is a multiple-party system, coverage is usually divided up among the political section's officers—often with the eager, extracurricular help of junior officers whose daytime hours are taken up with routine tasks. (One of these young men, in the writer's memory, was covering an evening rightist rally when he got backed by chance into a smoke-filled room and picked up some interesting tidbits before he was shooed out.) Finally, on E-Day minus one, all estimates are called in, the boss prays over them a while, then makes his predictions.

Few officers spend a major part of their careers as titular political officers, even after they get past the apprentice stage, but unless they go into an entirely different line of work their jobs will continue to call for political sensitivity—in international organizations, politico-military affairs, economic work, and so on. The interdependence of political and economic factors becomes more marked every year, and Foreign Service activity in the two fields is being made to mesh accordingly. At the same time, more and more FSO's are becoming interchangeably political and economic, and are the more valuable for it.

It should be noted that language-and-area specialists, those in the "hard" languages at least, fill virtually all the political and most of the economic officer jobs at the posts in their areas—not unnaturally, since, for example, a "substantive" officer with no Arabic would have little utility at an Arab post. Aside from mastery of the language *per se*, which in some cases may be relatively weak, the area specialist is steeped in the mores of his world and knows his way around in it.

By the time he reaches senior rank, the successful political officer (along with his economic colleague, unless the latter is a dyed-in-the-wool, one-subject specialist) will have the inner track to the next step up—program direction, with across-the-board responsibility as a DCM, a consul general, a deputy assistant secretary, a country director, or in a position of comparable dignity.

The Labor Attaché

The increasingly vital role being played by organized labor in world affairs was recognized in 1943 when provision was made for the addition of a labor attaché (or labor officer) to the embassy team. In recent years, the cooperation between the departments of State and Labor, as between State and Commerce, has become a generally productive and mutually satisfactory joint venture. The Foreign Service has the responsibility for labor reporting, while the Labor Department has the major say as to who will do that work—and is represented on both the Board of the Foreign Service and the yearly selection boards.

Labor, like Commerce, has the right to place its own people

in posts abroad, and occasionally does so via the Foreign Service Reserve. Most labor officers are regular FSO's, who fall into two general categories: old-timers who started life as regular labor men and joined the Service somewhere along the line, and regular examination-entry officers who have found the field interesting and have specialized in it—not deeply, in most cases, but at least to the extent of prepping in the subject and taking on two or more labor-officer assignments (not necessarily in succession). The old-timers are now dying out, but both categories have done well and have contributed their share of ambassadors to the Service.

There is no set rule establishing in which embassy section a labor officer shall work, but nowadays he is almost always found in the political section; at posts where the economic aspect of labor is paramount he may be placed under the economic chief, but this practice is becoming less and less prevalent. The economic section, and the AID mission with it, will often report intensively on wages, hours, labor disputes, manpower programs, cooperatives, and the like, but it is generally recognized that the work of the labor officer himself is essentially political. At posts large enough to support a full-time labor officer, he will almost always carry the title of attaché—and may have a full-time or part-time FSO assistant (sometimes a junior on rotation). At small posts, a political officer will usually do part-time labor duty. Big post or small, however, responsibility for labor affairs does not end with the reporting officer; everyone from the chief of mission on down has a representational duty to labor, as he does to commerce and industry, press and culture.

Table IV shows an "assistant information officer (labor)" in the USIS complement. The principal job of such an officer is to produce vernacular materials—mostly printed, but some audio-visual—under the guidance of the attaché for distribution in local labor circles. The labor information officer is a valuable adjunct in the continuing world-bloc struggle for labor men's minds. The AID staff, also, often has its complement of labor-oriented officers, generally interested in the manpower and training aspects of the picture.

With the increasingly important role of labor in shaping the political course of developing countries—old as well as new —the labor attaché has become a key officer at many missions. He is a star player in the election-guessing game, and on occasion he has been the only man at a post to be personally acquainted with the new leadership after a labor-based coup. Not only must he keep tabs on the many-sided movement for reporting purposes, he must also (discreetly, of course) be an activist in encouraging and supporting its democratic elements, through technical and other concrete assistance as well as through moral suasion and precept. In both, he may depend on wholehearted and very professional assistance from the American labor leadership, which itself provides not only technical assistance and training funds but also a considerable cadre of foreign affairs–oriented experts ("Have union card —will travel"). In one underdeveloped country, for example, a hard-pressed new government was seeking quietly to establish contact with American free trade unions, to ease its own unions away from the Communist-dominated World Federation of Trade Unions (WFTU). A well-connected labor attaché was able, quickly and without fanfare, to bring together representatives of the American Federation of Labor–Congress of Industrial Organizations (AFL-CIO) and the most effective of the local laborites; and the AFL-CIO, in turn, brought officials of the non-Communist International Federation of Christian Trade Unions (IFCTU) into the act. The ploy succeeded: the Communist element, sapped by corruption and political venality, gave way to an economically motivated free trade union group committeed to stability and progress. The United States does not win them all, of course, and sometimes the match becomes a stand-off between the forces of light and darkness. Nonetheless, American labor officers, backed by the American unions, have done a good job for their side in many parts of the world.

THE ECONOMIC SECTION

When Thomas Jefferson, first titular American Secretary of State, sent instructions to his sixteen consular representatives, he asked for "such political and commercial intelligence as you may think interesting to the United States." The kernels of economic information that dribbled in to Jefferson, who complained of their meagerness, have now grown into a mighty vine—and, as already noted, political and economic work have become the twin, intertwining rootstocks of American diplomacy. When the United States disposes of stockpiled tin, there are political repercussions in tin-rich Malaysia, Indonesia, and Bolivia, hence a political problem to three American embassies. When U.S. policy-makers set the goal of helping Korea to self-sufficiency through exports, Embassy Seoul has the job of reconciling this goal with nondisruption of the U.S. cotton textile market by Korean textiles.

By contrast with his political-officer colleague, the economic officer is usually (though not always) considered a functional specialist. Harr, in his 1962 statistical studies, uses as his distinctive criterion for specialization the situation of any FSO whose assignments during three points in time— 1954, 1958, 1962—were in the same field. On this basis, economic officers made up 18.1 per cent of his generalist group but only 15.3 per cent of his specialists. Generalist or specialist, the economic officer should have as a minimum the equivalent of an undergraduate major in economics (in which he at least learns the basic jargon) and, if he is going to specialize seriously, a year of advanced economic training.* Training or not, most economic officers tend to become more broadened

---

* The undergraduate major equivalent may now be obtained at the FSI's inservice "economic/commercial training" course (twenty-two weeks) which began in January, 1966, and by June, 1968, had graduated seventy-nine FSO's. An academic year of advanced university training (average in past four years: nine officers per year) helps meet what the FSI calls "the continuing and increasing need for officers who are sophisticated economic specialists in international trade and finance and economic development."

as they rise in rank, and they quite hold their own when the time comes to graduate to general executive responsibility.

The broad charter of the economic section of an embassy may be summarized as follows: advising the leadership on policies and guidelines for economic relations with the host country; analyzing and reporting on host-country economic conditions; negotiating on such matters as technical assistance, loans and investment, trade, finance, transportation, communications, and related matters; promoting American trade, consulting with and supporting American and local businessmen interested in two-way business relations with the United States; ensuring that all sections of the mission, other agencies as well as embassy, are briefed on economic conditions and trends that have a bearing on their activities.

There are, of course, all manner of specialized topics set forth in the ground rules for reporting. To select a few headings from the many listed in the *Foreign Affairs Manual:* Sino-Soviet bloc activities and relations; economic development in less-developed countries; economic-commercial treaties and agreements; restrictive business practices; public finance and fiscal policy; foreign exchange systems and rates; labor economic information (wages, hours, trends, and so on); labor in country development; socio-economic matters (health, education, housing and urban development)—plus, of course, the whole gamut of statistical economic reporting and trade promotion and protection. Periodic or "repetitive" reporting requirements are outlined in the Bureau of Economic Affairs' "Comprehensive Economic Reporting Program" (CERP).

Table IV shows, in addition to the titular economic officers, three commercial and one each transportation/communications, petroleum, and financial officers. Commercial officers are found at virtually all posts—or at least commercial work gets done. The role of the commercial attaché is taken up at length in Chapter VIII, since he is a chief protagonist in the story of service to the American public. Suffice it to note here that the State-Commerce agreement of 1956 has produced an harmonious and mutually advantageous interchange, and Commerce seems content to let State carry the brunt of its overseas work load.

The transportation-and-communication job, when it exists, may cover widely varying activities. At one post, it may simply entail handling day-to-day relations with airlines, cable companies, and the like, and reporting on developments of interest to the United States. At another, it may involve the active negotiation of agreements with the host country—or, conversely, dissuading the latter from agreements with other countries that are unfavorable to U.S. interests. Only where there is great volume and interest (political or economic) is it a full-time job. The incumbent is usually a middle-grade FSO who has applied himself to the subject and taken on the job (in which, it might be noted, he may often as not be called upon for a repeat performance at another post).

Another "sub-specialty" is fisheries and the fishing industry. The Department of Interior's Bureau of Commercial Fisheries is the interested agency, and has placed fisheries attachés at a few key spots; generally, however, the subject is covered by an officer of the economic section. Agricultural matters, too, may be farmed out to that section where there is insufficient volume or U.S. interest to justify the assignment of a representative of the Foreign Agricultural Service. (The work of the agricultural attaché will be discussed in Chapter VI.)

The petroleum officer (usually with attaché rank) is nowadays almost always an FSO, although his specialty comes under the Department of the Interior. As noted in Chapter I, Interior's Bureau of Mines gained the right in 1935 to maintain a service of mineral specialists abroad, then turned it back in 1943. State and Interior have agreed that most petroleum officer positions abroad shall be filled by qualified FSO's rather than by Interior officers. Qualification includes a four and one-half-month training period in the United States prior to posting abroad, an arrangement that has worked out very well, since experience has shown that a knowledge of foreign ways and a broad acquaintanceship among host-country petroleum people is usually more important than narrow, specialized knowledge of oil itself. For one thing, a petroleum officer must at times negotiate as well as report.

The same general arrangement with Interior is implicit in the reporting on minerals other than petroleum, although here the reporting load is seldom sufficient to warrant more than a cursory briefing and the gift of some background and reference materials. The writer knows of one young FSO assigned to an ore-rich country who just happened to be a trained geologist (no credit to Personnel, apparently). He was given the minerals-reporting job and did very well at it, but the field was not generally active enough to warrant specialization and he reverted to regular Foreign Service duties on his next assignment.

At a post where financial problems are sophisticated and complex, a Treasury specialist may be assigned, and may be expected to work in the economic section under the economic chief. If the financial work load is not that complex (and it seldom is), reporting will be handled by a qualified member of the regular economic section. The work of the financial attaché as a representative of the Treasury Department will be described in Chapter VI.

At a small embassy or consulate, the economic/commercial work may be handled by one officer—or even a part of one officer. At a middle-to-large post, the section will have its basic complement of economic and commercial officers plus whatever specialists the country work load may call for.

THE CONSULAR SECTION

Consular work at an embassy is performed by a consular section, headed by a titular consul general if the size of the post warrants it, by a consul if not. At a few superposts, there is a counselor for consular affairs, with supervisory responsibility for the constituent posts. Statutory consular functions fall into two broad categories: citizenship and protection work, and visa-issuance. The former category, with related duties in such fields as notarials and seamen's affairs, consists almost entirely of services to the American public abroad, and is discussed in Chapter VIII.

The processing and issuance of visas is a service to the host- and third-country public, and constitutes the major work load of any consular section or post (as of January 1968, 68 per cent). These documents may be either immigrant or non-immigrant visas, the latter valid for temporary sojourn. "Visitor's visas" are issued on a far larger scale than the immigrant type (e.g., 84 per cent of the 1967 work load at London, 93 per cent at Mexico City) but 60 per cent of all visa personnel are employed in immigrant work, which entails painstaking documentation, careful processing, and, at times, painful decisions.

The Justice Department's Immigration and Naturalization Service (INS) is responsible for enforcement of the immigration and nationality laws, but the admission of aliens seeking U.S. citizenship is controlled by visa regulations administered by the State Department's Bureau of Security and Consular Affairs at home and by the Foreign Service abroad. Final responsibility for the issuance or denial of a visa rests with the consular officer overseas. However, the visa (in Latin, *carta visa* means "document seen") is not in itself an entry permit, but only authority to apply for admission at the port of U.S. entry—and the INS may still find the applicant inadmissible. This happens seldom—in cases of doubt an officer will solicit an advisory opinion before issuing a visa—but when it does, somebody gets a black mark.

Most of today's senior FSO's—at least those who started at the bottom—have done a stint in visas, sometimes two or even three. They were birds of passage, however, with continuity and guidance provided by old-line consular specialists known then as noncareer vice consuls—many of whom stayed at the same post for years and years, and all of whom knew the visa regulations virtually by heart. Some of the younger of these men were Wristonized, but whether FSO or FSSO they remain a specialist group—numerically the largest after the administrative specialists—and the backbone of the visa service. Many a new FSO still does a visa tour, especially if assigned to a consulate, but, unless he is attracted to the work, it is unlikely that he will have to stay in it against his will.

The visa function is important to the United States—and, to the aspiring immigrant, vital. Procedures have by now been worked out whereby an applicant, through a mailed instruction kit, may assemble all his documentation before appearing at a consulate, then spend only one long day there being processed by skilled local employees. At the end of that day comes the last act—the moment of truth—when his assembled file has been reviewed by an American consular officer and he is called in for the personal interview and examination. If all goes well, the officer takes the applicant's oath and signs the visa. When that young officer stands before the American flag and tells the applicant to raise his right hand, he carries on his shoulders the dignity and authority of the U.S. Government.

Not all officers show themselves worthy of such dignity and authority, and very occasionally one yields to temptation—not necessarily in the form of an outright bribe, but at least in the use of influence for personal advantage. The fact that there have been only a handful of these in the history of the Service speaks well for the American fiber. Temptations can be great. For example, in the first years after the Chinese Red takeover, the Consulate General at Hong Kong was literally besieged by supplicants, and an Occidental entering the building faced heart-rending scenes as he fought his way through clutching hands and stopped his ears to offers of reward.

In some situations, desperate applicants, finding themselves quite ineligible, go off and quietly commit suicide. A few are not so quiet; one unsuccessful applicant in Latin America pulled out a live grenade and destroyed himself and a piece of the consulate just after the vice consul, luckily, had gathered his locals and made his escape. Refusal scenes can be dramatic and exhausting, but they are something a consular officer must earn to live with. Not infrequently there may be a sequel in the form of a congressional inquiry, prompted by constitutents who are friends or relatives of the rejected. These inquiries, fortunately, are handled on a common-sense basis by the congressman involved. (More will be said on this subject in Chapter VII.)

Nonimmigrant or visitor's visas pose a problem more of volume than of technicalities and blasted hopes. (In 1967, the embassies at London and Mexico City issued some 126,000 and 130,000, respectively.) Embarrassing situations arise, nevertheless. A powerful local politico or well-known savant wants to visit the United States—may even have been invited by a prestigious American group—but there are clearly documented Red marks in his record and he is ineligible under the provisions of the Immigration and Nationality Act. Exceptions are possible, and the U.S. Government is lenient in the matter of waivers of convenience, but these things must be approved at home and may take time. Meanwhile, there will be some bad moments for the consular officer, who must temporize tactfully until he can get the word. If the word is no— bango! another anti-American convert.

Most visa work is routine, even though much of it is done under pressure. Routine or no, the visa officer is in the front line when it comes to setting the American image before the host-country public. He is the first American official many of them have ever seen, and to them he represents the U.S.A. He, for his part, gets to know quite a bit about them, and he soon learns to communicate in their language. He has to.

THE ADMINISTRATIVE SECTION

Before World War II, the administrative section of an embassy usually consisted of a first or second secretary in the titular capacity and a junior officer who did the leg work, which included such taxing duties as standing over a local employee putting inventory numbers on chair bottoms and checking whether space was being occupied as listed. The same young man and his locals kept track of personnel and property, while a clerk-accountant (and his adding machine) paid the embassy bills and the staff. There was no large-scale "general services" operation, because there was nothing to service outside the chancery and the residence. If the first secretary's furnace broke down, his servants phoned a local furnace man; if he wanted an extra phone extension in his house, he or one of his minions wrangled with the phone company in person. As a general rule, no one except a VIP or a courier was "met." A young officer arriving in town by train, plane, or boat checked in at a hotel, washed up and donned a clean shirt, then made his way to the Embassy to report for duty.

The post-World War II expansion changed all that. Aside from sheer increase in numbers, many of the rank and file—if they had been abroad before—had been in or with the armed forces, where the business of watching over their every living requirement had become an occupation (often an end) in itself. Especially with the masses of civilian employees in occupied territories, a large amount of logistic support and administrative control was necessary (the lone-operator wolves were as much a problem as the flock-bound sheep) and it was not long before the "PX complex" rubbed off on the Foreign Service contingents. The metropoli were beset by shortages and black markets; the colonies and outposts were disrupted and logistically troubled. In most parts of the world, do-it-yourself administration was no longer possible and "administration for administration's sake" took over. Its practitioners, many of them recent graduates of the noncombatant army bureaucracy, piled up layer upon layer of paper work and shielded their operations with shibboleths only they could understand.

In due course, the counterrevolution set in. A pioneer band of regular Foreign Service officers, acting on the basis of "if you can't lick 'em, join 'em," applied themselves to mastering the mumbo-jumbo and took on administrative chores themselves. At the same time, some of the new empire-builders seemed to experience a change of heart, and became more of a help than a hindrance. By the time Wristonization got under way, quite a few of the "admin types" had become conditioned to Foreign Service teamwork and were ready for the FSO status they received.

Meanwhile, the movement for political independence was gaining strength in the world. Remote new outposts had to be opened, or expanded from one-horse consulates. As the Yankee invaders moved in on places equipped at best to support a small élite of colonial administrators and businessmen, government-supplied logistics became a must. The alternative of "living on the economy" was prohibitively expensive in many places (exchange rates were unrealistic and colonial employees were heavily subsidized) and the U.S. Government often found it cheaper and easier to build compounds and set up commissaries than to triple or quadruple living allowances. The regular Foreign Service continued to manage on its own in many parts—in Latin America as well as in Europe—but wherever such big affiliates as AID or a MAAG were installed, total logistic support was expected and had to be provided.

Although not a healthy development for American diplomacy (even the "new" type), much of the build-up was unavoidable. And the picture is by no means solely one of golden-ghetto living and the stuff of *The Ugly American*.* The general services sections of the Embassy and AID did yeoman, and at times heroic, service in keeping hundreds of Americans in the Kabul area fed, watered, and sheltered in landlocked Afghanistan during the winter of 1963–64—a winter that began with snow, ice, fires, broken pipes, and dry wells and ended with earthquakes followed by floods. At a Southeast Asian post, wells and septic tanks were dug, health measures instituted, a compound jerry-built (but built), and ingenious

* This book by Eugene Burdick and William J. Lederer shook up the United States about its overseas representatives. The picture it presented was exaggerated, but its effects not all unhealthy.

schemes devised to supplement what was laughingly called the local economy. (This did not, however, mean a life entirely free of water buffalo meat.) In Africa, several regional supply centers were set up in coastal cities, to cut down to weeks the former up-to-six-months' wait at interior posts for such items as diapers, office machines, and medicines.* The administrative officer in postwar Prague himself drove a truck to Nürnberg every two weeks for supplies. Embassy Helsinki served as procurement and personal-service office for Americans stationed in Moscow, furnishing such locally difficult items as paint, wallpaper, draperies, and replacement parts for American cars.

The administrative section in Table IV is believed typical for a fair-sized post; at a superpost, the elements would be more or less the same, but with more Indians per subchief. Where the administrative head holds the rank of counselor— usually as an FSO-2, sometimes an O-1—he may have a titular administrative officer under him (O-3 or O-4) to "run the shop" while he himself deals at higher and broader levels with the embassy leadership and the other-agency administrative chiefs. At a middle-sized post, there will usually be an FSO-4 or O-5 administrative officer. At a mini-post such as Rwanda (seven Americans including AID personnel), the whole administrative section may consist of one FSO-6 or O-7 (or FSSO equivalent).

The general services officer and his assistants do about what the title indicates—whatever is required in the way of repairs, maintenance, supplies, straw-bossing coolies, and so on. No GSO should be sent to an outpost unless he thoroughly understands the inner workings of a flush toilet.

Personnel officers, more often than not, are women. They

* The immensity of Africa's land mass, realized by relatively few people, is pointed up by the polite complaint of the president of a small, up-country republic. He was very grateful, he said, for the American Government's independence gift of a DC-3, but the plane took three days at its slow speed to get from his capital to the coast. Would it not be possible to replace the "Dakota" with, say, a small jet?

handle the considerable paper work involved in personnel transactions, but the good ones are also sympathetic souls attuned to the hopes and fears of their clients and ready to go to bat for them. The budget and fiscal (sometimes budget and management) officer presides over a small fiscal empire, which may include, in addition to a disbursing officer (paymaster), several American assistants and a host of locals and calculating machines.

The size of the communications set-up depends on the size, location, and work load of the post, but all handling of "classified" material—coding/decoding, filing, pouching/unpouching, as well as typing—must be done by Americans. At a small post, one clerk (or part of a clerk) may handle all communications work, doing the coding with a small, table-model "MOX" machine—and, even, today, with a "one-time pad" (OTP) in reserve for emergencies.* A large post will house bank upon bank of electronic monsters requiring a full-time telecommunications nursemaid to keep them happy and productive. Posts not having their own transmitting facilities can often lease a private line from the local posts and telegraphs, thus feeding their messages through it direct to destination. As for pouches, making them up can be heavy work, to which assigning a girl is ill advised; she only has to summon male assistance (not always willingly lent) come pouch day.

Before leaving communications, we should mention the problem of world time differences, which, especially in Europe and Africa, can be the bane of a communicator's existence—and of a substantive officer's as well. When it is 7 P.M. in Washington, it is 1 A.M. in Paris (and the Congo) and 3 A.M. in Moscow—yet too few officers in Washington seem

---

* OTP, slow but safe, is really a two-pad system—one pad in the sending office, its counterpart in the receiving. No two pages of a pad, or other pads, carry the same coding symbols. Each time a message is sent, that page is destroyed—and no page is of value to the enemy until used. Principal officers at out-of-the-way posts are well advised to learn the drill, even today. Many a crisis strikes when the one code clerk is absent, ill, or otherwise incapacitated.

to focus on these differences.* A panting desk officer who finally gets his crisis telegram cleared at 7 P.M. dashes off to the message center with a "Flash" or "Immediate," and shortly after 1 A.M., local time, a communicator and a political officer are roused by the post's Marine Guard with what turns out to be an instruction to "SEE FORN MIN IMMEDIATELY." At least one officer has suggested firing back a reminder that at the hour of receipt the foreign minister might not much welcome the idea of being seen.

Most posts from middle size up have a full-time security officer, in addition to the U.S. Marines (discussed in Chapter VI). He is charged not only with physical security but with investigations and clearances (for local employment, immigration, and so on). At certain centrally placed large posts, there are regional as well as post security officers; these men tour their areas and ride herd on the nonprofessional security officers at the smaller posts—usually the administrative officer but at times even the DCM. (During the McCarthy era, security officers could be and often were petty tyrants and witch-hunters, but all that has changed. Today's breed are solid citizens and full members of the embassy team.)

There are various jobs not listed on Table IV because they are usually filled only at superposts, e.g., such specialists as building superintendents. Also not mentioned are the representatives of the Office of Foreign Buildings (FBO), which is based in Washington but maintains regional officers at selected posts around the world. The FBO is responsible for acquiring, maintaining, and disposing of real property of the U.S. Government (houses, office buildings, warehouses, et al.) and its regional representatives ride their boundaries, inspecting projects and prospects lined up by their posts and keeping tabs on properties already acquired.

* It has happened at the highest level. During the Congo-Léopoldville crisis of 1961–62 the "Congo desk officer" was sometimes J.F.K. himself, and he seemed to have some of his best ideas around 9 or 10 P.M. To the President, ideas meant action, and action in such circumstances meant a long-distance call to his ambassador—at 3 or 4 A.M., local time.

As has been seen, the administrative officer presides over an empire of technicians. Not many of these aspire to the broader phases of diplomatic activity, although some do—and a few succeed. The rank-and-file, if happy in their specialties, can make a satisfactory career within the empire. Those who are not happy, or have just had a one-shot whirl at seeing the world, will probably leave the Service for other fields.

The administrative officer himself has undergone a metamorphosis during the past decade or so. In the bad old postwar days, there were a few "can do" officers, but many more who were expert in finding ways not to do things for others while operating the best of things for themselves. Today's administrative chief is a broad-gauge officer of proven executive ability, alive to the over-all U.S. interest. The writer knows offhand of six chiefs of mission who have been titular administrative officers, and of two others who have held senior administrative positions in the Department. Doubtless there are more.

THE CONSTITUENT POSTS

There is only one embassy per sovereign state, located in the capital, but in a well-established country there may be half a dozen or more "constituent" or subordinate posts. These are the consulates or consulates general, the latter being simply larger consulates in cities where there are important U.S. interests and activities.* In Germany, for example, there are six good-sized consulates general with bigger staffs and more varied duties than many a small embassy, while at several posts—notably Hong Kong, last of the great colonial holdings —the Consul General carries the rank of minister and his staff has responsibilities comparable to those of a diplomatic mission.

Whether he is a consul in charge of a two-man post or a

* There are no functions a consul general may perform that a consul may not. The situation is in fact slightly the reverse; because of the way certain U.S. states word their laws, there are legal functions that may be performed by a consul, or even a vice consul, but not by a consul general.

consul general over a hundred, the principal officer is the
Number One representative of the Foreign Service in his consular district—his Ambassador's proconsul or satrap. In this
preeminence, he has the edge on a "captive" consul general
within the Embassy, who is only a section chief. A principal
officer will naturally defer to his overlord when the latter visits
his district, but even then he continues in charge of "the
shop," in somewhat the same position as the captain of a ship
when the admiral is on board. If visiting Ambassador White
wants to send a cable from Consul Black's territory, he heads
it "From White" but signs it "Black."

The degree of a principal officer's independence within his
bailiwick depends on various factors. Chief among these are
such considerations as his accessibility or remoteness, the importance of his enterprise to the country-wide U.S. interest,
and the *modus operandi* of the chief of mission. Some ambassadors keep their consuls on a tight rein, others delegate
extensively—this in turn depending often on the abilities of a
consul himself. In most countries, it is the DCM who deals
with the constituent chiefs, unless there happens to be an
Embassy-based supervisory consul general.

The Department's ground rules (the *Foreign Service Manual*) make it clear that the consulates are expected to play a
very definite role in the political and economic reporting programs, and not to subordinate such work to other activities
excepting where necessary to ensure fulfillment of statutory
consular functions (visas, citizenship, et al.). A constituent
post may be directed to report on certain topics—notably
economic—to the Embassy rather than to the Department, to
enable the mission to consolidate and collate country-wide
reporting for a coordinated submission to Washington. The
principal officer, however, has discretionary authority to report directly to the Department whenever he deems it fitting
and necessary, and he is not formally obliged to send a copy
to his Embassy. (He seldom fails to do so, but there have been
some famous rows over "declarations of independence" by

principal consular officers.) Examples of topics generally reported directly: crises or emergencies, physical or political (earthquake, assassination); crucial or unexpected local developments (party in power loses by-election, Communists make friendly gesture); statutory consular emergencies (visa problem-case, dead American citizen); certain assigned periodic reports (monthly political summary of events in the district).

Particularly at a large consulate general, the principal officer (known customarily as "the CG") has, at his level, the same set of responsibilities for his district as the chief of mission has for the country. His Number Two, the deputy principal officer (DPO) is a junior counterpart of the Embassy's DCM. The Consul General has his section chiefs, his other-agency representatives, his "little country team"—and his problems of coordination, discipline, morale, and staff welfare.

In structure, a typical consulate general (or good-sized consulate) has the same five basic sections as an embassy—executive, political, economic, consular, administrative—but the staffing will usually be weighted heavily in favor of statutory consular functions. Political reporting is generally handled by the CG and his deputy, with certain topics and areas assigned on a voluntary-extracurricular basis to junior officers occupied with statutory duties. There is usually a titular economic/commercial officer, Number Three in the hierarchy, and a titular administrative officer. The commercial and administrative chiefs may have each a junior on rotation—or, at the largest posts, a regularly assigned assistant. Citizenship and protection work, excepting at big tourist-turnover consulates, may be handled by a chief of section (rank of consul) with one junior officer, the latter often on rotation. Visa work is the bread-and-butter operation of the average consulate and demands more staff, both officer and clerical—although most of the latter is local. At a post with a heavy immigrant and nonimmigrant work load, the number of visa officers may equal, if indeed not surpass, the rest of the officer complement put together.

The number and size of other-agency elements will depend on the nature of the work load and the location of the post. At a consulate near the Mexican border, for example, there may be representatives of Justice (FBI) and Treasury (Bureau of Narcotics) who work with their Mexican counterparts in controlling crime and contraband; there may also be representatives of Agriculture working on joint pest control and similar mutual ventures. These people are given office space and logistic support and are under the broad authority of the principal officer; they attend his staff meetings when in town and keep him generally informed of their doings. At a large, centrally located consulate general in Europe there may be a dozen or more foreign-affairs–oriented agencies represented, plus regional offices of such organizations as the General Accounting Office or the Internal Revenue Service, interested in domestic affairs abroad. And although they are not "other-agency," there will be Chinese-language officers at posts (consulates as well as embassies) where there are large communities of overseas Chinese. There will always be a USIS—often with branch information and cultural centers elsewhere in the consular district. In less-developed countries, the consulate staff may include district representatives of AID and/or the Peace Corps—and, in countries beset by problems of insurgency or other internal belligerency, provincial representatives of the Embassy's military elements.

All this gives a consul general plenty to do in the way of supervision and executive direction. His position, like that of the DCM, is reserved almost exclusively to senior FSO's of recognized managerial and representational capacity.* Like his ambassador, he must ride his boundaries, give speeches, tramp through the boondocks, play a prominent role in American and host-country club and social activity, handle congressional, press, and other visiting firemen, and make certain that his staff is not laggard in its duty toward the American image.

---

* There has been one exception known to the writer of a political appointee as consul general, and he has heard of one or two others—but they are rare.

If he has not served his consular apprenticeship as a junior officer, he will be well advised to do some homework in visas and citizenship—if only to avoid looking silly when an influential citizen buttonholes him with a simple question about his partner's nephew's eligibility for a visa.

Life at a small consular post is somewhat different. As at a mini-embassy, an officer may wear several hats and do his own leg work, but his responsibilities are often greater than those of an officer several grades his senior at an embassy or consulate general. Being a big frog in a little puddle has its advantages. An officer in charge of a hot spot will have reporting opportunities galore—and he may even have the distinction of being beleaguered, held hostage, or generally roughed up by less-developed elements. This always looks good on the record, provided the officer carries the situation off in the accepted Foreign Service tradition—and avoids death or dismemberment.

The principal officer at a two- or three-man consulate is still Number One U.S. representative in his consular district—the man who has the right to carry the Stars and Stripes and the thirteen-star consular flag on his official car, even though it be a jeep. Life is informal within a consulate, and a young principal officer may properly be Joe to his colleagues when *en famille,* even though they play up and snap to when the boss is on show.

THE SPECIAL MISSIONS

In Chapter II, we noted that Foreign Service officers, in addition to service in embassies or consulates or in Washington, might be detailed for duty with international organizations, commissions, or bodies—such tours of duty not to exceed four years unless extended by the Secretary. A few officers are assigned to various bilateral bodies such as the U.S.–Mexican International Boundary and Water Commission, whose executive secretary is customarily an FSO. Most jobs, however, are with the U.S. missions to multilateral international organizations. The number of these varies from time to time but for the past several years has been constant at nine, namely: the United Nations, New York; the Organization of American States, Washington; the International Atomic Energy Agency, Vienna; the North Atlantic Treaty Organization, Brussels; the Organization for Economic Cooperation and Development, Paris; the International Civil Aviation Organization, Montreal; the Mission to the European Communities, Brussels; the Mission to the European Office of the United Nations and other International Organizations, Geneva; and the Office of the Permanent U.S. Representative to the United Nations Educational, Scientific and Cultural Organization, Paris.

These missions are generally headed by high-level political appointees, but occasionally an FSO is named, for example, to the U.S. delegation to the OECD.* Below the top, Foreign Service people predominate—FSO's, FSR's, and a number of FSS secretarial employees. Officers need not fear getting outside the career mainstream, and many of the jobs are professionally interesting. The average FSO is nonetheless glad, when his tour is done, to get back to a line-officer's job and to membership in a country team. Only senior chiefs sit on that team as representatives, but every officer at an embassy or consulate is a member and contributes to its achievements—to which we now turn our attention.

* Charles W. Yost, a recently retired FSO career ambassador, was made Ambassador to the United Nations in 1969.

V

The Country Team, Coordinator of the U.S. Presence Overseas

The scene is an American embassy in the mid-1960's. It is 10 A.M., and the country team is gathering in the main conference room for its weekly meeting.

The team members stroll in and take their appointed places at the conference table, some of them carrying cups of coffee from an urn steaming invitingly in the corner. In the center, at the right of the place reserved for the Ambassador, sits the deputy chief of mission (DCM); it is he who will conduct the meeting. Across from him, flanked by a recording secretary, is a younger officer—the executive assistant to the Ambassador, one of whose duties it is to ride herd on the country team agenda and follow up on such action as the proceedings may call for.

Also present are two embassy counselors (political and economic), the AID representative, the counselor for public affairs (USIS), the CIA and Peace Corps representatives, the chief of the Military Assistance Advisory Group (MAAG), and the defense attaché (senior of the three armed services attachés). Other senior officers—the agricultural attaché, for example—may attend when matters within their sphere are up for discussion; it is on this basis that the Peace Corps is represented today. Finally, there is one very junior officer, whose job as staff aide to the Ambassador is rotated periodically— thus giving all FSO probationers the opportunity to sit in on

132

the deliberations of the Embassy's senior policy group. These persons comprise the country team, whose job it is to ensure that all available information and all available U.S. resources are brought to bear on the problems at hand.

The Ambassador enters, and the officers rise. He looks around with a quizzical smile: "Good morning, gentlemen—what have we on the docket for today?" The DCM hands him a copy of the agenda, calling attention to a slight change from the draft shown him earlier, and the team settles down to work.

The first item is the AID technical assistance program for the coming fiscal year, presented for approval. The AID representative reviews his proposals, questions are asked and details discussed. It is noted that the work of the AID secondary education specialist will complement and be made to dovetail with Peace Corps activity in the same field. The DCM has been checking the details of the proposed program and gives it as his opinion that it conforms to policy guidelines, noting that all elements of the team have been consulted and concur. The Ambassador agrees, and approves submission to Washington.

The DCM then asks the public affairs counselor to speak to the next agenda item—the matter of a new cultural center to be established by the USIS one block from the national university's main gate. The counselor, in making his presentation, recognizes the physical risks of such proximity, but says he and his colleagues believe them worth taking in order to be able to offer a convenient and attractive place for students' study and research—as well as for cultural events, possibly including political debates. The team is well briefed on the project, as there has already been considerable intramural discussion of the subject. The members are unanimously in favor of going ahead, and it is so recorded.*

The Peace Corps training report is next up for discussion. It

---

* As things turned out in this true case, problems of lapidation and graffitti were minimal but that of book-theft became fairly major.

is brief and satisfactory, as is a proposed Peace Corps questionnaire that has been circulated for the team's information, and the group passes to the final item on the agenda: the question of whether or not there is a Rightist coup in the making. Despite hot and cold rumors at all levels, the Ambassador has not been able to get much change out of the foreign minister or other senior officials, who blandly pooh-pooh such talk. They tend to tell the Ambassador what they think he wants to hear: that the people are solidly behind the social reforms of the government's "New Program," that the reactionary opposition cannot unite; that the military is firmly behind the government and the West, and so on.

The defense attaché says that the top military brass may indeed be with the government—the generals and admirals enjoy their position of favor and privilege—but it is becoming more and more evident that the officer corps below the topmost levels is not happy with the country's situation. The attaché has noted that the middle-grade officers are following political developments very closely indeed—for them—and adds that there have been significant shifts in the middle-grade command structure in certain key outlying military districts. (He has reported these to Washington and to the Ambassador.) The military assistance chief says that the reports of his officers on duty in the northern provinces confirm the attaché's observations.

The political counselor has a fairly firm report of clandestine contacts between well-placed field-grade troop commanders in the capital area and key civilians of the extreme Right, including two who are in exile in a neighboring state; the officers appear to be shopping around and assessing their chances. He further notes that, according to the labor attaché, the unions are not as happy with the New Program as the government seems to think they are, and that several labor leaders are known to have been flirting discreetly with the Right. The counselor does not yet see trouble at the door, but he gives the situation a fifty-fifty chance of becoming critical at an early date unless (1) the government pulls itself together and takes firm steps to protect its rear and (2) it makes visible concessions to the growing and general disenchantment with its New Program. The public affairs and economic counselors cite cases in point with respect to disenchantment, drawn from their recent talks with friends in various walks of life, from egg-head to hard-head.

There is general agreement that the situation is probably not much this side of the "Distant Early Warning" stage, as yet, but that it will bear careful watching. No one believes the government to be as oblivious of the portents as it seems to be, yet it continues to bumble along on its well-meaning, reasonably honest, but increasingly unpopular course. Meanwhile, there is the U.S. interest to be considered. Discussion on that score produces a clear consensus in favor of the regime in power, if only as the lesser of two evils.

The Ambassador, summing up, concludes that the possibilities for a coup must be taken seriously. He enjoins continuing vigilance on the part of his officers, and lays down several guidelines for the coordination of information. He goes on to say that the present regime, for all its faults, has given the country the nearest thing it has had to democracy for many a year, and that the apparent alternative—a return to dictatorship of the oligarchy—would not sit at all well with either the U.S. Government or the American public. He sketches out the substance of a telegram to Washington—with copies to certain nearby embassies—reporting the team's current estimate of the situation and giving his own ideas on what constructive steps the Embassy may unobtrusively take at this stage. The DCM designates the political counselor as drafting officer for the message and asks the executive assistant to work with him in coordinating the views of the country team.

The meeting breaks up at 11:10 A.M.

THE NIGHT THEY BROUGHT THE COLONEL IN

Not all country team meetings are scheduled in advance and not all follow a prepared agenda. One midnight in Caracas, in 1964, a visiting inspector received a phone call from the Marine Guard: "Sir, they've brought the Colonel in, and the DCM says would you like to come down to the Embassy and see the fun?"

The colonel, assistant chief of the air section of the Military Assistance Advisory Group, had been kidnapped by the underground Left when leaving his home for work three days before. This was the second kidnapping at the post within a year, in addition to such attentions as bombings, car-burnings, and threatening phone calls. One young secretary not only received insulting calls but had a pot shot taken at her from the street while she was leaning over the balcony rail of her penthouse apartment. In 1962, a bomb had gone off in an upstairs men's room of the chancery no more than thirty seconds after the political counselor had left it; one officer who happened to be nearby had his hearing permanently impaired. The terror, aimed principally at discrediting the United States and its role in Venezuela, was brutal and purposeful.

In the case of the colonel, however, the kidnappers quickly found they had a bear by the tail. The country team, on getting word of the abduction—which it did, fortunately, less than half an hour after the fact—went into high gear and kept on top of the situation during the eighty-six hours it took for the officer to be released. As command post, clearing house, and active liaison between Washington and the Venezuelan Government, the team played a key role in putting such heat on the kidnappers that they got rattled and dumped their captive far sooner than expected. The colonel, for his part, gave his captors a hard time through his quick wits and his refusal to be bullied. But all told, there were some bad moments for him and for the American Embassy when the Leftists made known a threat to link the colonel's fate with that of a Viet Cong terrorist then due to be executed in Saigon.

When the country team members reached the Embassy shortly after midnight, they found the lobby ablaze and flashbulbs flashing as the colonel, an arm around his ecstatic young wife, submitted cheerfully to an impromptu press interview.

Once that was over, he and his wife accompanied the team upstairs for a debriefing session. The management had thoughtfully provided something stronger than coffee and coke, and the two-hour interrogation was spirited but thorough. Both colonel and country team had the happy feeling of a test come through with flying colors.

THE COUNTRY-TEAM CONCEPT

The term "country team" first came into use in 1951 via the Clay Paper, an interdepartmental agreement based on the recommendation of General Lucius D. Clay, whom President Truman had asked for ideas on how to shore up the eroding prestige of his ambassadors. By this agreement, the chief of the U.S. diplomatic mission and the heads of the military and economic aid programs in a given country were to "constitute a team under the leadership of the Ambassador."

The country team, an evolutionary rather than revolutionary development in American diplomacy, is simply a management tool; it has no legal status nor any established *modus operandi*. Most chiefs of mission have found it a very useful vehicle for coordination and consensus, but it is only that. The Department of State has sensibly refrained from making the technique mandatory, recognizing that each ambassador must be left free to choose and use the coordination methods best suited to the needs of his mission—and that, whatever methods he may use, when all discussion is finished and all opinions are in, it is he who must make the decision and formulate the position.

The team concept evolved in response to a clear and urgent need. In the years after World War II, as the worldwide responsibilities of the United States multiplied, so did the number of its internationally oriented government bureaus and agencies. Everybody wanted to get into the foreign affairs act, and many did. At the same time, American military bases and installations, with sizable forces, were being maintained not only in occupied but also in allied countries.

On October 1, 1939, the career Foreign Service officer corps had numbered 833, including 114 recently amalgamated commercial and agricultural specialists. In July, 1945, the authorized strength was augmented from 860 to 1,160—then to 1,280 in 1947 with the first increments from the Manpower Act. Today, there are over 5,100 FSO/FSR's, but there are also thousands upon thousands employed by other government and private organizations working on foreign problems —many in agencies that either did not exist or were concerned almost solely with domestic affairs two decades ago. In the postwar years, the overseas missions of the U.S. Government soon passed from their traditional status—that of relatively compact diplomatic or consular units—to become small bodies surrounded by the multiple new arms of the overseas effort: semi-independent aid missions, military assistance groups, information and cultural services, scientific units, and others. With each agency having its own program and chief, its own expertise, and its own Washington principals to report to, the need for coordination, cooperation, and unified over-all country direction became critical. (See also Chapter VI.)

A further divisive element was added when a number of agencies wangled ambassadorial rank for their regional representatives in Europe. American ambassadors and free-wheeling special emissaries proliferated in the first postwar decade, and it was by no means unusual for a "diplomatic" ambassador to find himself on the outside looking in while important negotiations between other U.S. agencies and foreign governments were in progress.

In such a situation, the authority and prestige of an ambassador who was chief of diplomatic mission, accredited to a host-country chief of state as the President's personal representative, had to be reaffirmed. Presidents Truman and Eisenhower took strong steps in this direction, and, as the country team concept gradually emerged, the principle of "one country–one mission chief" was reestablished. In May, 1961, President Kennedy, in a letter to all his ambassadors in the field, unequivocally affirmed their country leadership—and President Johnson confirmed it after him. Pertinent highlights of the Kennedy letter were:

> I shall count on you to oversee and coordinate all the activities of the United States Government in _____.
>
> You are in charge of the entire United States Diplomatic Mission, and I shall expect you to supervise all of its operations . . . not only the personnel of the Department of State and the Foreign Service, but also the representatives of all other United States agencies. . . .
>
> Needless to say, the representatives of other agencies are expected to communicate directly with their offices here in Washington, and in the event of a decision by you in which they do not concur, they may ask to have the decision reviewed by a higher authority in Washington.
>
> However, it is their responsibility to keep you fully informed of their views and activities and to abide by your decisions unless in some particular instance you and they are notified to the contrary.
>
> . . . The United States Diplomatic Mission includes Service Attachés, Military Assistance Advisory Groups, and other Military components attached to the Mission. It does not, however, include United States military forces operating in the field. . . .
>
> Although . . . not in the line of military command, nevertheless, as Chief of Mission, you should work closely with the appropriate area military commander to assure the full exchange of information. If it is your opinion that activities by the United States military forces may adversely affect your over-all relations with the people or government of _____, you should promptly discuss the matter with the military commander and, if necessary, request a decision by higher authority.

The Kennedy letter, in the third paragraph of the excerpts given above, recognizes that important elements of the larger missions look beyond the Ambassador to Washington for staff, support, and guidance, and that their loyalties tend to lie in that direction. However, the Ambassador is clearly established as head of his team in the field.

The significant change that has taken place over the past few years is that a chief of mission is now called upon to manage programs, in addition to maintaining his traditional relations with the host government in such matters as representation and negotiation. Although he has the advisory resources of his country team, to be sure, he must himself also have a thorough understanding of the programs in order to manage them effectively. It is his job to keep in perspective the totality of U.S. interests and activities in the country of his accreditation, and it is he who must grasp all the implications of proposed courses of action and decide what is in the best American interest over all. Nevertheless, although he must not use the country team as a vehicle for decisions which should be his alone, he can lend weight to his own recommendations if he can say they represent the team's consensus.

ANATOMY OF THE TEAM

In practice, there are no set rules for the make-up or the activity of a country team. These matters must depend on the style and temperament of the Ambassador, as well as on such factors as the country situation, nature of the program, personalities involved, and so on. At some posts there is no defined membership, the team changing its composition to meet the requirements of the problems at hand. There are ambassadors who restrict basic membership to the heads of the AID and Defense Department components and discuss policy only. At the other end of the scale, one former chief of mission took the line that as the President's representative he was "above it all" and left it to the DCM to run team meetings, then report to him. At the smaller posts in Africa—where there may be five or six Americans in all, clerical help included—the term "country team" is but an honorific for the officer strength on board.

Typical membership at a fair-sized post, however, would normally include (in addition to staff aides and/or rotating junior officers) the DCM, the heads of the political and economic sections, the USIS, AID, MAAG, and CIA chiefs, and one or more of the service attachés. It may also include, sometimes permanently but usually *ad hoc,* such agency heads as the agricultural or financial attachés, and the Peace Corps representative if there is one. At posts where the security situation or other considerations demand it, the embassy administrative officer may also be a permanent member. The commercial and labor attachés are seldom regulars, since they work under the political or economic chiefs, but either may be called upon to sit in when a problem touching on his field is up for discussion.

As with membership, operating methods vary according to personalities and situations. When crisis supervenes, team meetings may come to resemble the diplomatic counterpart of a floating crap game. Thus, the case of the kidnapped colonel called forth the unremitting effort of the Caracas country team for as long as it lasted. During the 1958 emergency in Lebanon, the full country team met every day, wherever and whenever most convenient. For the three crucial days of the Brazzaville Congo revolution of 1963, the American Ambassador's office served as command post and clearing house while his country team—five FSO's, three agency heads, and two service attachés, plus junior volunteers—acted alternatively as leg men and consultative body.

Full-scale country team meetings are seldom held more often than weekly. At some posts, the chief of mission prefers brief daily meetings with key officers to the more customary agenda-based weekly or biweekly sessions. In either case, there are usually a number of ancillary subcommittee and task force meetings. Permanent subcommittees—e.g., on youth affairs, economic development, agriculture, intelligence, security—are generally made up of team members plus aides. Task forces, of one team member and a group of junior and middle-grade officers, address themselves to specific one-time problems. (At one post, where agrarian reform was a pressing problem, a team of juniors fanned out and paddled over the country's waterways to produce a body of basic information that had not been available until then to either the Embassy or the host government.)

Some ambassadors go in for committees more than others. As long as committee meetings are conducted on a business-like and productive basis, they can serve a useful purpose. The danger of becoming "over-committee-ed" is, however, something to be watched; the device must not be allowed to grow unwieldly nor to become a bureaucratic end in itself. Under no circumstances should an ambassador let the team or its adjuncts dilute his authority and slow down the decision-making process by wasting time on trivia. Properly run—and it almost always is—the country team can serve a very useful purpose as an advisory and planning body, as a forum for review, consultation, and consensus, and, last but not least, as the means of instilling a spirit of teamwork and cooperation into the mission as a whole. One of its most practical uses, in the writer's experience, is as an executive organ which, under the leadership of the chief of mission, sees to it that tasks are assigned to those who are best equipped to carry them out and then follows up to ensure that the tasks get done.

A COUNTRY-TEAM CONCEPT FOR WASHINGTON?

It is not within the province of a work on the Foreign Service, and its part in U.S. operations abroad, to go at any length into the problems of coordination in the government apparatus for handling foreign affairs in Washington. (Those problems have, in any case, already been the subject of many books and studies.) Nonetheless, it might be noted that by the early 1960's the success of the country team idea had become so well established that a number of observers were asking: if it works abroad, why not at home? It was pointed out, also, that the best cooperation among agencies in the field could not produce solid results unless there was a matching coordination among their opposite numbers back home. One of the Foreign Service's most able and articulate spokesmen, Ambassador

Ellis O. Briggs, put the problem neatly in his 1963 testimony before the Senate (Jackson) Subcommittee on National Security Staffing and Operations:

> What is needed, perhaps, is a change in Washington thinking, and here the analogy of the famous country team may be pertinent. The country team is a device whereby an Ambassador abroad obtains a consensus from among his senior colleagues, including the heads of the offices or agencies other than State that may be represented in that foreign capital—in other words, an advisory body—and when all the opinions are in, it is the Ambassador who has the responsibility for the decision. Similarly, in terms of Washington agency debate on a foreign affairs question, it should be the State Department—and not the Atomic Energy Commission, or the Pentagon, or the Department of Agriculture—that makes the final decision.
>
> I recognize that this millennium may still lie around a bend or two in the Potomac River. Nevertheless, re-establishment by the President of the primacy among executive agencies of the Department of State in matters of foreign relations ought to go a long way in the direction of creating more orderly Foreign Service operations.

The idea was much discussed and did, in due course, take shape. Early in 1966, President Johnson created the Senior Interdepartmental Group (SIG) and the Interdepartmental Regional Groups (IRG's) to work under the Secretary of State to administer and execute broad U.S. overseas programs. For the record, the Department of State was rather slow in seizing the opportunity thus presented, but by 1968 these interagency groups appeared to be developing as Washington counterparts of the overseas country team system.* In setting up these two groups to supersede the *ad hoc* interdepartmental task forces and working groups used during the Kennedy Administration to cope with most emergency problems, President

---

* While this volume was in the final stages of preparation, the SIG/IRG designation was dropped, but essential country-team style interagency cooperation on foreign-affairs decisions appears likely to continue under the Nixon Administration.

Johnson expressly assigned to the Secretary of State the authority and responsibility "to the full extent permitted by law" for the over-all direction, coordination, and supervision of U.S. Government overseas activities (excepting military operations). The key authority in these groups under the Secretary was vested in the under secretary and assistant secretaries of State, who were given full powers of decision on all matters within their purview and charged with the expeditious handling of foreign policy problems and the selectivity of areas and issues vis-à-vis resources, as well as with checking periodically on the adequacy and effectiveness of overseas programs.

Like the ambassadors overseas, the second and third level men in the Department today are called upon to master and manage programs as well as deal with the traditional aspects of diplomacy and foreign affairs. But it is important to remember that the Constitution put the President in charge of foreign affairs. It made no provision for executive departments except by implication: the establishment of these was left to Congress, which in setting up a foreign affairs department provided that the functions of its principal officer, the Secretary, were to be those which the President might assign him in his field and specified that he should conduct the business of his department "in such manner as the President of the United States shall from time to time order or instruct." The fact that the President in the twentieth century has delegated a portion of his decision-making authority only points up the depth of feeling in high-level government circles (which began during the Eisenhower Administration) about the need for coordination and over-all direction in the field of foreign affairs.

VI

The Embassy Family:
Interagency Relationships

We have noted in passing the role of the country team as keystone of interagency teamwork overseas. Not all is sweetness and light, to be sure, but the system has served its ends well and the posts abroad are generally more free of interagency strife than is the case in Washington. Country team participation builds up a certain solidarity among its members, through shared experiences in dealing with the host government on the one hand and the Washington complex on the other.

Still, each agency representative has his spiritual home, as well as his career interests, in his own home office—and each home office has its own axe to grind. The other-agency members of the country team, and the smaller units not entitled to full membership in it, acknowledge the Ambassador's primacy and respect his overlordship as chief of mission. They keep him informed about their work, invite his comments and take his advice, seek his support where it may help them, and are generally guided by him in matters of conduct and form vis-à-vis the host country. Yet their dependence on him is limited at best: they consider themselves members of his team but not of his staff—and most have their own reporting lines to Washington.

This reality is one which both parties recognize, but it need not unduly hamper over-all effectiveness. A chief of mission has the authority he needs to pull his team together and make it pull together, thus giving cohesion, focus, and impact to the U.S. effort. The degree of his success may vary from post to post, depending on situations and personalities, but the general pattern of other-agency activity is fairly uniform. Let us now consider the individual operations of these agencies, and their relationships with the Ambassador and his staff.

THE MISSION AND AID

Many people, including not a few in overseas service, think of U.S. foreign economic aid as having begun after a certain Secretary of State made his "Marshall Plan" speech and a certain President proclaimed the Truman Doctrine in 1947. They forget that the United States gave foreign aid on a fairly massive scale after World War I through Herbert Hoover's American Relief Administration (established by executive order in February, 1919) and, in World War II, through Lend Lease and the Middle East Civilian Supply Program. The United States then participated in United Nations Relief and Rehabilitation Administration (UNRRA) programs and in several post-UNRRA improvisations before Marshall Plan operations got under way in 1948. And in Latin America, aid at the technical-assistance level began in 1940 with the programs of the Institute of Inter-American Affairs. Thus, U.S. assistance to others began a half century ago and has had fundamental continuity for over a quarter century.

Yet, in recent years, the U.S. foreign aid program has been in trouble. In 1968, despite an able presentation by the AID administrator and an eleventh-hour plea from the White House, Congress cut a modest $2.9 billion request—the smallest since the Marshall Plan was launched—by over $1 billion. For a time, it appeared that there might be no program at all, despite the fact that in the preceding fiscal year, 96 per cent of all commodities financed by AID were purchased in the United States and a number of U.S. industries stood to lose substantially as a result of Congress's action.

The lawmakers were admittedly intent on getting economy-mindedness into the record back home during an important election year, and foreign aid is a program without a constituency. But their action was not based on political considerations alone. The idea persists in many quarters that foreign assistance is a give-away program and/or an attempt on the part of the United States to wet-nurse the world. Yet for all its troubles and shortcomings, the program has been a major instrument of U.S. policy since World War II—and, on the whole, remarkably successful.

The Agency for International Development (AID), since its inception, has operated as an autonomous arm of the Department of State, headed in Washington by an administrator with the rank of under secretary of State.* Some 13,000 of its 15,000 employees, plus an additional 2,000 hired under contract, work overseas. In the field, an AID mission is headed by a country director, who ranks with the counselors of embassy and is a key member of the country team. At a post with a fair-sized aid program, the Ambassador must maintain close and constant contact with his AID director—not only in connection with the ramifications of the program itself, but also because it is the director who is responsible for the work performance and personal conduct of the AID employees and their dependents. His task in this respect is not always easy.

The AID mission† comprises two principal elements: the civil servants who make up the bureaucracy and the technicians who handle operations. The former, by and large, are an

* AID is the name given the fifth U.S. aid program since the Economic Cooperation Administration (ECA) was launched in 1948; in between came the Mutual Security Agency (MSA), the Foreign Operations Administration (FOA), and the International Cooperation Administration (ICA). An operational difficulty with the acronym is that in telegrams, which are encrypted without reference to capital or lower-case letters, it is not always easy to tell whether what is meant is the agency (AID) or its product (aid).

† AID groups refer to themselves as "missions," as do the military assistance groups discussed later. These should not be confused with the diplomatic mission headed by the Ambassador, which represents the U.S. Government overall. When used in the lesser sense in this book, the term is qualified (e.g., "aid mission") unless the meaning is unmistakable from the context.

experienced cadre of "aid officers," some of whom have been in the foreign assistance business since World War II. They recommend operational and programming policy, produce most of the paper work (translating English into AIDese), and ride herd on the technicians.

The latter group, technical-assistance experts on direct hire or contract, play an important representational role since it is they who deal with the people of the recipient country. Their considerable numbers reflect the shift in emphasis from the sophisticated advisory role of the Marshall Plan in Europe (long since phased out) to a quite different program aimed at transmitting technical know-how to remote and underdeveloped parts of the world. These technicians, generally speaking, have earned the status of experts in their fields, but have known little of life abroad. To succeed in their overseas assignments, they must be psychologically well balanced and able to adjust to unusual living conditions, since most aid of the technical type has its operating locus in less-developed areas. The job of an AID recruiting officer is not easy, and he can never be sure how even an apparently ideal choice will perform under fire. A well-grounded agronomist, fluent in the local language and enthusiastic about the job, may turn sour because he disagrees with the AID policy for his program, while a monoglot mechanic, communicating by sign language and example, takes to his job immediately and runs a successful program.

From the viewpoint of the Ambassador and his staff, the problem of coexistence with AID is twofold. First there is the problem of adaptability, or the lack thereof, on the part of the AID employees and their families. Whereas a small, remote embassy may have managed to get along quite comfortably by its wits and its Foreign Service know-how, once a big military assistance or AID mission arrives there must be virtually total logistic support. Commissaries are set up, ready-made housing is provided—usually in the form of a compound— and one more Little America is established. Second is the problem of relative size. If the AID group is not disproportionate in numbers to the rest of the official community, chances are that it will "join the family"; if the agency's mission is a huge one, it will probably keep separate. In either case, if the "embassy types" strike the "AID types" as being clannish, the latter will react by becoming more clannish themselves.

The twenty-man AID component shown in Table IV (Chapter IV) is a small one, and would be smaller were it not for the existence in the sample country of an important public safety program employing eight advisers (police). It should be noted that the Latin country picked as generally typical for the purposes of the discussion in Chapter IV is not one of the fifteen "concentration countries" on which over 85 per cent of AID's worldwide effort is focused. There are, however, a number of such countries in Latin America, as there are in South and Southeast Asia. In concentration countries, it is not unusual for the AID staff to outnumber embassy, service attachés, USIS, and Peace Corps headquarters staff combined. In Southeast Asian countries where it operates, the AID presence is overpoweringly large—owing, of course, to the special Vietnam situation, which spills over into Laos and Thailand. In Laos, there were in early 1968 three and a half times as many AID officers as there were embassy and other-agency officers put together—and over 80 per cent of the AID people were quartered in the capital.

The foregoing comparisons do not take into account the U.S. military presence, other than the service attachés, but they do point up the problem faced by an ambassador and his senior colleagues—including the AID leadership itself—in riding herd on hordes of technicians and lesser AID bureaucrats. One countervailing device, gaining increment of late, is that of having the FSO heading the economic section double in brass as deputy AID director—and sometimes as director. Another is the stationing of resident foreign aid inspectors at posts with programs large enough to carry with them the danger of slippages and kickbacks, both foreign and domestic.

The problems of control and of keeping peace in the family

are never easy, but if the Ambassador is on top of his job and the AID chief on top of his, a *modus vivendi* is worked out. Regardless of factional jealousies and individual idiosyncrasies, all hands—even old-line Foreign Service types—recognize by now that foreign aid, albeit reduced and more closely supervised than in the lavish past, has come to stay as an instrument of policy, at least for so long as poverty and hunger continue to pose a threat to world stability and world peace.

THE DEFENSE ESTABLISHMENT OVERSEAS

The role of the U.S. defense establishment in the operations of the diplomatic establishment is largely limited, insofar as duty assignments go, to the activities of the armed service attachés and the military assistance advisory groups (MAAG's). Before we turn our attention to these, it might be well to comment briefly on the U.S. peacetime military presence abroad as a whole.*

When the ends of diplomacy were accomplished solely through government-to-government contacts, American overseas representation was small. As the world evolved through the twentieth century, representation broadened—first gradually then rapidly, and not only on the civilian but also on the military side. In this era of total diplomacy, U.S. military representation abroad is no longer limited to attaché service and staff exchanges. Aside from the activities of military assistance groups and other advisory missions, U.S. representatives operate as part of coalitions, and this calls for coalition military planning—hence, augmented military staff. Finally, the non-combatant troops stationed overseas as coalition support play a representational role themselves. In Europe particularly, this role must be controlled and guided—both positively, to serve American policy ends, and negatively, to minimize friction that might obstruct achievement of those ends.

Service in an international command and troop-community relations are a matter for the respective staffs and troop com-

---

* This excepts Vietnam. The type of operation being discussed here is what might be called noncombatant military support.

manders; the Ambassador is not in the line of military command—although, as noted in the Kennedy letter excerpts (Chapter V), it is his duty to ensure that troop activities do not damage over-all relations. By contrast, the activities of the service attachés and the military assistance advisory groups *are* within his responsibility.

The Service Attachés

Aside from ceremonial duties, the principal function of the military attaché (army, navy, and now also air) has always been "observation," or the gathering of intelligence—even in friendly countries, one must gauge the strength of one's allies —but, like other diplomats, he is expected to do so in a "correct" manner. An incorrect attitude, such as bribing officials and/or stealing documents, passes over the line into espionage, and he who is caught at that stands to be declared *persona non grata* (in effect, deported)—as happened to Captain Franz von Papen, later to become Chancellor of the German Reich, when he was military attaché at Washington in 1915. Nowadays, it happens frequently behind the Iron Curtain, where all diplomats—but particularly service attachés—may be subjected at any time to the exposure techniques at which Communist countries are so adept.

Until after World War II, an ambitious career officer rarely sought attaché duty. Allowances were so meager that independent means were virtually a necessity, G-2 itself was a stepchild operating on a shoestring, and service out of the career mainstream was not good for promotion prospects. A small band of professionals was nonetheless built up, composed in the main of reasonably well-to-do officers who had a flair for intelligence work, languages, and refined living. Not all were effective, but a few were outstanding—notably the U.S. military attaché in wartime Berlin, who accurately foretold what the *Reichswehr* was going to do in 1940. (His warnings were largely disregarded till after the fact.)

In the postwar period, the entire American intelligence

community, the military included, was put on a sound professional basis. Civilian and military intelligence services grew apace, in close coordination but at the same time in competition. In this environment, attaché duty gained in stature. Able officers were assigned to it, entertainment and maintenance allowances were generously increased, and those chosen for the duty were given intensive training in both language and the intelligence function. Attaché service is still not a "career line" for officers—more than one tour of duty is rare—but a number of noncommissioned officers do claim it as a specialty and make a career of it. This group, providing needed continuity and know-how, includes many with foreign background and language fluency.

As of January, 1968, before the balance-of-payments problem began to take its toll, there were some 400 officers serving as attachés or assistant attachés in the three services. Before and during World War II, there were only military (army) and naval attachés—some with flying officers on their staffs—but once the Air Force had become independent (September 18, 1947) it lost little time in sending its own attachés abroad. In July, 1965, on the advice and recommendation of various authorities including the Jackson Subcommittee, the position of defense attaché was established. He is the senior attaché at a given post, chosen usually because his service is the most active in the country concerned. He does over-all reporting in addition to reporting for and running his own section—army, navy, or air.

Attaché duties include representation as well as reporting. They do a good bit of representational work on their own—vis-à-vis the host-country military and their third-country attaché colleagues—but they are also a plus for the Ambassador in his ceremonial duties. The officers generally have good figures and good manners, and their dress uniforms lend dash to any ceremonial group. Attachés are on the diplomatic list as a matter of course. Within the mission, their diplomatic precedence may vary according to the desires of individual ambassadors, but the norm is that attachés rank with but after counselors, assistant attachés with but after second secretaries (in both cases, irrespective of the military rank they may hold). In practice, about all this boils down to is who stands or walks where when the whole group is on show.

Protocol and ceremonial apart, a well-connected attaché can be invaluable to his Ambassador, not only as adviser on local military affairs but also, in many countries, as a prime source on the political ambitions of the host-country officer corps—which, all too often, lead to the overthrow of governments. In smaller countries, the service attachés are often accredited but not resident, living in a larger capital of the area and visiting their "constituent" posts periodically—or on demand in times of crisis. Army and air attachés are now listed at most diplomatic posts. It is the air attaché who maintains and flies what is known by courtesy as the embassy plane, since the Ambassador and his staff get a good bit of use out of it. (Not for junketing, it should be noted.)

Naval attachés, of course, are of service only where there is sufficient water to sustain a host-country fleet, or at least a flotilla. Where they do function, they earn their keep. In the Mediterranean and the Far East, particularly, the movements of U.S. fleets can mean hundreds of headaches to a diplomatic mission: the arrival of one aircraft carrier and its satellite vessels means shore leave for thousands of men with hundreds of thousands of dollars' ready cash in their pockets—and, nowadays, like as not, may also mean a series of antiwar demonstrations to add to the general confusion. (More welcome from the diplomatic point of view are the good will visits of several small, hand-picked task forces, usually to underdeveloped nations. These programs are tailored to the countries visited, in advance consultation with U.S. embassies; officers and men are trained in the basics of public relations, and incidents are few. The one drawback is that, though much entertaining is done on board, no liquor is served by the U.S. Navy. This has bewildered many dignitaries of new Africa, accustomed as they are to the free-flowing hospitality of their former colonial masters.)

By and large, the service attachés (and their wives) are a hand-picked, compact group and fit easily into the Foreign Service milieu. Almost without exception, they consider themselves part of the diplomatic establishment and under the orders of the Ambassador, and they get along well with the embassy officers. The presence of a MAAG or other outsize military mission, on the other hand, cannot help but make for problems of control, coordination, and coexistence.

The Military Assistance Program

The United States is providing military aid on a multibillion-dollar scale to make its allies more effective members of its military coalitions—and, in some cases, for reasons of political expediency. Such aid may provide not only weaponry and equipment but also advice and training in the use of it, this in a program carried out both in the United States and through missions overseas. In recent years, U.S. missions have also given advice and training in such activities as counterinsurgency and "civic action" (use of host-country forces in public works and similar activities).

The Military Assistance Program (MAP) grew out of the Greek-Turkish aid program of the Truman Doctrine, by which the United States took over from the United Kingdom the obligation of bolstering those countries' defenses in the face of Communist pressure. The United States now maintains military assistance advisory groups (MAAG's) to carry out its military assistance functions abroad in about forty-five nations, and provides minor assistance to another five states where MAAG's are not maintained. The program embraces more countries than any other military activity save the attaché program, and the officers assigned to a group are naturally far more numerous than the attachés. In January, 1968, more than 5,000 military personnel (about 2,200 officers, 2,500 enlisted men, and 400 U.S. civilians) were serving in the MAP abroad. Of these, about 2,000 performed training functions and another 3,000 advisory and administrative tasks. Typically, the head of a mission is a general or flag officer, although he may be a colonel or navy captain at smaller missions. The senior officer of each service has diplomatic status.

In Latin America, there are about a dozen American military missions that long predate the MAAG's. Their tasks have to do with training, which varies from country to country. After MAP was established, the United States concluded special agreements to permit the assignment of MAAG duties in addition to former training responsibilities. The military assistance organizations in countries such as Greece, the Philippines, Saudi Arabia, and Turkey also have designations other than MAAG (e.g., Joint U.S. Military Assistance Group—JUSMAG).

To the Ambassador and his staff, the presence of a MAAG poses what is in effect a military counterpart of the problems posed by a large AID mission—an outsize group, its members dispersed and often working in highly specialized fields, and with a general tendency to keep to itself. The group commander usually maintains an office in the chancery, and he and his section chiefs keep abreast of embassy and other-agency activities, but the MAAG rank-and-file are seldom seen in embassy circles.

All this is understandable. The MAAG chief accepts the primacy of the Ambassador, and is happy to give the benefit of his unusual vantage point to the over-all effort of the country team, but his work does not easily lend itself to ambassadorial control. The MAAG's job is highly operational, it has its own lines to the Pentagon, and it tends to dispute the right of the Ambassador (or any outsider) to come between it and its home office. Despite the explicit phrasing of the Kennedy letter, not a few MAAG chiefs look upon themselves more as area commanders than as officers attached to a diplomatic mission.

Withal, the MAAG men in general are a credit to the

United States as they work with their host-country counter-parts in fields of mutual interest and absorption, although a few, especially those working in outlying districts, sometimes embarrass headquarters through free-wheeling interpretations of U.S. policy. (These few are hard enough for the MAAG chief to control, let alone the Embassy.) One of MAAG's most difficult jobs is talking the local brass out of expensive but useless (to them) prestige items—e.g., cruisers, where what are needed are shallow-draft patrol craft. When a MAAG re-fuses such status items, it sometimes happens that another power steps in and provides them.

A great propaganda asset of the United States is its ability, and readiness, to lend quick and massive disaster relief. In countries where there is no U.S. military command, the Am-bassador relies on his attachés and/or his MAAG for logistic arrangements. A classic example is the rescue and rehabilita-tion operation carried out after the Skopje (Yugoslavia) earthquake of 1963. Through the good offices of the air at-taché, the U.S. Air Force flew in mobile hospitals, medicines, tents, blankets, and food within hours after disaster had struck. At the other end of the scale—in size of operation—an Air Force plane may land in a minuscule republic to evacuate one small peasant child in desperate need of specialized medi-cal treatment not available in her country.

The U.S. military presence overseas presents drawbacks to diplomacy, naturally—not only in matters of high policy but also, at times, in people-to-people relationships—but the pres-ence is, in the writer's view, an over-all plus.

THE EMBASSY AND THE CIA

Aside from its recent bad press in the matter of subsidizing educational and cultural activities, the Central Intelligence Agency has been called an "invisible government" and ac-cused of making and executing foreign policy on its own. It is criticized harshly by those to whom secrecy is undemocratic and un-American, while many traditional diplomats—conforming to an attitude that is probably as old as diplomacy it-self—have looked askance at extracurricular operations and preferred not to know what their shady-side colleagues might be up to.*

The CIA is, in fact, a productive and hard-working agency of the U.S. Government, staffed by loyal, able Americans charged with the coordination, evaluation, and dissemination of the national intelligence product—and not with making policy. For all its 007 image, the agency's so-called covert operations are a relatively minor part of its over-all activities; a far greater part is the analysis, in Washington, of published, unclassified documents gathered from all over the world. (In this connection, it is interesting to note that the Soviet intelligence community is said to maintain that it can fulfill 95 per cent of its U.S. reporting obligations solely through reading information published openly in this country.)

Created in 1947 along with the Department of Defense and the National Security Council, the agency's principal operating authority lies in the Central Intelligence Act of 1949, which among other things permits it to protect the confidential nature of its work and makes provision for operations abroad. By the late 1950's, however, CIA activities were getting out of hand in some parts of the world, and this problem was high among those which led President Kennedy, in 1961, to send out the May 29 letter mentioned earlier. The Kennedy letter gave every chief of mission, for the first time, the right (and in fact the obligation) to know everything his CIA people were doing—although not always the way in which they were doing it. A CIA station chief may tell his Ambassador that he is about to investigate a certain local politico's relations with the Soviet Embassy—the Ambassador may even ask him to do so—but there will be no discussion of how the station chief plans to go about it. Similarly, he will show his

* Louis XIV's famous ambassador François de Callières, for example, warned that diplomats should maintain a discreet distance from the activities of their undercover agents.

reports to the Ambassador and designated members of the staff but he will not name the sources of his information—simply describing these briefly to place them in the scheme of things. The system works fairly well at most posts most of the time, but there can be spectacular blow-ups and general unhappiness when someone gets caught or is exposed.

Practically speaking, in day-to-day operations the CIA representatives are members of the embassy team, well thought of or not according to their individual abilities and personalities. During the past decade or so, there has been a noticeable improvement in what might be called the diplomatic plausibility of the people sent out. Professional competence apart, the CIA men (and their wives) are almost without exception socially presentable, culturally alive, and well equipped to fit into the Foreign Service milieu.

The problem of "cover" is something else again. At small posts, where the one CIA man spends a good bit of time at an overt job such as commercial reporting or consular work, there is no problem. However, at a large post, owing to CIA ground rules, the contingent sometimes dwells in the seclusion of wings or attics—often with bells, bolts, and buzzers shielding them from the run-of-the-mine embassy staff. Were it not for this isolation, the average CIA officer would be indistinguishable from his FSO colleague, at least to 90 per cent of the general public. As it is, all the local employees—and not a few outsiders, including the host country's Foreign Office people—peg him immediately. Visiting firemen are sometimes bemused when they hear locals refer casually to Mr. So-and-So as "our chief spook."

The agency's considered answer to this appears to be: "So what? They'll be identified sooner or later, anyway." The agency may be right. The important thing to the Embassy is that the CIA pull its weight on the country team (which it does) and preserve appearances in public (which it almost always does). In a reasonably friendly country, the local gentry are not particularly bothered by the vagueness as to just what young Jonesmith does in the U.S. Embassy as long as he is good company and can discuss local issues intelligently. In an unfriendly country, anyone in the U.S. Embassy, be he the lowliest voucher clerk, is a spy—or at best a pawn of unspeakable interests. One thing the recent "spotlight CIA" has achieved, it may be said, is to cut down on the opposition's vocabulary requirements. In the past, a hard-working street demonstrator had to master such jawbreakers as "despicable dog of a demoplutoliberaloid, monocapitalist Yankee!" Now he simply screams "CIA!"

THE USIS ROLE

From the end of World War II till 1953, the U.S. Government's overseas press and propaganda arm was under the Department of State in much the same manner that AID is today. On August 1 of that year, the United States Information Agency was established by authority of the President's Reorganization Plan No. 8, as approved by Congress, and on August 20, 1968, the Act providing the USIA with a career officer corps was signed into law.* The agency in Washington receives guidance from the Secretary of State on U.S. foreign policy—consultation to this end goes on continuingly at various levels—but that is about the extent of the Department's involvement in USIA affairs. Abroad, where the agency's 220 posts in 105 countries operate under embassies and consulates as the United States Information Service (USIS), the situation is somewhat different. Although, strictly speaking, the Foreign Service role is comparable to that of the Department in Washington—i.e., providing guidance on policy and ensuring that USIS activities conform to it—in practice relations are generally close and activities complementary under the over-all authority of the chief of mission. At all posts where it conducts a program, USIS is not only a key element of the country team, but, ordinarily, very much a member of the embassy family.

* See *The United States Information Agency,* op. cit.

It is the writer's belief, based on general observation and on particular experience as an FSO doing a tour of duty with the pre-1953 USIS, that this general rapport developed largely after the USIA had broken loose from the Department of State. When the information and cultural service was under the Department's authority, relations at overseas posts—and in Washington as well—were often strained and prerogative conscious. As sometimes happens with nations themselves, once the restless colony had won its independence it began to look more warmly on the mother country—and the warmth became reciprocal.

At any well-run post, embassy officers are encouraged to participate in USIS programs, particularly those of the binational centers (see below). An ambassador or consul general can give the USIS enterprise a boost by lending his presence and patronage to its affairs, but the advantage is mutual and both sides profit. All USIS materials and facilities, including motion pictures, are readily available for the Embassy's political and other activities, while everyone gets good mileage out of the program under which American artists perform and professors lecture abroad. Embassy, USIS, and other officers share in the selection of persons invited to visit the United States—both students on scholarships and host-country leaders on travel grants—via the State Department's exchange-of-persons program. The youth affairs program is a country team effort, chaired usually by a senior embassy officer, but the Information Service, with its resources, does most of the leg work.

Table IV (Chapter IV), in its USIS section, shows a counselor for public affairs, an executive officer, an information officer and two assistants, a cultural officer and three assistants, a trainee, and two binational center officers. At some posts, there is a deputy public affairs officer, in which case there may or may not be an executive officer—depending on the size of the operation. Let us examine the role these people play at the post.

The counselor for public affairs, whose title at most embassies is simply public affairs officer (usually called the PAO or USIS director), has in his charge the two basic USIS tasks: first, to gauge and to advise the Ambassador on the impact on local public opinion of American policies and actions; second, to make American policies and programs understandable—and, if possible, palatable—to the people of the host country. To achieve these objectives, he has two principal operating arms, informational and cultural, which we shall take up shortly.

It goes without saying that the PAO must be an effective executive, not only to get the best out of the resources at his command but also to put his agency's best foot forward in dealing with the Ambassador, the country team, and American and host-country leaders. A PAO may have come up via the information, cultural, or administrative route, but the odds appear to favor information and a journalistic background. There is also a sprinkling of PAO's who started as Foreign Service officers and switched to the Information Agency when they found that was their métier. Whatever his career channel, the USIS chief must be tough minded and politically oriented. Today's programs are based on realism, not art for art's sake or the love of a bleeding heart.

The deputy PAO, when there is one, plays a DCM-type role—sometimes with administrative duties as well. In any case, the duties of the executive officer are largely administrative, but not in the strictest sense, since basic housekeeping and bookkeeping chores are handled by embassy personnel through an interagency arrangement known as joint administrative support—such support being reimbursed on the basis of a mystical man-hours-spent formula, which is haggled over once a year by all agencies represented at the post.

The information officer is the press-radio-TV-movie man, and he has the considerable resources of USIA Washington at his disposal. News and feature material, both staff-written and purchased from commercial sources, goes out at the rate of

12,000 words a day over a worldwide radio-teletype system for post distribution to key newspapers and periodicals. Photographs, cartoon strips, and USIA pamphlets reach a public of hundreds of millions every year, as do the documentaries, newsreels, and short subjects produced by USIA's motion picture service. Five major slick magazines are published, including two separate language editions for sale in Russia and Poland. Three "regional service centers"—in Beirut, Manila, and Mexico City—publish another eighteen magazines in fourteen languages, as well as pamphlets, posters, and photo exhibits. The agency maintains over 7,500 motion picture projectors for its own showings and for loan to others.

The cultural affairs officer (CAO) will usually have an academic background and sometimes a Ph.D. He must not only be *persona grata* in university and intellectual circles— and be prepared to deliver a discourse or turn out a monograph on command—but he must sometimes do a hard-sell job in the face of heckling by students and others. Furthermore, he will be well advised to check with the political section before deciding whom to trust among the many-hued intellectuals he must deal with.

It is the CAO who acts as key man in the State Department's cultural exchange program, which sends American artists and performers abroad. (One of the best "cultural" presentations the writer ever hosted was a small track and field group—half white, half black—which came to the Congo. The young men were gentle, kind, and approachable and quite won the Africans' hearts, especially those of the worshipping small fry who flocked around them wherever they went.) The performing artists' program is generally excellent—its cast has ranged from Louis Armstrong and Duke Ellington to Isaac Stern and the Juilliard String Quartet—but the top performers are in such demand, and travel arrangements so complex, that it is no simple matter for a post to get the attractions it deems best suited to its public. A standard complaint heard by the inspectors is that the CAO, with the Ambassador behind him, put in well in advance for the University of Illinois symphony orchestra but was practically forced to take in its stead the Cozy Cats Combo. (An absurd situation developed in the Middle East, where the Arab countries complained that the list of choices contained too many Jewish artists—barred to them, of course—while the Israelis grumbled that since these performers could not come to Araby they skipped the whole area, Tel Aviv included.)

The cultural affairs officer is also coordinator of the ex-change-of-persons program, which, like cultural exchange, is run by the State Department in Washington but administered by the USIS in the field. As mentioned above, this is an Em-bassy-wide project when it comes to the selection of students and leader-grantees (the latter are chosen from politics, indus-try, and labor as well as from arts and sciences) but the CAO pulls the action together and his assistants do the leg and pa-per work. Finally, under the PAO, he has advisory and super-visory responsibility for libraries and English-teaching, to which we now turn our attention.

Table IV shows a director, binational center, and a director of courses, binational center; at a smaller post, one man would wear both hats. Until a few years ago, these officers were "grantees" hired on a contract basis, but when a number of them showed interest in continuing the work they were taken into the USIA and given FSS status (without which they had had no tenure or seniority rights). The centers—there are over 130 worldwide, more than 80 per cent of them in Latin America—are joint enterprises between the United States and the host country, administered by a binational board, with the degree of USIA support and participation varying according to country and situation. In Latin America, most of them are self-supporting—indeed, many are well in the black—through the minimal fees charged for English and other courses. It is almost unbelievable how many people still want to learn En-glish; the centers attract as many as a quarter million enrollees a year. Affluence has brought a considerable improvement in the cultural-center plant: whereas twenty years ago most of the "institutes" were housed in drafty old properties, today there are many spanking new structures of chrome and glass, functionally designed for the purposes they serve—with ample library and classroom space plus social rooms and a theater-cum-auditorium.

Not all libraries are housed in the more than 130 binational centers. In addition, there are over 220 libraries, information centers, and reading rooms scattered through some ninety countries. The USIA estimates total yearly attendance at more than 25 million. Over 2 million books are on the shelves, and many more are distributed to libraries, institutions, and individuals—the last generally as year-end gifts, for representational purposes. Many a principal officer has had good reason to be thankful he could give such gifts, both to institutions and personages.

The role of the press attaché, a USIS officer assigned to handle the Embassy's press relations at certain larger posts, will be discussed in Chapter VIII, but one other USIS responsibility should be mentioned—that of coordinating overseas exhibits, especially at trade fairs and "expo's." When it is simply a matter of providing an American exhibit, the USIS exhibits officer (usually one of the press or cultural assistants) will do the necessary. Typical of these were the full-scale replicas of the Gemini space capsule, on the road for years and always with waiting lists. More often than not, however, there will be a trade fair tie-in. In such cases, the commercial attaché does the spade work at the professional end, with American business on the one hand and the local authorities on the other, while the exhibits officer lends his logistic know-how to getting the space prepared and the stand set up. When the fair or exposition is a large one, the USIS may assign special staff to it—as may Commerce, too. The USIS, of course, will use any trade fair or similar occasion to include a bit of free-world propaganda on its own.

The activities and institutions described above have been presented in an embassy setting. The whole operation is, of course, repeated, on a scale proportionate to the size of the post, at a consulate or consulate general—with the difference that at the constituent posts instructions and materials often come from the USIS chief at the Embassy (in this context referred to as the country public affairs officer, or CPAO) rather than from Washington. The head of USIS at a consular post is known as the branch public affairs officer (BPAO) to the Embassy, but not necessarily to the local gentry. He as well as the branch CAO (sometimes one and the same) may use a consular title or make up his own. One impressive CAO with a German university Ph.D. decided on *Kulturreferent.*

Not all provincial centers, libraries, and reading rooms are tied to the presence of a consulate in town; a number of BPAO's have more outlying dependencies under them than the Embassy has under it. Some may be simply reading rooms —mini-libraries presided over by one or two locals—while others may be full-scale binational centers, complete with governing board and bank balance. These are generally supervised and periodically visited by the BPAO, as well as by any other USIS or consulate officers who pass through town. The binational plant at a constituent post, or even at a subconstituent town of that post, can be quite impressive, especially if an affluent and booster-minded American business community gets together with well-heeled and equally patriotic local industrialists in a matching effort to outshine nearby and rival cities. The binational principle has paid off in more ways than one—as, indeed, has the whole USIS enterprise.

THE PEACE CORPS REPRESENTATIVE

It is not within the province of this chapter to go into the activities of the many thousands of Peace Corps volunteers at work around the world. Their goals and achievements have been well publicized, but the very nature of their mission keeps them out of and away from the formal diplomatic establishment.

Obviously, however, a Peace Corps volunteer (PCV) is not sent out of the United States directly into Cocalandia to roam the countryside without guidance or support. These are provided by a country headquarters staff—sometimes supplemented by field staff outside the capital—its size and scope scaled to the number and location of the PCV's in operation.

These officers, some of them ex-PCV's themselves, keep in touch with their charges on the one hand and maintain liaison with the Embassy on the other. The chief Peace Corps representative is not necessarily a full-fledged member of the country team, but he is free to come and go and usually attends meetings when matters within his sphere of interest are on the agenda. He must preserve a delicate balance in his relations with the embassy and its affiliated agencies, keeping himself informed of what they are doing (and vice versa) while avoiding the appearance of being in the embassy's pocket. Even if he never goes near the chancery, in some countries his operation will be tagged "CIA" by the adversary. Thus, with all good will on both sides, relations are kept to the minimum necessary.

This arrangement does not mean that there is no contact between embassy and volunteers. In Africa, the American Ambassador may accompany the president of a small republic fifty miles upstream to dedicate a schoolhouse built by PCV's with local help. In Latin America, a consul general may join with the governor of a province in inspecting a Peace Corps clinic. Also, in the outlying areas, it is not unheard of for resident PCV's to form friendships—purely unofficial—with young FSO's assigned to the consulate of the district. Contact or no contact, it is inescapable that the volunteers get the idea of what the Foreign Service is all about. Of the 520 examination-entry officers statistically studied in Table II (Chapter II), fifty—or almost 10 per cent—were ex–Peace Corps volunteers.

THE AGRICULTURAL ATTACHÉ

As noted in Chapter I, the Department of Agriculture in 1930 gained congressional authorization to attach its own specialists to diplomatic missions abroad. The Act that set up the Foreign Agricultural Service (FAS) stated in its enacting clause that it was "for the purpose of encouraging and promoting the agriculture of the United States and assisting American farmers to adjust their operations and practice to meet world conditions." The State Department could veto proposed nominations of attachés, but no provision was made for the chief of mission to control their activities abroad.

In the unification of 1939, the FAS was brought under the general Foreign Service, but the arrangement did not work out as well as it did with Commerce. Agriculture officials are reported as believing State took on the agricultural function in good faith, but lacked the resources to do the job. In any case, post-World War II domestic pressures were building up to dispose of U.S. agricultural surpluses then accumulating, and, in 1954, Congress reinstated the Foreign Agricultural Service —to develop markets for American farm products and gather economic intelligence on foreign demand for and competition with those products. Agricultural attachés assist U.S. exporters in making contacts, and keep close watch on foreign-consumer reception of U.S. products; if American farmers or professional agriculturalists travel abroad, the attachés are at their service. The FAS, in association with AID, also promotes the surplus utilization program for farm commodities under P.L. 480. (See also Chapter III.)

Agricultural attachés do not normally advise foreign governments on how to improve their agricultural research and practice—that is generally an AID function—but the Department of Agriculture's research service sends some of its people overseas to administer foreign agricultural research programs financed through P.L. 480. The research service also places selected employees abroad—for the most part professional entomologists—to work on pest-control and do research on insects, predators, and parasites that might threaten American agriculture. A joint U.S.–Mexican pest-control program functions the length of the border and has been signally successful.

The Foreign Agricultural Service considers that persons interested in becoming agricultural attachés should have a background in agricultural economics and agricultural marketing; the successful applicant is normally a graduate of an agricultural college. Overseas duty is on general Foreign Service lines: two years abroad followed by home leave, the typical pattern being three two-year tours abroad followed by two years in Washington. The FAS believes an attaché can spend most of his time in the field for up to twenty years without impairment of his ability as a specialist. Knowledge of a language or an area is not deemed essential to assignment overseas, but the successful attachés usually do acquire a language, then tend to spend more time in that language area than elsewhere.

The agricultural attaché is of course under the over-all guidance and authority of the Ambassador, and sits on the country team. He enjoys diplomatic status, as does his assistant if he has one. The writer, through the nature of his own assignment pattern, has known relatively few agricultural attachés—six or seven at most—but by curious coincidence two of these started their careers abroad as examination-entry FSO's. Both had had some agricultural background, got interested in the work, and happily transferred to it.

TREASURY REPRESENTATIVES

Like the Department of Agriculture, the Treasury Department maintains a separate foreign service on a modest scale. In 1930, when the FAS was authorized, Treasury had a number of customs officials abroad, and these began to be referred to as treasury attachés. Like the agricultural attachés, they were attached to diplomatic posts, but there was no provision for control of their activities by the chief of mission. When the unification of 1939 took place, Treasury was a significant exception. Acting under its very broad authority to use proceeds from the Exchange Stabilization Fund "for any purpose in connection with the provisions of this Section," the Department began to place a few financial experts abroad—first in

London in 1939, and since then elsewhere in western Europe, in southern Asia, the Far East, and Latin America. Known as Treasury representatives, they operate under the Treasury's Office of International Finance.

Treasury representatives observe and report on financial and monetary developments where these are too complicated or sophisticated to be handled by a Foreign Service economic officer. The "financial attaché" of Table IV is a Treasury representative, granted attaché status because he must negotiate with host-country financial officials. He uses embassy communications channels and has an office in the chancery—sometimes with an assistant, who may be another Treasury man or an FSO. He is a senior member of the embassy economic section, and unless he is an exception is well integrated into the Foreign Service establishment.

High finance is not the only Treasury activity represented abroad. The Internal Revenue Service (IRS), the Bureau of Customs, and the Bureau of Narcotics all maintain small overseas operations, sometimes at consulates as well as at embassies. Over a dozen customs representatives are assigned to key world cities; they are, so to speak, the early-distant-warning watch on U.S. ports of entry. A dozen or so narcotics agents are stationed abroad for their particular form of traffic control; they operate under cover and work closely with host-country enforcement officers. The duties of an equal number of IRS officers are somewhat less exciting; they are assigned to key overseas posts to aid U.S. taxpayers (citizen and alien) in fulfilling their tax obligations. Operating under the terms of established tax treaties, they aim principally at protecting taxpayers from double taxation but also keep an eye out for tax liabilities.

Although these officers depend on the chief of mission and the Foreign Service only for over-all guidance and logistic support, most of them—including the narcotics men—attend staff meetings when they can, keep the principal officer generally informed of their doings, and integrate socially. It is said that both State and Treasury officials consider relationships to be good, and the writer—from his own experience with titular Treasury representatives as well as with those of the other three services—entirely agrees.

THE ATTORNEY GENERAL'S MEN

The Justice Department is regularly represented abroad by two groups: legal attachés and officers of the Immigration and Naturalization Service (INS).

The primary function of legal attachés (or legal officers, if attached to consulates) is to carry out liaison activities overseas related to the domestic responsibilities of the Federal Bureau of Investigation (the FBI) in both the criminal and security fields. They work with local law-enforcement agencies, and their activities do not conflict with those of the intelligence community. Legal and assistant legal attachés are special agents of the FBI, attached to Foreign Service posts and enjoying diplomatic status. By far the largest contingent is stationed in Mexico—in consulates as well as at the Embassy— working with the Mexican police on problems stemming from the common border. It is not unusual to see the hard-eyed features of one of America's ten most-wanted glaring from the back page of a Mexican daily, and once during the writer's time one of the wanted was caught (in Mexico City, not in Acapulco).

With its 6,000-member staff of special agents, the FBI has no problem in finding able and well-adjusted men for overseas assignment. If knowledge of a particular foreign language is required, an agent with that skill is picked. Today's legal attachés fit easily and well into Foreign Service life.

In Chapter IV, it was noted that an applicant for immigration, even though issued a visa, might be found inadmissible by the Immigration and Naturalization Service at the port of entry. At a number of key "immigration" posts that danger has been obviated through the stationing of resident INS officers. A few such officers were sent abroad as early as 1924, to act as technical advisers to consular officers. The need for them disappeared in time, but with passage of the Displaced Persons Act of 1948 the INS was again called upon and sent twelve inspectors to European posts; the refugee relief people preferred to have their selections rejected before departure rather than after arrival at a U.S. port. This activity expired in due course, but in 1957, when the Attorney General was given the right to waive certain standards of inadmissibility, State and Justice agreed to establish regional INS offices in a number of key world centers—and also, in Canada, Mexico, Bermuda, and Nassau, "pre-inspection offices" for persons traveling to the United States.

The INS contingent has been a welcome addition to the Foreign Service family. It is a comforting thing to a visa officer to have the other half of the immigration operation represented on the premises and prepared to produce a decision—yea or nay—in cases of doubt.

OTHER AGENCIES

In addition to the departments and agencies mentioned above (and Commerce, Labor, and Interior, which are taken up elsewhere), there are a number of organizations whose overseas activity is more narrowly specialized but who are, nevertheless, members of the foreign affairs community.

The Atomic Energy Commission sends scientists abroad wherever agreements reached on the basis of the Atomic Energy Act of 1954 provide for exchange of nuclear information (and at times materials). These regional AEC "scientific representatives" may assist the Ambassador with diplomatic or other reporting functions related to atomic energy, but they generally limit themselves to technical reporting and fostering cooperative effort between the United States and other countries.

The Federal Aviation Administration (FAA) has a two-fold interest overseas: the civil aviation attaché function and the FAA's flight standards service. Civil aviation reporting is done almost entirely by FSO's, but since 1963 a few FAA (and Civil Aeronautics Board) employees have been assigned as FSR attachés on regular overseas tours. The FAA's aviation safety officers and facilities-inspection personnel are stationed at certain key Foreign Service posts to inspect aircraft, flight personnel, and facilities used by U.S. flag carriers. They generally get along well with host-country officials, and their inspections have brought about many technical improvements.

The U.S. Public Health Service (USPHS) has people stationed at a number of posts—those which process the great majority of immigrants to the United States. Their units at embassies and consulates are staffed by commissioned officers of the USPHS and/or local physicians on contract; they examine immigrant visa applicants for mental and physical health. When there is no resident USPHS or local doctor, the examinations are done by a physician selected by the applicant from a panel approved by the Department of State. Most Public Health physicians are willing to give staff members medical advice, and emergency treatment when necessary, but they all frown on being thought of as "the embassy (or consulate) doctor."

A number of other civilian agencies have limited representation abroad. To name several by way of illustration: the General Accounting Office (regional control of U.S. Government activities); the National Aeronautics and Space Administration (tracking and data-acquisition); the National Institutes of Health (foreign research and administration of research grants to foreigners); and the Environmental Science Services Administration (weather observation stations across the border).

The dependence of such representatives on a Foreign Service post varies according to nature and location of operation, but most of them expect and get logistic support and all are under the nominal authority of the Ambassador. By no means all the "other agencies" mentioned in this chapter are present in one country, to be sure, but big embassies may run to twenty or more and even a consulate general, if it is strategically located, may find itself hosting five, ten, or even more. Technical specialties and logistics apart, the question whether the representatives integrate socially depends principally upon themselves but also, to a considerable degree, on the style of the post—and that is set by the principal officer (and his wife). "Minority groups" who have kept to themselves under an aloof chief of mission may find themselves drawn by his warmer successor into full-scale participation in post activities—or, of course, vice versa.

The Marine Guard

And now, to the dessert—the Marine Security Guard. Whether raising the first 50-star American flag with impeccable polish and precision at a July 4 ceremony, patiently checking chancery security late at night, or defending U.S. lives and property during a hostile demonstration, the U.S. Marine Corps is at home in the Foreign Service establishment and has long been its welcome associate.

Since the day in 1805 when the American Consul at Tunis, William Eaton, enlisted the help of a small U.S. Marine detachment and set out from Egypt with thirty-eight Greeks and some 300 Arabs to retake Tripoli for a dethroned pasha,* the USMC has come to the aid of the Foreign Service on many an occasion. Whether or not political historians may judge some of these occasions approvingly, the marines themselves landed to protect legations and consulates from riot and revolution, ran diplomatic despatches through fighting lines, and rescued stranded American officials—not only in Latin America but also during the Boxer Uprising of 1900 in Peking. It was not until 1948 that marines were detailed for embassy guard duty on a regular basis, but the basic authority was

---

* The pasha, Hamet Bey, accompanied the expedition. When Derna had been occupied he presented the commanding officer of the U.S. Marines, Lieutenant P. N. O'Bannon, with an ivory-handled Arab sword—the ancestor of the slightly curved dress saber, with ivory "Mameluke hilt," that USMC officers wear today.

granted by Congress in 1932 and a detachment helped open and staff the new American Embassy at Moscow in 1933.

The first American a visitor is likely to encounter on entering a U.S. chancery will be a clean-cut young man in the uniform of the U.S. Marine Corps. Today, there are marine security guards at some ninety Foreign Service posts, including some of the larger consulates general. At embassies the size of those in London or Paris, with various buildings to be covered, the detachment may number as high as 35. (There are 100 or so at Embassy Saigon, but at the time of writing that could hardly be called a typical Foreign Service post.) The small regulation unit is five men—four "watchstanders" and a noncommissioned officer in charge (the NCOIC, frequently called the "Gunny," because many are gunnery sergeants).*

The noncommissioned officer in charge is often married, with "wife at post"—this is the preferred USMC policy, to lend stability to the operation—but the watchstanders must be single and remain so for the two-year tour. Assuming permission is granted, a Marine may marry at the post after arrival of his relief; needless to say, the young men are considered quite a catch by the female population, both local and American, and not a few return to the States as benedicts.

At four posts, worldwide—Frankfurt am Main, Panamá, Beirut, and Manila—there are "Regional Marine Officers," rank of major or lieutenant colonel, with area supervisory responsibilities. The RMO's were formerly assisted by sergeant majors, but they now have junior commissioned officers. The duties of the latter are largely in personnel work, and in 1968 two of the four were women.

The Corps dates its creation by the Continental Congress as of November 10, 1775, well before American independence

---

* Even smaller units have been known. When the U.S. diplomatic mission in Laos opened for full-scale business in late 1954, the only two marines to arrive for some months stood what they called a sleeping watch—twelve hours on, twelve hours off, with one cot in the chancery and one (not two) in the legation's bachelor quarters.

was declared, and November 10 is a red-letter day at Foreign Service posts lucky enough to have a detachment. The Marine Corps ball is full-dress occasion, its high point the cutting of the birthday cake. The first piece of cake goes to the youngest marine present, the second to the eldest, and both pieces are eaten with ceremony.

For the USMC, "embassy duty" is a volunteer's assignment, for ranks from lance corporal to sergeant. Most of the volunteers have either extended their enlistments or used them as reenlistment options. Selection standards are high, and successful applicants do six weeks at the Corps' "embassy school" in Washington before going on post. Discipline in the detachments is strict, but few have to be sent home prematurely (1968 figures: about 5 per cent). The Marine Guard's job is a demanding one. Its members are charged primarily with the security of the post's classified material—they oversee the after-hours char force, then check all safes, doors, desks, wastebaskets, and so on—and secondarily with the protection of U.S. Government property and the lives of U.S. employees. At the same time, they must keep up on military subjects (through extension courses) and on physical training—and they are always on display to the host country, on duty or off. They represent not only the United States but the American Embassy, and if there are U.S. military elements in the area they make it clear that they are under the orders of the Ambassador, not the military. They are truly the elite of an elite corps, and the Foreign Service is proud to have them in the family.

VII

The Service and the Hill

It has often been said that an institutional weakness of the Foreign Service is its lack of a "public" at home—no domestic constituency, hence no voter appeal to commend it to Congress. The Department of Commerce has the U.S. Chamber of Commerce and the National Association of Manufacturers behind it, the Labor Department has the unions, Agriculture has the American Farm Bureau Federation and other groups, but State has the support of no active pressure group at all. Aside from this lack, the Department and the Service are chronically susceptible to public and congressional mistrust because they are thought of, however inaccurately and unjustly, as "representing foreigners."

Relations with "the Hill"—hearings and briefings on substantive legislation, world events, policy, security, and the like—are handled by the State Department's Office of Congressional Relations, which not only rides herd on the considerable volume of congressional correspondence and related paper work, but also acts as intermediary in arranging for the taking of testimony from departmental and Foreign Service witnesses. (Appropriations legislation is handled separately by the deputy under secretary for administration.) The Secretary, of course, is the chief witness (some twenty-five appearances a year) but the Foreign Service also plays its role, with ambassadors and other high-ranking officers—either on duty in Washington or brought in from the field—being called upon to testify. The exercise, though often grueling, can also be beneficial. An interesting viewpoint on the subject has been advanced by the Honorable James W. Riddleberger, retired Foreign Service officer and holder of the revered rank of career ambassador, who made the following observations in the course of a wide-ranging article in the May, 1968, issue of the *Foreign Service Journal:*

> One of my colleagues said to me, I think it was in Belgrade one night, some years ago, that he really pitied American ambassadors because they were burdened with the necessity of appearing before committees of Congress. As you know, in most European countries it is the minister and his parliamentary secretary, to use the British phrase, who carry all of the interventions within the Parliament. With us, of course, the system is altogether different. We can be and are summoned before committees of the Congress, even though we are non-political. However, in looking back over it, I cannot honestly say that I deplore this experience, however difficult it may have been at certain times. I said to my European colleague: "It is perfectly true, of course, that we are exposed to hearings and questioning that may make it more difficult for us to execute our function when we return to our post. But at the same time the average American ambassador frequently has a domestic political experience that is denied to most of his foreign colleagues. We are compelled by the very nature of our Constitution and government to take account of and to take into very careful account, the attitudes and the feelings within the Congress. I think it makes our role somewhat more difficult in many respects, but I cannot say that I deplore it, and the advantages compensate for the difficulties."

The advantages do indeed compensate. Congressmen must be sensitive to opinion back home, and they respond almost seismographically to vibrations of indignation, alarm, or other waves of emotion about some aspect of foreign affairs or the men who conduct them. It is therefore well that the representatives of the working Foreign Service get a chance to tell their side from time to time, not only with respect to policy and appropriations but also, particularly, on matters concerning organization and structure—testifying at hearings on amendments to the Foreign Service Act, for example, or giving testimony in support of the USIA career bill. Leading members of both the Senate Committee on Foreign Relations and the House Committee on Foreign Affairs—and of several other committees and subcommittees as well—have taken an abiding, sometimes even proprietary, interest in foreign affairs organization and personnel. These gentlemen have come to know the Service well, and although they can play the gadfly when they feel there is a need for it—and some have their personal prejudices—their approach is generally friendly and solution seeking. The Foreign Service people who deal with them, for their part, learn the limits of their domestic political base at first hand, and this knowledge can provide a useful guideline in their work both at home and abroad.

Relations with Congress in Washington, however, are only incidentally part of the Foreign Service job. Relations abroad, through direct as well as indirect contact, are something else again. With the re-emergence of Congress, since World War II, as a major factor in American diplomacy—not only because of its Constitutional prerogatives but also because so much more money needs to be appropriated for the expanded U.S. role overseas—the visit from a member, or members, of Congress has become very much a part of Foreign Service life.

CODEL DOE. SEN AND MRS DOE AND STAFF ASST ROE ON SCHEDULE, DUE SALAMANDRIA THUR APR FIRST AAA FLIGHT 123. RE YOUR X-456 SEN APPROVES PROGRAM BUT ASKS ENSURE EARLY NIGHT FRI DUE DAWN DEPARTURE SAT.

CODEL (Congressional Delegation) flags immediate attention. Upon receipt of the above telegram from a post up the line, Embassy Salamandria starts final preparations for the two-day visit of Senator John Doe and party. It is happy that the Senator has approved the proposed program, even while realizing that fatigue and caprice may play a role in changing it before the visit is over. The call on the Prime Minister and the visit to the National Assembly should go all right, as should the Ambassador's and the Foreign Minister's receptions on Thursday and Friday, but the party may easily beg off on such events as a dispensary visit and a trip through Salamandria's pride, the cement works. Host-country eager beavers have pressed these visits on the Embassy against its better judgment, but it has taken a chance since Senator Doe is known to be always ready to do his bit for public relations.

As things turn out, the visit does not go at all badly. Mrs. Doe has a touch of the local ailment, and is thinking more in terms of a private visit to the dispensary at the chancery than of a public visit to one of the host country's, and she balks at the very thought of the cement works, but the Senator is game and holds up his end in good style.

The substantive part of the program goes off as planned. After the Senator has had a chance to meet the embassy staff and digest the information sheets prepared for him, the Ambassador's briefing begins. Each member of the country team speaks his piece, and the Senator and his assistant ask questions. Before the session ends, the Senator contributes a little briefing of his own, giving the embassy group a useful survey of current political trends and developments back home. In the late afternoon, the Senator and the Ambassador call first on the Foreign Minister, then join forces with the latter for a visit to the Prime Minister. There is an earnest (and at times edgy) discussion of current problems in U.S.–Salamandrian relations, with the Ambassador's executive assistant acting as interpreter. (The Foreign Minister speaks passable English; the Prime Minister does not.) Light refreshments are then served, many photographs are taken, and the Senator grants a brief, stand-up press interview (his second of the day, the first having been at the airport). That night, the Ambassador gives his reception, attended by leading Salamandrians, the diplomatic corps, and the small American community—with special attention shown to anyone from the Senator's home state.

Next morning, the Senator meets with the Speaker of the National Assembly in the latter's office (with warm beer offered at 10:30 A.M.), then accompanies his host to the Assembly floor to be introduced and say a few words to the deputies —in English, through an interpreter. Mrs. Doe, meanwhile, has been taken on a shopping tour by the embassy ladies, and there are purchases to be packaged and mailed to the Senator's Washington office. Richard Roe, the staff assistant, has spent the morning conferring with several of the country team and following up on matters of special interest to the Senator.

Lunch is a family affair, and includes the two embassy staff members who hail from the Senator's state. After lunch, there is some time for relaxation, then off to the dispensary and the cement works. The Ambassador has taken the precaution of sending his executive assistant ahead as advance man, to make sure no changes have been rung in either program. This pays off: at both stops, the embassy officer spots several added features and diplomatically scratches them on the plea that the Senator's schedule is very tight. This plea is literally true, since the Ambassador has neatly contrived to move forward the hour of the Foreign Minister's reception so that the Senator may have his early night. By 9 P.M., the party is back at the residence for a much-appreciated bowl of Chinese soup with toast and American coffee, after which the Senator and the Ambassador spend a relaxed hour rehashing and evaluating the visit. Next morning CODEL Doe is up betimes and, after several stops en route to the airport for "just one more picture," is ready to hit the trail again. Once the party is airborne, Embassy Salamandria phones the next post in line (a short hop) to announce departure on schedule and confirm the Senator's views on his upcoming program expressed by cable the day before.

Not all congressional visits go off so smoothly, of course, and not all CODEL's are so small. A few legislators like to "lone-wolf it" without even a staff assistant, let alone a wife, but many travel in packs and require considerably more organization—especially in contingency planning, since there will almost invariably be at least one congressman who wants to do something not on the program, or just strays off the reservation. Fortunately, the old maxim of "practice makes perfect" plays a role (though not of course to perfection) on the Foreign Service side. In the immediate post–World War II era, with congressional travelers spread all over, many visits were devoted more to hedonistic junketing than to statesmanlike fact-finding—while the Foreign Service, new to the job of handling such visitations, often muffed it through sheer nervous anxiety to please. Then came the ordeal of McCarthy, which made the Service more nervous and the Congress more hard to please than ever. In due course, things evened off, and as the Service regained confidence it also acquired more know-how in the care and feeding of CODEL's. The lawmakers, for their part, came to take their travels more in stride and their role more seriously.

Nowadays, it is unlikely that a senior Foreign Service officer will have got as far as he has without having gone through many congressional visits, including not a few repeaters. The writer himself was host to the same Senator three times, in different parts of the world. He will never forget the spectacle of the honorable gentleman, sitting in water up to his middle with a broad grin on his face, and demanding to be thoroughly photographed before allowing himself to be succored. He had been visiting an AID project where, because of an ill-advised choice of location, the premises had been flooded with the first monsoon rains. The Senator had not purposely fallen off the narrow planking that was the only access route to the site, but once in the water he made the most of an opportunity to dramatize his opposition to the project for his report to posterity.

In recent years, Congress has had more recourse to the useful device of sending out staff assistants on fact-finding missions of their own, especially if the situation calls for personal contact but not necessarily for the presence of a congressman in person. The congressional staff assistant of today is an able professional, often an expert in his own right, and in some cases may actually be the drafting officer on the project he has come to look into. Although these aides are given every co-operation and fittingly entertained, their presence does not put nearly as much strain on a post's facilities as does that of a full delegation.

They also cost less. Congressional travel is financed out of a special fund set up by statute for that purpose. The Treasury Department controls all currencies owned by the United States abroad. Treasury transfers funds from these accounts into a special account administered by the Department of State, which estimates what funds will be required in a given fiscal year. When the funds run low in any country, Treasury is notified and it sets up additional funds for congressional travel. In some instances, it may be necessary to use American dollars to purchase the necessary foreign funds for this purpose.

Even during the postwar "roaring '40's"—when it might take a post weeks or even months to pick up the pieces after a congressional visit—the institution of the globe-trotting congressman had its benefits for American diplomacy. Legislators who had quite frankly come just for the ride could not help but learn something of the problems and attitudes of the countries they visited, and observe at first hand the problems American diplomats faced in their efforts to achieve U.S. goals in those countries.

It also paid off at home. Many an intelligent senator or representative who had formerly taken a rather parochial view of foreign affairs could no longer ignore the realities when the time came for roll call. When he himself had had on-the-spot acquaintance with the people of other nations—and had debated with their leaders, at times rather warmly—he could not simply dismiss their problems by sweeping them under the rug.

None of this means, of course, that the institution of legislative travel has made all congressmen omniscient and right-thinking, nor sold them all down the line on the Foreign Service itself. The latter will probably continue to provide Congress with a convenient public whipping boy, and continue to have trouble getting the funds to operate in the manner to which it would like to become accustomed. Nonetheless, the Congress and the Service have come to know each other better, and each now realizes that the other is not always the monster he once took him to be.

URGENT
A CONGRESSIONAL—FOR IMMEDIATE ACTION
A reply or written acknowledgment must be made within
Three Working Days . . .

Like the term CODEL, this minatory message in red on yellow, when affixed to a piece of correspondence, means quick action, or else.* The whole Foreign Service establishment, but especially the consular element, spends a good bit of its time on "congressional interest" cases. These have to do in the main with visa matters—the immigration of constituents' relatives or friends—but may also concern protection cases and, less frequently, business and commercial affairs. The total volume of the Department's congressional correspondence more than doubled between 1960 and the beginning of 1968, from 11,200 to 26,481 pieces a year.

The typical pattern of the correspondence routine is as follows: the constituent writes (or talks to) his Senator or Representative, the latter writes (or talks to) the State Department, and the Department—if it does not have adequate information to provide an answer directly—passes the case on to the post, normally by air, but if necessary by telegram. The post has three days from date of receipt to make a reply—definitive if possible, interim if not—which it sends in most cases

* There is no statutory punishment for a failure to comply. The offender is simply left in an empty room with a loaded efficiency report, thus given a chance to take the honorable course and select himself out.

directly to the congressman, with copies to the Department. The congressman in turn passes the post's second copy to his constituent, who may if he chooses correspond directly with the post thereafter.*

On the consular side, if the matter is a "protection case"—for example, a constituent worried about the welfare and whereabouts of a traveling relative believed mislaid—the post will set to work along the lines described in Chapter VIII and do what it can to get a quick solution. Generally, however, congressional interest centers on immigration, with the greatest volume coming from those lawmakers with large minority constituencies—some of whom always want to bring kith and kin from the old country. Often, as noted in Chapter IV, the congressman's aid will be enlisted when the constituent's candidate for immigration has been found inadmissible and refused a visa.

In most matters of visa interest, the post will be on top of the case and able to answer forthwith. Some cases, however, can present thorny problems and require considerable effort and consultation; in such instances, an interim reply will be sent, to let the congressman (and the constituent) know that action is under way. Fortunately for the Service, the congressman himself almost always has a common-sense approach, and merely wants to see to it that his constituent gets an answer. Naturally, no member of Congress expects—or wants—a consular officer to twist any laws, regulations, or policies on his or his client's behalf; this is usually made clear by the wording of the original letter of inquiry, for example, "You may be confident that whatever consideration you give this

---

* The problem of world time differences mentioned in Chapter IV can arise here, too. A Texas millionaire interested in the immigration of a German chemist to work for him receives his copy of the post's reply, signed by the principal officer—and, being a Texas millionaire, puts in a person-to-person call to Germany forthwith. If the principal officer is at home, the call will like as not catch him at dinner or later; if the caller is impatient (as he often is) this means rousing the duty officer and/or the visa chief and having them get to the files and call Texas back before the end of office hours, U.S. Central Time.

request commensurate with your policies will be greatly appreciated." He does, quite rightly, expect expeditious and equitable handling of the case—and, if the answer must be no, a reply worded in a manner to help soften the blow to his constituent.

Congressional correspondence on commercial matters—principally concerning trade opportunities for and trade complaints of constituents—generates less volume because, unless the matter is vital enough to warrant bringing up the big guns, businessmen usually deal through the Department of Commerce or correspond with the post directly. Most "congressionals" in the commercial field stem from the complaints of individual constituents who, as tourists, have had trouble either in getting promised delivery of goods paid for or with the quality of goods delivered. A Foreign Service post is perfectly willing to check on such matters in order to oblige, whether the request comes through Congress or directly from the interested party, but must make it clear that it is not itself a collection agency (see Chapter VIII).

UNCLASSIFIED

TO   : Neumania, Salamandria, Upper Tarzania
FROM   : Department of State
SUBJECT : Travel of James Brown
REF   : CA-1234, April 1, 1968

Congressman John Smith of South Dakota has informed the Department of the travel plans of his constituent, James Brown of Deadwood. Please extend appropriate courtesies and assistance, if called upon.

Although not strictly commercial in nature, a fair bit of correspondence is also devoted to congressmen's recommendations of constituent businessmen traveling abroad and, often, combining pleasure with a little busman's holidaying. In such cases, the routine channel is through the Department, which will send a circular airgram* to all posts on the traveler's

* The "airgram" was introduced as a means of bypassing the traditional diplomatic despatch in cases of urgency not warranting a telegram. It

itinerary. (This may also include a word on his credit rating, which is customarily noted when a business traveler approaches the posts via the departments of Commerce and State.) At times, however, a senator or a representative may write the principal officer directly to commend his dear friends the Browns for special consideration. In cases of routine notification through channels, the post will generally leave it to the traveler to report on his treatment, or not (unless, of course, something has gone wrong and explanations are in order). When a member of Congress has taken the trouble to write personally, however, it behooves a principal officer to follow suit with a personal acknowledgement—and to put himself out a bit more for the visitor when he arrives.

Correspondence apart, there is nothing like personal contact to smooth a post's path in its relations with Congress— and especially a post with a chronically heavy load of "congressionals." A principal officer en route to such a post will be well advised, during his prepping in the Department, to go over the post's file of congressional correspondence, pick out the congressmen who account for most of the traffic, and call on them. This courtesy often pays off, not only though the original impact of a show of interest, but also—much more so —later on at the post. When the going gets rough (as it sometimes can, on thorny problem cases) a relationship of personal acquaintance and mutual confidence can help a great deal.

This truism, in fact, might be generalized to cover the whole story of the Foreign Service and the Hill.

---

eschewed the long-windedness and niceties of form (such as "I have the honor to report") and was given priority in airmail delivery and in distribution. Its venerable forebear was soon supplanted entirely, and in today's usage the airgram is generally called a despatch (or instruction, if it goes out from the Department). In the process, of course, its original claim to priority handling has been lost. Long-windedness has returned, and all that is left is a traditional despatch without the niceties.

VIII

The Embassy, the Consulate, and Americans Abroad

This is a recording. The Consulate General will be closed until Monday morning at 7:45 A.M. If you have an emergency, please call the duty officer, Vice Consul William Beck, on Monterrey 3-06-50. I repeat: this is a recording.

It was 2:40 A.M. on a Saturday as Bill Beck, stumbling sleepily toward the phone and hoping it wouldn't wake the baby, sighed to himself, "I guess the duty's begun." The voice at the other end was American, and upset. "Is that the American Consul? I want the American Consul. This is Joe Jones—Joseph J. Jones of Cincinnati, Ohio. We've been in sort of an accident and they've taken my wife to the hospital and the Mexican cops are holding me at the police station in, uh, hang on a minute—in, uh, Villa Guadaloopy . . . yeah, that's right, Route 52 to Mexico City."

"O.K., sir, don't worry, we'll do our best to take care of you. Better let me talk to the police."

Bill had easy Spanish, and after a few minutes' talk with the desk sergeant learned that Mr. Jones, traveling at a fair clip, had plowed into one of the casual cows that made night driving down the long, straight highway a menace; that neither Jones was seriously hurt, although there was a bit of blood and Mrs. Jones might have some broken bones, that damage to the car was not extensive, but the vehicle was not in condition for onward travel even were this permitted; and, finally, that Mr. Jones appeared to have adequate insurance and was not under arrest but must remain at the station house till he could get a lawyer and settle the paper work. Bill located the list of lawyers that all duty officers abroad keep handy and read off the names of three residing nearby from which Mr. Jones might make a choice. He also asked whether the desk sergeant knew Doña Matilda Maloney at the Motel Victoria in neighboring Matehuala and, on learning that he did, asked that she be called if any problems arose. He then talked once more to Mr. Jones, reassuringly, and promised to keep in touch.

Twenty minutes later, Vice Consul William Beck was in his office at the Monterrey Consulate General, writing up his notes and checking the duty officer's handbook; he had served his rotational tour in the citizenship and protection section, and knew the drill pretty well, but his present duties were administrative and he thought it well to make sure he was not forgetting anything. He then called the Guadalupe police back and learned that (1) lawyer Martínez Gómez had been reached and was on his way to the station and (2) Doña Matilda Maloney was already there. Word from the clinic was that Mrs. Jones had only cuts and bruises and a cracked collarbone, and could travel when necessary; Mr. Jones, meanwhile, was partaking of beer and sandwiches brought by Doña Matilda and seemed as relaxed as could be expected under the circumstances. Bill chatted with Mrs. Maloney and thanked her warmly. Then, ten minutes later, the lawyer called to say that Mr. Jones's insurance was in order, all was under control, and the Señor Cónsul could go back to bed.

As noted in the preceding chapter, the Foreign Service does not have a domestic public in the generally accepted sense. Nor is "service to the public"—so large a part of many Cabinet departments' business—an activity of the State Department except in such relatively limited fields as the issuance of passports, the handling of welfare and whereabouts cases at the U.S. end, and the work of its public information services, which furnish materials on foreign policy to educational organizations and institutions, provide visiting speakers, and organize foreign policy conferences and briefings for interested citizens.

Abroad, however, service to the public is a major concern of every Foreign Service post. Aside from relations with the host country (which entail a variety of services to all strata of the local society from the humblest visa applicant to the foreign minister and, on occasion, the ruler himself), an embassy or consulate engages in a wide field of activity involving aid, counsel, and services to American citizens abroad—tourists, transients, and residents.

Such services fall principally into two traditional categories: consular and commercial. In these fields, domestic interests do enter the picture, but on an individual rather than a group-interest basis. Typical examples: Joe Jones's accident, relatives vitally concerned with the fate of a missing American, or in the immigration of a sister, cousin, or aunt from the old country; businessmen in search of trade information, or seeking redress in cases of fraud. A third category of service, equal in importance but by its nature smaller in scale than consular and commercial work, is assistance to the American press, both itinerant and resident. Finally, although not "services," there are the post's social and cultural relationships—principally with resident Americans but also, on occasion, with transients.

"I Want the American Consul"

Consular services to Americans in foreign places cover a broad range, from such simple operations as the renewal of passports, taking of affidavits, or issuance of Social Security checks to the frequently complicated and sometimes gruesome business of protection and welfare work. Not all the millions of U.S. citizens who travel abroad come through their adventures unscathed. Some are stranded or become destitute, others fall ill or are injured. Many lose their money or their passports—some even their wits—while a number run afoul of the local law (in some cases innocently, in others not at all). And every year, Foreign Service posts throughout the world must cope with their quota of compatriot eccentrics.*

Vice Consul Bill Beck's fictional weekend duty, although no picnic, was light in that there were no deaths or serious incidents. Over a million Americans travel into the interior of Mexico every year, and it is inevitable that some get into trouble. The Monterrey consular district covers four good-sized Mexican states, and it is often out of the question for consular officers to make it to the scene in an emergency—Matehuala, for example, is a good five-hour drive from Monterrey—but it has long been the Consulate General's practice throughout the district to cultivate and maintain an unofficial auxiliary of resident Americans, like Doña Matilda Maloney, willing to lend a hand when compatriots get into trouble.

At the Monterrey CG's Monday morning staff meeting, Bill, as duty officer of the week, would have spoken first. His report: "Well, the weekend was pretty standard. Another American couple ran afoul of the livestock near Matehuala. Our friend Auntie Matilda took care of it for us, God bless her—nothing serious, luckily. One young lady stranded—I got her a bus ticket to the border, with money from the kitty. And—oh, yes—another compatriot caught with the goods by the narcotics boys. They nabbed him heading for the border with half a kilo of grass. He's already been interrogated and has confessed; I visited him in the poky last night and got him to pick a lawyer—Rodríguez Peña."

Bill's stranded young lady, in good health and spirits but out of funds, would be given the address of the nearest Health, Education, and Welfare office across the border and told that

---

* In Laos, the writer once spent a bemusing week with the problems of an elderly American Buddhist monk from Yonkers, who had come to pass the summer visiting Southeast Asian monasteries and decided, almost on arrival, that he had made a mistake. Among other things, he complained that his issued robes "itched" him.

HEW would pick her up from there at the end of the bus trip paid for out of a modest fund kept going by the American Society of Monterrey.

Although consular responsibilities include the repatriation of indigent compatriots, Congress has not appropriated funds for this purpose.* Where there is an established American community, as in Monterrey, keeping a small welfare kitty going usually presents no problem, but in small and remote posts, more ingenuity is called for; some hold fund-raising affairs, and one small embassy in Southeast Asia was for a time able to keep its kitty going by selling the wood in which supply shipments came crated. Usually, however, the indigence to be coped with is temporary, as when a tourist has been robbed or loses his belongings in a hotel fire. In such cases, the post immediately notifies his friends or relatives back home and asks for funds.

The delinquent Bill Beck reported had been caught with marijuana, bought to be smuggled and resold in the States, would probably have been good for a year or two in the local penitentiary, although he might be the beneficiary of a gubernatorial pardon at year's end. American citizens who break Mexican law are subject to its penalties. All the Consulate General is expected or permitted to do is to keep in touch and see to it that they do not lack for normal comforts, have competent legal advice, and receive every consideration to which Mexican law entitles them.

In 252 embassies and consulates scattered around the world,† American consular officers like Bill Beck stand ready to help their fellow citizens with routine or emergency problems. Americans abroad expect a great deal from their consuls, and they get it, but travelers sometimes have an exag-

---

* Funds are available, on a loan basis, for the evacuation of American citizens from a foreign country when it is determined by the Ambassador that they should leave and they are without resources for transportation.

† Throughout this section, the terms "consulate," "consular officer" and the like refer either to the consular services unit of an embassy or to the corresponding element in a constituent post (consulate or consulate general).

gerated idea of what an American passport entitles them to and are vexed when they find there are limitations to what a consul can do for them. He may not, for example, cash checks or act as an agent, attorney, or in a fiduciary capacity in their behalf—although he can and does advise them how to obtain such services. To the surprise of some tourists, he is not empowered to perform marriages—although he can, in his official capacity, witness a wedding and issue an impressive-looking "Certificate of Witness to Marriage." Marriages performed abroad have whatever validity the law of the country gives them, but many Americans attach great importance to a consular officer's presence at such a ceremony. There is a story, possibly apocryphal, of an American missionary in China who, when officiating at an American wedding, climaxed sonorously with "In the presence of Almighty God and of Vice Consul John Smith, I now pronounce you man and wife."

If an American lands in jail, a consular officer will visit him if he desires it, talk to him in private, and arrange for legal assistance. The Consulate sees to it that Americans are not discriminated against because of their nationality, advises them of their rights as U.S. citizens, and generally assists them to get a fair deal. However, a consular officer may not use his position to influence the outcome of a case, and he is bound by the universal rule that the legality of an act must be determined by the law of the country in which it took place. Actually, an officer will usually do everything short of engineering an escape to ensure fair treatment for his countrymen. (And the writer knows of one case in which a consul general had to fight off an offer by overzealous compatriots to do just that: engineer the jailbreak of another American.)

In practice, any competent consular officer will have built up cordial working relationships with the local police, health, and other municipal and institutional authorities. If a countryman runs afoul of the law, or is injured or victimized, a well-connected consul is in a good position to ensure that he gets the best possible break. Harmonious relations can be fostered at no greater cost than simple friendliness and consideration; nonetheless, an occasional luncheon or cocktail invitation helps considerably, and, in the writer's opinion, too little thought is given to the consular working level when available representation funds are being doled out.

Assistance Rendered in Death Cases

With so many present-day Americans traveling and living abroad, a number will die away from home; in 1967, the figure was over 6,000. It is the consular officer who cables word of the death to the Department of State, which in turn notifies the family and asks for burial instructions and funds to cover costs. If the deceased is to be returned home for burial, the consular officer makes the necessary arrangements and sees to it that the body is cleared to depart the one country and enter the other. It is he, also, who prepares the "Consular Report of the Death of an American Citizen," which is generally accepted as an official proof of death.

These are the formalities, and when death is "peaceful" little more is required than to keep the paper work moving and take possession and dispose of the deceased's personal property. (The consular officer is charged with this responsibility by U.S. law, when there is no legal representative of the deceased on hand.) In cases of sudden death and tragedy, the picture is quite different. Had Mrs. Jones been killed, or had there been other serious complications, Bill Beck would have had to get down to the scene as soon as he could—and in the event of a more extensive tragedy he would have roused his boss and called for reinforcements. When a plane carrying 117 travelers from Atlanta, Georgia, crashed near Paris a few years ago—with no survivors—all available embassy hands were pressed into service to work around the clock with French and airline officials (plus a special FBI team and the Mayor of Atlanta, flown in for this purpose) to expedite identification and push through the work of disposition of remains.

Even disposing of a deceased compatriot's effects can cause problems at times. With no next-of-kin on the scene, these possessions are taken over temporarily by the Consulate. At a busy post, where several such cases may be pending at a given time, the protection section can look more like a baggage room than a consular office. The matter of inventory and accountability, moreover, is not always a cut-and-dried affair. Pilferage before the Consulate's representative can reach the scene is always a possibility: on one occasion, a valuable diamond ring, which the crash victim was reported to have been wearing the night before, was nowhere to be found—and the police who had been first on the scene swore they had never laid eyes on it. (In this case, fortunately, the culprit was later turned in by one of his fellow officers.)

Welfare and Whereabouts Cases

American consulates around the world are asked to trace nearly 1,000 lost Americans each year. In extreme cases, and where staff can be spared, a consular officer may go after the missing man himself. Such was the situation several years ago in Ecuador, when two Americans were reported missing after setting out to climb the Sangay Volcano, most active and dangerous in the Andes. A consular officer at Embassy Quito received his orders from the Ambassador: "Go find 'em." He organized a search party, which included Indian packers and two Ecuadoran mountain climbers, and headed for the wilderness, where army search patrols were already at work. From the last remote hacienda, the base of the volcano was two days away—one hard day on horseback, eighteen hours on foot the next. The party came upon one of the missing men, exhausted and barely conscious after six days without food, at the end of the first day. The other, who had insisting on pushing on alone against what were in fact impossible odds, was never found— although the party kept up the search for ten more days, during which it got lost itself for a time.

In the annals of the Foreign Service, there are many such instances of performance above and beyond the call of duty, and by no means all of them have happy endings. A young officer in the Central African Republic traveled 2,700 miles over rugged trails and through jungle savanna and marshland, trying to follow up a lead in the case of an American student missing in a dugout canoe. He later wangled the use of the Republic's only helicopter and spent days overflying likely looking islands, then made one more trip to the area with friends of the student who had come from the States—only to learn in the end that the alleged sighting report had been a cruel and malicious hoax. The student was never found.

Few posts have the staff to spare for such large-scale exploits as these, or even to develop leads beyond routine checks, but they do have a well-set procedural pattern that has proved generally effective. The consulate provides inquiring relatives with a list of reputable private investigators and, when circumstances warrant it, enlists the aid of the police. If any relatives or friends of the missing person are known to be in the country, consular officials will check with them. When an itinerary can be obtained, a check will be made of the places he was due to visit—while another is made with the immigration authorities. In some countries, especially those behind the Iron Curtain, cooperation may be poor; in others, cooperation may be good but records poor; in still others, cooperation and records may be excellent but there may be just too many ports of entry through which an American citizen could leave or enter the country. Withal, the record of the Service in the matter of locating the lost and strayed has been a good one.

Reasons for disappearance may range from amnesia to kidnapping to just plain taking a powder, but, as often as not, the hide-and-seeker has been on a binge and has temporarily withdrawn from circulation—or, indeed, has been withdrawn by the local gendarmery. In the latter event—when a tourist gets too boisterous, for example—good relations between the consul and the police usually bring about a friendly phone call to "come and get him," rather than an entry on the police blotter.*

Emergency Evacuation

The evacuation of Americans in time of crisis is a recognized responsibility of all Foreign Service posts, and emergency plans are developed and kept current on a mandatory basis. Although posts are no longer permitted to canvass for American citizen registration—this was considered bureaucratic busybodiness by some—it is inescapable that whenever and wherever there is trouble in the offing the number of citizen registrations multiplies manyfold.

During the 1967 Middle East crisis, more than 30,000 Americans were moved to safe haven in a mass evacuation never before equaled for speed, scope, and efficiency—and this with hardly a ripple of public notice. As the *Foreign Service Journal* commented wryly at the time, since modern-day journalism requires a sharp focus on as few individuals as possible no one will ever hear the details of how 30,000 American men, women, and children escaped from the danger zone (many with only hand luggage), how the word to move out was passed in Cairo in the middle of the night, how an overland convoy moved through the desert from Iraq to Iran, or how so many evacuees piled up in Rome hotels that they began to interfere with the tourist pleasure of other Americans untouched by the crisis. The *Journal* noted one common reference running through the accounts of the escapees: "the American Consul." The term as used covered virtually everyone in the American missions involved in the evacuation,

* Good police relations paid off rather differently when the writer was Ambassador at Brazzaville. Early in the morning, after a much-publicized reception at the residence, he answered a phone call that turned out to be from the police. The desk sergeant said cheerfully: "Ah, *bon jour, Excéllence*, we have had your houseboy Nestor with us overnight. He is still a bit hung over, but I think he will survive—though his uniform may not. If you will be good enough to send the chauffeur Pierre down here with 500 francs (US $2) we shall be happy to let you have him back."

from ambassadors to code clerks. It was not a *consul ex machina* but hard-working, hard-pressed Foreign Service people who managed the evacuation.

Vessels and Seamen

The consular officer has a special and traditional duty with respect to seamen; it is, in fact, the oldest major consular function and dates back to the days of Benjamin Franklin. Working conditions "before the mast" have improved considerably since the days of the clippers, and a captain may no longer "shanghai" bodies or dump undesired hands ashore in foreign ports. Every time a crew member leaves or joins a ship, he must be signed on or off the ship's articles in the presence of a consular officer, and seamen's affairs account for a good part of the work load at seaport consulates.

The activity referred to in the consular manual under the heading "Vessels and Seamen" is usually routine in nature, involving friendly greetings to ship's captains, processing their "Marine Notes of Protest"* when necessary, safeguarding ship's papers during layovers and, occasionally, processing the signing on or discharge of American seamen. There are, however, times when the duty gets more lively, as when a ship docks with a seaman in irons or when a sailor on shore leave goes on a spree and has to be sprung from jail or miss his ship.

Reflections on Consular Duties

Most consular services, though useful, are fairly routine. Consular officers take depositions from witnesses abroad for use in American courts and authenticate such documents of public record as birth, marriage, and death certificates, adoption and divorce papers, deeds, and other legal papers. Consulates, of course, also issue and renew American passports, distribute Social Security and veteran's checks, register American citizens on demand, and perform a variety of personal

* "Having experienced rough and boisterous weather and fearing damage to the ship and cargo . . . ," and so on.

services. All this can become pretty humdrum after a time, and rare is the officer—junior or senior—who does not welcome an occasional crisis. No one relishes being roused in the middle of the night to cope with the battered remains of a cracked-up compatriot, but it does enliven things a bit—and it helps the officer to feel more a part of the Foreign Service tradition of business-as-usual under unusual conditions.

As American industry broadens its foreign clientele and partnerships, more and more businessmen and attorneys realize they need a consular officer to have a document executed, an affidavit sworn to, an individual's testimony taken, or copies of public records obtained and authenticated. In commercial and economic affairs, the consular section, if properly run, will coordinate its activity with the post's commercial and economic officers; consular and commercial services often overlap and complement each other.

This development is interesting, in that it appears to be bringing closer once again a traditional relationship which once held the terms consular services and commercial services almost synonymous. When the eleventh-century European merchants began to establish themselves commercially in the Middle East, flag followed trade rather than the reverse. Unwilling to submit to local law and justice, these merchants devised a special regime for themselves, i.e., the appointment of magistrates familiar with the national laws of the foreign traders, to represent them before the local authorities. The merchants fixed it so they could choose one of their own colleagues for this office, and called him their consul. If several trading-nation groups were present, there were several consuls. Later, with the growth of inter-European trade, cities soon began exchanging consuls among themselves. These officials, appointed by the state rather than by the merchants, were principally charged with the settlement of trade disputes, whether by land or sea (*consules mercatorum; consules artis maris*).

Almost from the beginning of foreign business ventures by

U.S. citizens, Yankee traders not only expected active support from their consuls—they demanded it. By the turn of the nineteenth century, more and more American businessmen were going abroad to look into potential markets, and beginning to meet their consuls personally. Most of these consuls were, unfortunately, spoils-system types. Disgruntled, many businessmen complained to their congressmen of the quality of the representation. Their influence was considerable. It helped with the Act of 1906, and a well-known professor of international affairs, writing in the 1920's, noted that the Foreign Service merit system—which peaked in the Rogers Act—owed its success in no small measure to American businessmen with foreign interests who wanted the consular service strengthened and spurred their congressmen accordingly. For a time, consular and commercial services were so close that today one Commerce Department veteran recalls having served in the "Consular-Commercial Office" of the State Department.

THE COMMERCIAL ATTACHÉ AT WORK

In regard to the principle of a single representation abroad, the Department of Commerce has shown no visible separatist tendencies since it reamalgamated its foreign service with that of the State Department in 1939, after several years of existence apart. A State-Commerce agreement in 1956 expanded personnel interchange between the two services, the work of a joint task force in 1966 further strengthened the alliance, and an ancillary agreement, in 1961, stressed the need of and made provision for a commercial specialist program. For some years, FSO participation in commercial work has been considerable: as of the end of January, 1968, there were 135 Foreign Service and 22 Commerce Department officers doing such work full time abroad, while 27 FSO's were on detail at Commerce in Washington. In addition, there were 150 FSO's in jobs that contributed substantially to trade expansion support. The relationship has been generally harmonious and mutually profitable, and the office of commercial attaché has become a key position at Foreign Service posts.* Basically, the attaché's work involves, on the one hand, services to U.S. businessmen interested in foreign trade and, on the other, assistance to foreigners interested in doing business with the United States—i.e., the obverse and reverse of the coin of American world trade.

The history of the Foreign Service reflects a continuing effort by State and Commerce to improve their relations with and services to the American business community. Abroad, the keystone of the relationship is a fund of mutual confidence and cooperation between the Embassy and the American community. The Ambassador and his officers must play a leading role—many mission chiefs hold periodic give-and-take sessions with community business leaders—but it is the commercial attaché and his staff who foster and maintain such relationships from day to day, in the office and out of it. If the town has an American chamber of commerce, the attaché should be active in it, and while he must ration his time between compatriots and host-countrymen, he must not favor the latter to a disproportionate degree. Good embassy-community relations benefit both sides: the attaché can often get as much help and information from resident Americans as they can from him.

The activities of commercial attachés around the world today involve many a business drama:

• In a western European capital, the U.S. commercial attaché confers with an official of the ministry of trade, a personage with whom he has frequent personal and official contact. The attaché has learned of proposed legislation, inspired and provoked by the powerful wine lobby, to ban the sale of a

* Normally, the head of the commercial unit at an embassy is given the diplomatic title of commercial attaché—or counselor at the largest posts. Commercial officers assigned to consular posts use their consular or functional title: consul, vice consul, or commercial officer. In the interest of simplification, the term commercial attaché will be used to refer to all heads of commercial units, regardless of diplomatic or consular status.

popular American soft drink on the grounds that it contains a noxious chemical. He argues that it would be only fair to have the liquid tested chemically before judgment is passed, and the official cannot disagree. In due course, a test proves the charge to be baseless, and the legislation is dropped.

• A worried American businessman is seated in the office of the commercial attaché at an embassy in southern Asia. His story, alas, is a familiar one. A dealer in animal hides, he began importing consignments from a man known to him as "Sheikh Mohammed." He had inspected the first several shipments and found them up to standard, then relaxed his vigilance and began allowing his warehouse to accept shipments without examining them. Some months later he found he had been paying fancy prices for worthless trash. *Question:* Who is Sheikh Mohammed and where can he be found? Can the attaché help? *Answer:* At this late date, unfortunately not— although the attaché still dreams of catching up with the elusive sheikh and bringing him to book. Had the businessman taken the precaution of checking with the World Trade Directory report (see page 207), which the attaché had filed on "Sheikh Mohammed," and which was available in Washington, he would have learned that the name was one of many aliases used by an unscrupulous fly-by-nighter who changed names and whereabouts as fast as he could exact his toll, then fold his tents and move on.

• A routine communication comes to the desk of the commercial attaché in Tokyo: a prominent West Coast chinaware manufacturer is interested in an arrangement to sell the chinaware products of a Japanese firm on the U.S. market. The format of the communication is routine, but the attaché does not treat its substance as such. Aware of the excellent reputation of the American firm in its field, and alive to the potentialities of such an alliance, he devotes considerable time and effort to bringing the American company together with one of Japan's most prominent china manufacturers—the makers of "Noritake." The result has been a major and mutually profitable business commitment, and Noritake has become a respected brand name in the States.

• In a Latin American capital, a solid-looking citizen enters the Embassy's commercial reading room, looks around tentatively at the neatly arranged American newspapers and periodicals, trade journals and directories, and eventually picks up a specialized directory on electronic products. The young receptionist, a local girl of good family who enjoys her job with the Embassy, has had her eye on the visitor and goes up to ask whether she can be of help. He tells her he owns a radio-television business and is eager to branch out into the latest fad—portable transistors. How does he go about making a connection with a U.S. firm, with a view to either a licensing arrangement or a dealership? The receptionist suggests he might wish to talk with the commercial attaché, whose office is right down the hall, calls her boss, finds him in and receptive, and ushers the visitor to his office. The attaché is polite and attentive, and takes down the basic data, but the visitor's name vaguely rings a bell and he is noncommittal insofar as immediate action is concerned; he will be in touch with the gentleman soon. Sure enough, a file check confirms that the man is—well—a bit shady. (His senior local could have told him that right off, but at the time he was out chasing down data for a World Trade Directory report.)

• In the same Latin American capital, a similar situation develops, but the visitor is "on the up and up" and wants to go to the States to make his connections personally. In this case, the attaché will probably issue him a "commercial invitation" on behalf of the Secretary of Commerce.* This invitation welcomes the visitor to the Bureau of International Commerce and to the Department's field offices, and informs him that these offices will be notified of his interest and his

---

* At many posts, a direct tie-in has been established between the visa section and the commercial unit. Local businessmen applying for visitors' visas are handed a letter signed by the commercial attaché, noting that his office is right upstairs (or wherever) and he would be delighted to meet the prospective traveler and render any assistance he can.

itinerary and will be ready to help in locating U.S. business-men interested in establishing trade connections in his field. Notice of the impending visit will further be published in the Commerce Department's weekly *International Commerce,* which has a wide distribution in the American business world.

Trade Promotion

The above examples illustrate to some degree how the attaché promotes U.S. foreign trade through reporting, correspondence, and personal contact. Many of his reports to Washington eventually reach a large American business readership, while direct correspondence with individual businessmen often helps answer specific questions or supply information not readily available from the Commerce Department at home.

Although he must remain an independent and unbiased observer, it is essential that the attaché develop access to all reliable channels of information, never having to depend on a single source but being able to weigh and analyze data from different sources with different points of view—not neglecting the political factor, which in the world of trade today may often as not influence the commercial/economic decision.

In the writer's view, the principal *raison d'être* of a commercial officer is his usefulness as a catalyst between the business interests of the United States and those of the host country. To maintain this usefulness requires personal contact—constant contact with a variety of groups. As mentioned earlier, the commercial officer must have the friendship and confidence of the American business community and play a substantial role in its activities. He must equally be *persona grata* at both the ministry of trade and the foreign ministry, as well as with the leading bankers, businessmen, and trade and industrial associations of the host country. Finally—and perhaps most importantly—he must get to know and understand the host-country people and be able to interpret the national mood. All this makes for an active life and demands an outgoing personality. The effective commercial attaché is never a deskbound automaton, poring over piles of statistics in order to grind out reams of replies to queries from Washington. (If he is any good, he will have a well-trained local staff to take most of such work off his hands.)

Nonresident American businessmen fall generally into two categories. First, there are those who have no particular problems but just want to pay a courtesy call and make their presence known. This type will probably call first on the Ambassador or principal officer, who in turn will summon his commercial chief—and often, incidentally, offer appropriate hospitality on his own. Secondly, there are those—transients and newcomers—with problems. Aside from the feckless who get taken by the "Sheikh Mohammeds," anyone new to trading abroad may run into situations entirely outside his experience. Transactions that would be wholly private at home often involve government or quasi-government participation in many countries, and a private trader simply cannot get off the ground without assistance. In an oil-rich Arab state, for example, it takes an experienced and well-connected embassy officer just to map out strategy and guide his countryman through the labyrinth of Arab bureaucracy—even when both parties recognize a deal to be advantageous and are anxious to do business.

The attaché may not himself execute selling or purchasing contracts or act as an agent for an American firm, nor discriminate in favor of one American firm against another, nor give out information on competitors. But from his broad knowledge of the local market place he can often help a compatriot quickly find a suitable local representative or other contact. He can provide briefing and documentation on the general economic, commercial, and political situation in the country, its policies affecting trade and investment, and its plans for economic development—or, in case of need, data in depth on particular imports or exports in which the U.S. trader may be interested. He may also arrange suitable local appointments, as noted above. What he may not do is vouch for his own countryman's reputation, technical competence, or financial standing—unless he has had advance notice of these.

Advance notice will usually come through regular channels, along with information on the visitor's plans, if the post is notified of the impending visit through the Department of Commerce in Washington. Because the assistance requested by most businessmen does require advance preparation, the latter will save everyone's time if they give such notice—to allow the attaché to brief himself on the enterprise involved, gather the necessary data and, when pertinent, pass word of the businessman's visit and objectives to suitable local interests.

Trade Protection

It is the attaché's duty to be watchful on behalf of the commercial interests of the United States and its citizens and to report any evidence that such interests are being discriminated against. If a problem is at the governmental level, a well-connected attaché can usually solve it amicably, formally or informally. Problems between American and foreign businessmen are more common, and here the ultimate responsibility rests with the parties themselves—but the U.S. Government has a valid interest in helping promote a settlement and may offer, but not insist on, its intermediary services. The offer is usually welcomed, and the mediation often successful.

Nonetheless, the Foreign Service is not a collection agency for either American or foreign traders, and much correspondence is devoted to dispelling this common misconception. A commercial unit can and does supply information on reputable attorneys and collection agencies and tries to clear up misunderstandings—sometimes through getting the parties to accept arbitration by a private group such as a chamber of commerce. Anything the post can do to help settle trade disputes improves relations, leads to continued business, and creates a better climate for U.S. trade.

Trade Missions

The past decade has witnessed the growth of the useful and constructive device of the traveling trade mission, a cooperative venture of American business and government that establishes person-to-person contact between U.S. and foreign businessmen. Trade missions are usually made up of four to six businessmen of recognized stature in their fields, accompanied by one or two government officers. These gentlemen, who volunteer their services and work without compensation (excepting expenses) represent the U.S. commercial community as a whole and not merely their own business interests. More recently, another type of mission has developed, organized by industry, unsubsidized but nominally sponsored by the Department of Commerce. Since the members pay their own way they are free to do business on their own, and generally visit countries with more developed and lucrative markets.

Trade missions, especially the "official" ones, are often but not always tied in with U.S. participation in international trade fairs. Such participation, through U.S. national exhibitions, is a joint government-industry effort given permanent status by Congress in 1956, to tell the story of free institutions as well as promote two-way trade (and, on one famous occasion in Sokolniki Park, a two-way "kitchen debate" between Messrs. Nikolai Khrushchev and Richard M. Nixon). When there is a trade-fair tie-in, the mission sets up headquarters at the fair grounds; otherwise, usually, at the local chamber of commerce or a similar association. In either case, it uses the American Embassy or Consulate as a logistical and operational base.

The post's job begins well before the mission arrives and continues after it leaves—first in preparing the ground, later in riding herd on the necessary follow-up work. A full-scale briefing is given the group on arrival, usually presided over by the Ambassador—or, at a consulate, by the principal officer—with the commercial attaché playing the key action role.

Trade missions, fortunately, bring representation allowances with them, although the post willingly makes available its residential and other entertainment facilities.

Any assistance the post can render is more than repaid by the enhanced effectiveness trade missions impart in providing a practical and high-caliber consultation service to local business and industry. The writer has hosted six such missions and helped with others; the teams have been uniformly broad-gauged and well prepared, and their activities have benefited not only our commercial-economic work but also the U.S. image in general. Moreover, by stimulating an increase in American exports, they help out considerably with the balance-of-payments problem.

Commercial Reporting

A large part of the work load of any commercial unit lies, of course, in its reporting. Since this services the public only impersonally, the writer will limit himself to commenting briefly on the principal reporting requirements. They are:

World Trade Directory Reports. Reliable commercial intelligence on prospective trade connections abroad. The worldwide file contains some 120,000 active WTDR's (of nearly a half-million prepared) which may be purchased from the Department of Commerce at $2 each. (It was this type of report that the victim of Sheikh Mohammed should have consulted.)

Trade Lists. Information on firms engaged in a particular industry. Available at $1 each, or may be consulted free of charge at the Commerce Department or its field offices.

Trade Contact Surveys. Canvasses of local agents, distributors, manufacturers or suppliers, prepared selectively on specific request.

Trade Opportunities. Reports prepared whenever the attaché discovers a bona fide opportunity for an American manufacturer, exporter, importer, contractor, engineer, or other businessman to establish commercial relations with a responsible party abroad. These are published in the Commerce Department's weekly *International Commerce*. A recent addition to this type of service is the "commercial investment newsletter," being put out by fifty-two posts as of early 1968 and available to American businessmen in the United States.

The commercial unit also contributes to the post's regular economic reporting program, which generally calls for one or more of the following types of principal reports: a biweekly economic review, from selected areas; a quarterly, semiannual, or annual economic trends report; a semiannual or annual politicoeconomic assessment.

The economic trends report—by definition an integrated statement of the situation and identifiable trends in a given country, with an evaluation of implications for the United States—has its focus on American business interests, actual or potential. It is unclassified (though classified addenda may be submitted when necessary) and available not only at home but also at the posts, to any American or local businessman who may be interested. Copies are available in the commercial unit, and at many posts it is sent out to a mailing list. In one Latin American capital, a prominent local newspaper translates the report into Spanish and publishes it, often on the front page.

All this reporting requires legwork and research, digging and delving. Even though the attaché has a full-time American assistant and/or a junior officer on training rotation, he must lean heavily on his local staff—not only for covering the market place and searching out and collating statistics but for a goodly amount of first-drafting, which the attaché can check for facts, style, and English before it is put in final form. The writer has worked with and inspected a number of "commercial locals" and found them, with very few exceptions, to be loyal, able, and industrious—an asset to the U.S. image abroad. The American businessman, principal beneficiary of their efforts, owes them a debt of gratitude.

GENTLEMEN OF THE PRESS

New Delhi, 1962. The Red Chinese "invasion" of India has just begun. Within a few days of the first headlines, big names rally 'round—Mr. Averell Harriman and a jetload of political and military experts, the American commander of CINC-STRIKE, the British chief of staff. British, American, and Indian chiefs meet constantly. Other jets full of American weapons touch down at Calcutta.

At the same time, inevitably, still other jets are disgorging representatives of the world press. The American contingent includes correspondents from leading metropolitan dailies, news magazines, press and radio-TV services, and others. Although they are ready and willing to exploit any sources they can turn up, it is to the American Embassy that they will look for the word on what is going on and what the United States is doing about it.

The key man in this situation is the press attaché, a USIS officer who has had experience as a member of the working press. It is he who will handle the horde: bona fide experts on the crisis area, truly famous writers, electronic journalists encumbered with equipment and helpers, instant experts who have read all about the country and the problem on the plane trip over, nonentities whose editors owed them a trip to a "big story." The attaché has already shooed the local employees out of the commercial library at the rear of the Embassy, anticipating a demand for frequent briefings, and sessions are soon being held two or three times a day—sometimes with the Ambassador or other embassy officers participating, sometimes with the attaché carrying the ball by himself. There follow hectic weeks for all concerned, but the attaché and his colleagues manage to do the job expected of them: to get across to the American people, in terms the Embassy wants it expressed, the story of what is going on—insofar as the Americans know what is going on—and to provide such background material and logistic assistance as the press may need (including help in getting the electronic journalists' tapes and films out of the country).

Titular press attachés are found today only at the larger embassies such as London, Paris, Bonn, New Delhi (and now, Saigon). They are customarily USIS officers with journalistic backgrounds, on special detail because the recognized regular target of the USIS in the news field is the host-country press and radio-TV. The degree of influence a press officer may have on the visiting or locally assigned American news fraternity depends in large measure on the press attitudes of the Ambassador and his senior staff. Nonetheless, a good press attaché—as spokesman for the Ambassador and the Embassy but also as one who enjoys informal, personal relationships with his clients—can have a direct and important influence on the picture Americans at home get, through their press, of the Foreign Service and its conduct of U.S. foreign relations abroad.

Aside from his day-to-day relations with resident American correspondents—and with descending hordes in times of crisis —the press attaché must handle the itinerants. These range from notable newsmen passing through to small-town editors traveling on their own or on cooked-up "press tours," which can be written off at income-tax time. With this latter category, an attaché can be of great help to a chief of mission. Few of the itinerants have serious problems, but they all expect service: the big names usually want an interview with the Ambassador, which the attaché can arrange for a convenient time while sizing up the visitor and his wants beforehand; the unsophisticated need not only briefing but also basic and careful guidance (this in the Embassy's interest as well as in their own).

At medium-sized posts that have no press attaché, the "American" job may be handled by the USIS press officer, an embassy officer, or a combination of both. At small posts without any regular press officer, where there are seldom resident American correspondents and where U.S. newsmen come to town only for special stories, it is usually a senior embassy officer—or the principal officer at a consulate—who deals with them and sees to their needs. The writer has done this duty often, and found the "regulars" to be a cheery and knowledgeable lot (with some outstanding exceptions, of course). A half-dozen or so took up in-and-out residence in beleaguered Hanoi during the French crisis of the early 1950's, and they were good company indeed: they did drink up the hoarded Scotch, but they paid their way by bringing in lots of news and telling lots of stories.

The care and feeding of correspondents can take stamina. A former New Delhi press attaché tells of a Christmas luncheon he gave for a group of press corps friends. The commander in chief of the Indian army was due to drop in later in the day, around 6 P.M., for cold turkey. Lunch, served on the lawn beginning at 1:30 after many Martinis, was a long drawn-out affair. At 6:30, the general arrived, to find the hard core of the press corps still on hand and singing Christmas carols. The commander in chief got little attention as he stripped scant pickings from two turkey carcasses.

Most American journalists—visiting or resident, at large posts or small—like to get the official U.S. view on current issues and compare notes on shifting fact and rumor. The degree of association between press and embassy depends to a great extent on the individual correspondent. Most of the newsmen welcome a friendly give-and-take from which both sides profit, but there are always those who distrust "embassy types" and those who cannot be trusted with off-the-record classified information. The great majority respond to a forthcoming approach and honor the unwritten gentleman's agreement that governs such relationships. As with the commercial attaché and the business community, it is often the case that an embassy officer can get more help from a correspondent than the correspondent can get from him.

A sound and friendly working basis between an embassy

and correspondents can pay off in unlikely ways. Shortly after the 1948 election had returned Truman to office, his wife and daughter and a yachtload of VIP's stopped over in Habana for a day's visit from Miami. They were ready and willing to do their representational duty, but first Mrs. Truman and daughter Margaret wanted to do some unobtrusive shopping. This outing was arranged discreetly, and all was set with the shops; the ladies were to mingle with the regular shoppers, with a minimal escort and with no fanfare or publicity. They set out on foot and were about to turn into a well-known plaza when the embassy press officer, who was one of the two escorts, had a presentiment and ran ahead. Sure enough, there was old Jack, a resident American news service representative, all set up with cameraman, lights, and sound. The escort rushed up to him and pled: "Please, Jack, not now—later! Just this once, give us freedom *from* the press!" The correspondent, a good friend, bowed with mock courtesy, waved his battery away, and granted the fifth freedom—just before the ladies came into view.

THE EMBASSY AND THE COMMUNITY

This chapter has gone at some length into consular and commercial activities, and to a lesser but commensurate degree into press relations, because these are the fields in which contact with and service to Americans is part of the job. Political and economic officers, generally speaking, center their overseas interests on the political and economic affairs of the host country and on the people involved in such affairs, masses as well as leaders. The various branches of the administrative complex are occupied with housekeeping problems, mainly within the office itself but also in contact with such local officials as customs and public utilities people and with contractors, haulers, shippers, and purveyors. This does not imply indifference to or aloofness from the doings of their countrymen. Although the economic officer does not serve American business in the sense that the commercial officer does, he must maintain regular contact with resident leaders and give their views and interests a prominent place in his reporting. Then, too, the writer recalls the administrative officer at a smallish post who, on learning that a visiting American was getting what the officer considered an unfair rate of exchange for his transactions, marched right down to the government bank to get the visitor a fair deal—and did.

The degree to which social relations are maintained between official and unofficial Americans abroad depends largely on the situation at a given post. In large European cities, where there are thousands of American citizens resident (not to mention tourists) it is unlikely that the two groups will rub shoulders excepting on set occasions—or on a mutually selective, individual basis. At small posts where there are few Americans (in Brazzaville there was a resident community of two) relations tend to be more personal, at times intimate.

In places where the American community is large enough to support an American society, club, or similar association, an ambassador or principal officer should have honorary membership in it—and is in fact usually the honorary president *ex officio*. The officers and wives of the staff, for their part, are encouraged to play a role in American community activities, and usually do. Aside from social and recreational considerations, the community groups often help out in such ways as providing a welfare fund (as noted above) while many of them engage in good works on behalf of the host country's underprivileged.

In some cases, embassy people (particularly wives) tend to associate overmuch with their compatriots—especially when they are not easy in the local language—and in so doing shirk their duty to the people of the host country. This separatism is not encouraged, but it is sometimes hard to control. As with business relations, the official representative must ration his social time between countrymen and host-country people— the mix to depend on the situation at a given post and on the rank and official interests of the officer concerned.

A public relations–minded ambassador or principal officer will keep a watchful eye on this aspect of the Foreign Service job. Under no circumstances should the American community —resident or transient—be given grounds to feel that its official representatives are aloof, or uninterested in their activities and welfare. It must be said that there was a good bit of this standoffishness in the old days, but in the writer's experience —and he believes it to be representative—those days are over.

IX

The Rough with the Smooth

The scene is an embassy residence garden, the time shortly before sundown on July 4, almost any year. While servants and American volunteers scurry about on last-minute errands, the DCM is calling together the various working groups set up for the occasion: combined greeters and VIP escorts, sound-controllers, food-controllers, bar-watchers and bouncers, et al. Other units, such as the food and decorations committee (usually wives) and the invitation-writers (wives and secretaries), have already done their chores.

"O.K., are we all here? Combined greeters?"

"Yes, sir, present and combat ready."

"All right, Joe, you all know your duties, but be sure to get the names straight and sing them out. One thing I do want to stress: Keep the receiving line in motion! We receivers will do our best to cut off the chatty types before the line silts up, but it's up to you taker-offers to get them out of our hands and into circulation—then back to duty on the double. Who's catching the President, and when do we expect him?"

"About 6:30. Tim Dunnigan is posted at USIS across from the palace, and will phone us from there when the motorcycle cops start revving up. As for the President's escort, I thought Captain McClintock. Both colonels are in the receiving line, and with Major Burns off on TDY he's our only available set of aiguillettes. If you'd rather not have a uniform . . ."

"No, no. The captain will do fine. All right: bar-watchers and bouncers?"

"Here, sir, may it please your honor."

"Cut the comedy, Baldy. You know the drill. Keep the drink trays moving, and above all, keep the servants sober till after clean-up . . . . Ah, here's the Ambassador. Good evening, sir; good evening, ma'am."

"Good evening, Ted. Good evening, everybody. Confusion keyed to the hour, eh? Everything looks fine."

Thus go the last-minute preparations for a small embassy's big moment. Planning for this particular affair had begun in late April, with a request to all staff members for names of those it would help their cause to have invited, while at the same time the previous year's lists were hauled out and checked for departures, defections, or continuing desirability. Since that time, July 4 had never been far from anyone's mind.

Most posts hold their national day celebrations during the evening cocktail hour, although some prefer high noon. Large missions may put on several different affairs—for example, a midday baseball and hot-dog picnic organized for and sometimes by the American community, plus a diplomatic reception in the evening. Since most smaller and some middle-sized posts must depend on the garden to supplement indoor space, the possibility of rain is something to worry about; lucky the mission whose dry season falls in July. In India, the United States' independence is celebrated in the cool season, on a date close to an appropriate national holiday such as Washington Birthday.* Whatever the hour or the date, the official purpose of a national day celebration was originally and still is to receive the congratulations of diplomatic colleagues and host-country well-wishers.

By the 1950's, especially in Europe, big pushes had become customary, and July 4 was linked in the American tourist's mind with free-loading at the embassy—leading Secretary Rusk, not long after he took office, to issue an instruction on

* The British have long celebrated the monarch's birthday (their national day) on a date of convenience. This was recently changed to the second Saturday of June—which is fine in England, where the big event is a parade. Posts abroad have discretion to alter this to another day—say Friday, where weekend exodus is the rule—or another month, for reasons of climate. Some posts now celebrate on the Queen's actual birthday, April 21.

Fourth-of-July affairs that in effect gave an "out" to any principal officer not wishing to hold a party, or at least not wishing to host a knock-down drag-out. Not only was the patriotic value of the latter doubtful; the price tag was high. Duty-free liquor or no duty-free liquor, food was a major item—even when embassy wives banded together to produce great piles of sandwiches—and the outlay for a relatively modest affair could wipe out a post's whole representation allowance for the three-month quarter, or more.

Despite all this, most principal officers continue to want a Fourth-of-July affair. Aside from the fact that their diplomatic or consular colleagues celebrate their national days and the United States would look cheap without one, the event offers a useful opportunity to cultivate the friendship of the many minor (some not so minor) officials, purveyors, and the like, whose good will is operationally desirable but who would not normally be invited to the Big House—and to whom an engraved invitation with the seal of the United States embossed upon it is something to be kept in a memory book.

Such attentions can pay off throughout the year, but seldom can results have been more "instant" than the time a USAF plane crew was in trouble for landing at an African airport without clearance, owing to a cable mix-up. The assistant air attaché was dispatched posthaste to the airport to see what he could do with the local air traffic chief, a testy and status-conscious bureaucrat who could be difficult enough without provocation. When the attaché reached the traffic office, he found the gentleman wreathed in smiles and with hand outstretched. "You are from American Embassy, yes? Look, just this morning I receive invitation from your Ambassador!"—and out of his pocket came an embossed July 4 card. There was no trouble about the day's irregular landing, nor in future dealings with that air traffic office.

OF PARTIES AND PRIVILEGES

July 4 is by no means the only occasion for diplomatic entertaining, of course. Congressmen, editors, businessmen, ath-

letes, researchers, Washington bureaucrats—the list goes on
and on, even at relatively tourist-free outposts. Then there is
the diplomatic corps, and the host-country hierarchy, to enter-
tain and be entertained by. For a Foreign Service hostess, this
second category does not always mean dazzling the Prime
Minister or the Crown Prince at dinner; it can also mean tedious teas with little ladies who speak virtually nothing but
Chingchin or Kikiki. Yet diplomatic party-giving has a definite place in the scheme of international comity (as it does
domestically). It is an important way of winning friends and
influencing people—and woe betide the representative of his
country who refuses to play the game.

Social high life, time-consuming though it can be, is only a
part of what comes under the general heading of representation. There are inaugurations, dedications, fairs, exhibitions,
contests, and what-not-else at which the United States must be
fittingly represented.* The Service is always on display, always
on duty, and always aware of it. Officers and their wives not
only open bazaars, attend and deliver lectures, hold discus-
sions, and generally show the flag in the metropolis; frequently,
they do the same in the provinces.

Fatiguing forays into really remote areas, where a for-
eigner's visit is such an event that he is the center of more attention, and attentions, than he could comfortably care for,
are also a part of *la vie diplomatique*. Often, it is on such occasions that a greater degree of diplomacy (read courtesy)
may be called for than at the ruler's palace or the Malvolian
Ambassador's residence. If squatting on the haunches with village elders is called for, squat on the haunches. If a betel-
chewing session is in order, chew betel (but do not disgrace
yourself, or your country, by missing the little gold or silver
spittoon that is passed ceremoniously from hand to hand). It

* Not necessarily always by Number One or Number Two. According to
the nature of the affair, middle-grade or junior officers may be sent to
"represent"—but they must make it clear that they are there in the name of
the principal officer, not in their own right, and see to it that they are
treated accordingly.

is not only in the so-called underdeveloped areas that representational duty can tax the constitution; in Germany, for example, where speeches are long and many, the prized accomplishment for those with a low boring point is to be able to sleep with the eyes open.

Not until the diplomatic service was joined with the better paid consular service in 1924 did Congress make any pretense of providing a living for diplomats. Since that time, with growing national awareness of the importance of foreign affairs —and with greater participation of "average" people in the conduct of these—salaries and allowances have risen to a respectable level. Not so the important representation allowance: an American chief of mission and his top aides are still at a disadvantage vis-à-vis their Great Power colleagues (including the Russians) because the amounts doled out for general representation (in effect, reimbursement of business expenses) are well below what the others get, let alone the sums paid by American private enterprise to be suitably represented overseas. Congress has recognized in its authorizing legislation the obligation to reimburse extra cash the Foreign Service must pay out to do its job, but all too often the amounts actually appropriated fall far short of what must be spent.

Diplomatic privileges and immunities are a help, but by no means the bonanza that some seem to think. What they largely boil down to, in dollars and cents, is the duty-free importation of household effects and possessions, food, liquor, tobacco, and one automobile. More important plusses are government-paid housing, either in official quarters or through a housing allowance; a cost-of-living allowance for posts where prices are substantially higher than in Washington; government medical care in cases of accident or major illness; and an education allowance to defray extraordinary expenses of elementary and secondary schooling, plus one round trip for dependents enrolled in U.S. schools. There is also a minuscule "transfer allowance" to help care for additional clothing expenses in moving from a hot to cold or cold to hot zone, but it does not begin to cover the innumerable extras in even the simplest of such transfers.*

It is often the disruption as much as the expense that causes problems in a transfer—new schools, new house, new house current, and so on—but uprootment becomes a way of life to the Foreign Service family. What is harder to get used to is what the packers and shippers can do to one's things. The wives of overseas business representatives, who face the same problem, have a saying: "Three moves equal one fire." Heavy insurance also becomes a way of life, but insurance cannot replace all of what is lost, destroyed, or hopelessly damaged— and no amount of money can console for the loss of the silver wine-taster presented on a memorable occasion, or the small rocking chair that every child in the family has enjoyed since the day great-grandfather had it made for grandmother. Even though disaster only strikes every third or fourth move, when it does strike it can be shattering. One newly arrived officer at a Middle East embassy was idly watching a ship unloading, from his office overlooking the harbor, when a block-and-tackle broke and a large lift van plunged into the water. He later recounted the episode to his wife and they commiserated with some "unfortunate souls"—only to learn later in the day that they were the unfortunate souls. The embassy family rallied 'round with loans and gifts, and in several weeks the couple were able to camp out in their rented house, but the wife was in a state of shock for months: furniture, silver and chinaware, pictures, books, linens, everything, ruined beyond hope of salvage.

That such accidents do not happen more often is surprising, especially when one considers the moving resources available at some of the more remote posts. The writer recalls vividly the 1955 scene in Laos when his Chevrolet was brought across the Mekong on two pirogues lashed together, then

---

* It should be noted that all these allowances are paid for duty overseas only. Employees assigned in the United States normally get nothing but base salary.

hand-pulled up a fifty-degree mud incline by dozens of yelling coolies. ("Recalls vividly" refers only to the beginning and end of the operation; he had his eyes closed in prayer all through the pull-up.)

Petty thievery, and some not so petty, is another fact of life in service overseas—as is the constant attrition through breakage, deterioration, and loss occasioned by the ignorance, inattention, and indifference of local domestics. Aside from carrying a good all-purpose insurance floater, the best defense against all this is probably to learn and embrace the philosophy of the Sermon on the Mount: "Lay not up for yourselves treasures upon earth, where moth and rust doth corrupt, and thieves break through and steal."

One substantial financial auxiliary in the present-day Service is the hardship differential, a salary increment paid at posts where there are unusually difficult living or health problems, or both; depending upon the degree of hardship the amount may vary from 5 to 25 per cent.* The hardship differential was instituted for staff corps personnel not long after World War II, to help induce them to accept less attractive postings, but until 1955 FSO's were ineligible—on the grounds that they went where they were sent, and no backtalk. They did, however, get time-and-a-half retirement credit (which can amount to more in the long run) and they still have that option. Chiefs of mission have no choice; they must take the time-and-a-half. The differential has been quite a help in getting less desirable posts staffed. There are many who seek such assignments—FSS as well as FSO—especially when expenses have been heavy and retrenchment is a must.

As mentioned earlier, the liquor privilege is also an aid to Foreign Service living. It means not only exemption from host-country import taxes but also from excise tax in the country of purchase: for example, bourbon from the United States, Scotch from the United Kingdom, wine from France,

* Under conditions of exceptional hardship there are also the so-called Vietnam amendments of 1967, described at the end of Chapter I.

at something less than half the over-the-counter price in those places. (The deal is roughly the same as that of the overseas army installation's "Class VI" package store, although with more chance for discriminating choice.) None of this means that Foreign Service people succumb to the temptations of bargain booze and "go dipso" en masse. They need more liquor and cheaper liquor, because serving it is expected of them—on almost every occasion and on an unstinting scale— as it is expected of every other diplomatic mission, with the begrudged exception of those from teetotal regimes. Representational *raisons d'être* apart, the average American visitor (including members of Congress, despite their annual howls for the record over what they call "the whiskey appropriation"*) considers embassy entertainment, and drink therewith, to be one of his civil rights. Some seem to feel that since they are taxpayers it is they who have paid for it; it does not occur to them that their host pays taxes too, and that the four double bourbons they have put away were not just drawn as government rations. The diplomatic liquor privilege may sound alluring to the outsider, but no one ever got rich on the money he saved buying refreshments for his guests at a discount.

It has, unfortunately, to be admitted that a few do get a bit rich via another channel—by black-marketing liquor, tobacco, and even foodstuffs acquired from commissaries or other privileged channels. In one major Latin capital, where a fifth of Black Label fetched up to $30, the embassy commissary firmly stamped its name on every bottle sold—yet a sharp-eyed inspector, sitting at the bar in a big hotel and letting his glance wander over the bottle display in front of the bar mirror, made out the embassy stamp on a bottle of John Haig. The barman had no idea how the hotel had got it, but said with a shrug that it was not the first.

What we now frown upon as black-marketing was not always seen so black. In medieval times, it was not unusual to

* More than one Foreign Service wife has sternly required her husband to find out how visiting Congressman Doe voted on the whiskey appropriation before deciding how much and what quality of drink to set before him.

wink at an envoy's bringing in merchandise from his native land, otherwise barred by prohibitive protection measures, for sale on the host-country market to help defray the expenses of his mission. Even today, some smaller and poorer republics, rather than pay allowances on a scale they are unwilling to afford, look the other way in the matter of their own representatives' use of diplomatic privileges to import things duty free (e.g., watches, liquor, cigarettes) for illegal resale rather than personal use.

Such practices are, of course, strictly and explicitly forbidden to the Foreign Service establishment overseas—as is the black market in currency—and punishment for those caught can be severe. (Where possible, offenders are "terminated.") Current control and accountability measures have proved generally effective, fortunately, and the "crime rate" has gone down considerably since the postwar years. Without wishing to appear overly "holier than thou," the writer would note that most of the trouble that still exists appears to come from free-wheeling temporary elements unwilling to accept the self-discipline of the established career services. Most regulars soon recognize the validity of the precept *"Aliis licet; tibi non licet,"*—"others may; you may not."

OF LINGO AND LOCALITIS

There is nothing like protracted exposure to an exotic atmosphere to make it lose the aura of romance that adventure novels and travelogues have built around it. The well-adjusted Foreign Service couple soon sheds such illusions and accepts things as they are—in underdeveloped Jujubura as in Paris—without going all xenophobic or succumbing to "localitis." Of the two, the latter—defined by a Foreign Service wit as the belief that one's post is the navel of world affairs—is probably the more dangerous. Localitis can come from overspecializing, overempathizing, or just plain soft-headedness. Whatever the cause, it makes for a loss of perspective, not to say slanted reporting.

Much has been heard of late about the need for specialization—it has been touched on earlier in this book—but concentration on conditions and opinions among the Miniputians must not lead an officer to lose sight of conditions and opinions in the United States, let alone the U.S. interest in Miniput. It is all very well to steep an officer in the language, mores, prejudices, and inhibitions of a civilization, but these must not be allowed to rub off on him to such extent that they warp his judgment and, in effect, lead him to "go native." He must not forget which side he is on. It is for this general reason that a hard-shell Arabist will be given a change of pace—in Latin America or Europe, for example—after several consecutive tours in the area of his specialty. Critics of the Service find it odd, and even reprehensible, to assign an officer to Buenos Aires after he has spent ten years in Japan immersing himself in Japanese language and culture. Nothing odd or irrational about it at all. If he has been in Japan that long, chances are it is time he got out for a change.

The line between overempathization and soft-headedness is one of degree—and, of course, personality as well—but this form of localitis is also to be avoided if one is to serve one's country in a professional and effective manner. "Do as the Romans do" is a good general rule of conduct (as noted earlier in this chapter), but it can be overdone. An ambassador or one of his senior officers may properly participate with village elders in the solemn rites of a special occasion, and share whatever bizarre concoctions they consume, but participation must be by formal invitation, with duly heralded arrival and with stately exchange of courtesies. Primitive people are highly protocol-conscious. Younger officers are somewhat less bound by formality, but they too must observe the niceties.

The problem of language is one often oversimplified. An FSO returning from Africa is bemused at being asked whether he speaks Swahili and then not being given a chance to explain that, in the particular country he has just come from, there are three major languages—none of them Swahili—and over fifty dialects but that, since none of these have written forms (except in simple phonetics worked out by the missionaries), official as well as commercial business is done in French (or English or another European language). In a developing ex-colony every officer, from the Ambassador on down, should command a half-dozen or so polite phrases—more if possible —for what might be called the courtesy of the country,* but the people he normally deals with are well educated in a European language, are proud of it, and would be at least put out, if not insulted, were a diplomat to try doing serious business in a native tongue. (Compare the day when M. Isvolsky, the Tsarist foreign minister, would have been outraged if addressed in Russian by a foreign ambassador.) The only African-language officer assigned to Congo-Brazzaville in the early 1960's (luckily also fluent in French) confessed that, aside from his occasional village trips, about the only chance he got to use his Munukutuba was in listening to local vernacular broadcasts—and Munukutuba, one of several *linguae francae* of the area, by no means covered all of those.

Hard languages with an established official public—Arabic or Japanese, for example, or Turkish or Iranian—are, of course, a different matter. There is a large and continuing need for expertise in even more exotic tongues, which, fortunately, the Foreign Service has managed to fill to a creditable degree. A rather common misapprehension, unfortunately reinforced by *The Ugly American,* is that of Soviet diplomacy's large-scale mastery of the languages of Southeast Asia. In fact, at the time the Burdick and Lederer book was written,† the Soviet Embassy in Rangoon, to cite an example, had only one Burmese-language officer—young Aleksandr Kaznachayev, who later defected to the United States—and there was jealous competition for his services among the four mutually mistrustful embassy branches—political, economic, security, and military. (Note that, according to Table III, Chapter II,

* But care must be taken not to use, say, a Lari phrase in M'Bochi territory. This would be a graver solecism than speaking Romanian in Hungary.
† See also Chapter IV, p. 122.

the Foreign Service of the United States today boasts thirteen Burmese speakers.)

Not all officers can or should be trained in such specialties, to be sure. The fact is that with two or three of the so-called world languages—French, German, Spanish, Italian, and Portuguese (in addition to English)—one can make himself understood in virtually any part of the developed world, and in most of the less developed. Every FSO should have at least one language other than English—preferably more—but the important thing, in any language, is that he be a "communicator."

One caveat: it is generally not wise for a diplomat to be perfect in a foreign language. He should be able to read with rapid comprehension and converse with intelligent fluency—and idiomatically enough to understand the punch line of a joke—but if he sounds exactly like a native he risks losing his credibility as a representative of the United States.

OF HOUSING, HEALTH, AND OTHER HAZARDS

We have discussed representation, and we have discussed what might be called misrepresentation. What of the setting in which such activities are carried out, and how do Foreign Service people live? Let us look first at housing.

Quarters vary considerably from country to country and post to post. Several years ago, the principal officer in Florence (a consulate, not a consulate general) lived in an immense stinking pink palazzo, while the first resident ambassador to the Chad lived, and worked, in a small and unimpressive villa; for the months it took to ready the chancery, he and his two officers had to wait for breakfast to be removed before they could use the same table for desk space. A code clerk in Rangoon may have more comfortable accommodations than, say, the assistant visa chief in Paris. What type of housing the new arrival gets depends on what the place has to offer.

Availability aside, there are certain more or less established patterns and norms. A principal factor is whether housing is

individually rented through a quarters allowance or is government-owned or -leased—the latter category breaking down in
turn into separate private dwellings or U.S.–run compounds.
For purposes of the present discussion, unless otherwise noted,
we shall be dealing with the problems of Mr. and Mrs. Average FSO and FSS—neither the lowliest nor the mightiest. Ambassadors and principal consular officers have their problems,
too, but they are assured of the best available in government
quarters, and receive an official residence allowance to cover
domestic staff and other expenses over and above what they
would spend were they not in charge.

Compound living—the "golden ghetto" so often inveighed
against—is not all bad. Where a large Yankee invasion moves
in on a small ex-colony, construction by the U.S. Government
is often the only sound solution. Neither is this solution all
good, obviously, since it makes for an incestuous type of community living and inhibits free circulation among host-country
people. Most FSO's and their wives overcome this obstacle,
but obstacle it is.

Compounds come in many shapes and sizes. In Bonn and
Frankfurt am Main, where they were built principally to give
much-needed requisitioned housing back to the Germans,
there are row upon row of neat, modern apartments with one,
two, or three bedrooms (even a few with four) and with public and social buildings. In Rangoon, where a second secretary
took his courage in his hands and seized an opportunity to
contract for properties of British interests pulling out after
1948 independence, the compound comprises a group of spacious and stately houses around a lake. In post-independence
Vientiane of the mid-1950's, AID (then the ICA) joined with
the Lao government in constructing a glorified hutment (the
units began to decay almost before they were finished) while
the embassy built its own town-edge "Silver City"—a cluster
of boxlike, tin-sided "pre-cuts" in which not even a kitten
could be swung. (Both compounds were roundly criticized on
all sides, and with reason, but the fact remains that if there

were to be more than a dozen or so Americans in Vientiane, something had to be built, and quickly.) In Saudi Arabia, both Embassy Jidda and Consulate General Dhahran are housed in spacious grounds that include not only attractive modern bungalows—with stands of special evergreens viable in sand—but also a large chancery and other office and public buildings. In some places, the embassy contracts for whole apartment buildings or has them built on a long-leasing arrangement.

Compounds, of course, are a boon to management. Every thing is centralized and uniform, standard government furnishings are handily interchangeable and repairs easily controlled—all the comforts of an army post. Since units come furnished, new arrivals can usually move in immediately, which saves the government a special temporary housing allowance (up to ninety days) as well as the permanent quarters allowance. The compound also tends to suppress the type of individuality expected of the Foreign Service, but most families soon acquire enough pictures, *objets d'art* and other distinctive possessions to lend cachet to even the most uniform of quarters.

More serious than uniformity is the already-noted inhibition of free intercourse with the host-country community—not only through making it more difficult for Americans to get out and around but also, in many places, through making the local people reluctant to visit inside an American ghetto, which is an unwanted form of exterritoriality. In 1958, during the flurry which followed publication of *The Ugly American,* a high-level and high-minded commission studied the problem at State Department request and came forth with a series of well-reasoned recommendations—chief among which was that senior officers with recognized representational responsibilities (political and economic officers, PAO's, and the like) be moved out of compounds and into town. Some of the posts with compounds embraced this recommendation and speedily submitted suggestions and estimates—at which point the Department apparently began to realize that such moves would cost money, and the recommendations were shelved.

Although its psychological and representational advantages are manifest, private housing—leased or government-owned—can present many problems, and not only in less-developed countries. Chief among these is doubtless that of plumbing, a field in which other nationalities—the Latins notoriously, but even to some extent the Nordics—are less interested than are Americans. When the State Department's Foreign Buildings Office (FBO) contracts for the purchase of a palatial local residence for the American Ambassador, the contract does not necessarily guarantee W.C. performance. Lighting fixtures and appliances, and the current to keep them going, are often a major headache. Generators can supplement a weak municipal electric system, but sometimes whole walls have to be torn out and faulty wiring redone. (It is always well to keep a supply of candles and kerosene lamps handy, in any case.) Leaky roofs are another nuisance, with buckets to be brought out whenever the weather turns a bit inclement. Yet most chiefs of mission and senior officers prefer the relative discomforts of roomy traditional construction to the sort of thing that certain American architects, commissioned by the FBO, have dreamed up for Foreign Service habitation. Unfamiliar with the usages of the job, and apparently unwilling to take advice, these experts tend to confuse diplomacy with hotel-keeping.

At posts where housing is in reasonably good supply, there is a variable mix of government and private leasing. In many less-developed countries, houses or apartments suitable for junior personnel may be available but priced out of reach. In such cases, the U.S. Government, rather than triple or quadruple quarters allowances, may assume responsibility for the leases. In Europe and Latin America, private lease is the general rule for all but the top echelon with heavy representational responsibilities, for whom government-leased or -owned quarters are provided to the extent feasible. As for the rest, most families—and especially the FSO's—manage somehow to set up establishments suited to their needs and adequate for the entertaining for which their local situation may call.

A second major logistical factor in service abroad, along with housing, is that of the local standard of living and way of life. Can employees live comfortably "on the economy" or must they import even the most ordinary necessities? Are there well-stocked food shops, or must one depend on group orders (commissary or free-lance) for virtually everything but scrawny poultry, vegetables and fruit when in season, and lettuce that must be washed in chemicals lest it be the product of deadly night soil? Are there laundry and dry-cleaning facilities, or does a wash-amah take the clothes down to river's edge and beat them on rocks with a stick?

Such questions lead in turn to the quality and availability of domestic service (which, incidentally, *is* a necessity of diplomatic life, whether homebodies choose to believe it or not). In a developed capital, a junior or middle-grade family may have one all-purpose house servant (or a part-time one) with extra help in for parties, whereas in a less advanced capital the same couple may need three or four—say, gardener, cook and houseboy, plus night watchman—to get the same (or less) work done, and with the lady of the house "walking behind them" to boot. Three retainers for a young couple may excite envy back home, but it does not mean nearly as much as it sounds—simply that the local life is so geared that they are an unfortunate necessity. The cook, for example, would die rather than make a bed, and the houseboy would quit rather than warm a can of soup.

Good servants are still obtainable in Europe, if one is lucky and patient, but their ranks are thinning as the older generation passes on. In the ex-colonial areas they are not as easy to come by, or even to train, as we are told they were in the great days of empire. It is easy enough to take on a stable of shuffling supernumeraries, but willing ability is another thing. At a small post in Southeast Asia, a young British diplomat's wife managed to hire a good Chinese cook and was the envy of the corps—till one day he disappeared. For days she muttered darkly about getting her hands on that unholy celestial, then suddenly he reappeared as if nothing had happened. When a friend asked what she had done about it, she said, "My dear, I almost kissed him, I was so glad to have him back!"

The same young lady, incidentally, was casually unrolling a rattan porch screen, with the baby in her other arm, when she found a live cobra asleep inside the roll. She is not at all sure what happened then, but believes she must have waked it with her screams and caused it to go elsewhere for its nap. Snakes, lizards, geckos, bats, gooey slugs, and king-size rats—these and other wildlife help make a tour in the tropics interesting to naturalists and hunt-loving pet cats, but not always to the lady of the house.*

Health is a problem at many posts, but naturally more so in the tropics, where malaria, amoebic dysentery, and other ailments are endemic, and hepatitis a constant threat. Modern wonder drugs have done much to alleviate the rigors of such illnesses and hasten the cure, but people serving in unhealthful areas must still watch what they eat and drink and keep current on inoculations and preventive medication.

The problem of drinking water and other beverages comes to the fore, particularly, in the matter of representation. One may boil and filter at home—and even brush his teeth in purified water—but what is one to do, say, at an Asian provincial governor's reception or an African village chief's welcoming ceremony? One cannot, without risk of giving offense, insist on drinking out of one's own bottle or canteen, or refuse all offers of hospitality liquid or solid. In the Far East, there is often the resource of tea, for which water must be at least

* Some comic relief is afforded by the tiny chameleons, called by such onomatopoeic names as chee-chaw or chin-chuk for the little yak-yak-yaks they expel when inflated with air. These small creatures lurk behind pictures or near wall lamps, whence they stalk then pounce on flies and other insects. Their catch per stalking-hour is insignificant, but they are fun to watch and nice to have around—although some wives complain that they are not housebroken.

minimally boiled, but there is no sure defense against the questionable little cakes and other goo-goodies. (What the working Arabist goes through as all in the day's work is better left to a language-and-area specialist's handbook.) The only answer is to take all possible precautions, prophylactic as well as after the fact, and hope for the best—or else stay at home. Many a dedicated diplomat has given his digestion for his country.

As for the handling of more serious diseases and injuries where adequate medical facilities are not locally available, the Service has made considerable progress in recent years—principally via better organized emergency evacuation to suitable treatment areas. No longer need there be undue delay because of red tape; it is strongly impressed on chiefs of mission that they themselves have the authority to issue any travel orders and arrange for any transportation that may be called for in case of emergency. In the fiscal year ending in July, 1967, the cost of medical travel cost State alone (AID and other agencies apart) almost a quarter-million dollars; half that travel was from Africa, either to army hospitals in Europe or to the United States.

The medical complement of the Department of State and the Foreign Service comprises 35 medical doctors, 29 nurses, and 5 laboratory technicians. Of these there are 28 doctors, 26 nurses, and 4 technicians stationed at posts abroad, the overwhelming majority in Africa and the Far East where local facilities are generally less than adequate. The doctors having regional responsibilities number 24, including 1 who covers Central America from the Washington base. At some posts, non-State doctors fill the bill; at this writing, for example, the assistant air attaché in Moscow is an M.D. who has joint medical and military duties, while in Manila, and also in Djakarta, a U.S. Navy doctor aided by a corpsman handles embassy cases. Of late, moreover, there has been an increase in civilian interagency cooperation—notably on the part of Peace Corps physicians but also, in some areas, on the part of the U.S. Public Health Service—where formerly there was separatism. Especially in Africa, a spirit of neighborly helpfulness seems to be growing.

The situation is different, of course, in Europe, most of South America, and other areas where perfectly competent local doctors are available (although resident Foreign Service people may be accepted at U.S. military installations under exceptional medical circumstances). Even in the less developed countries, there are usually some facilities, and doctors capable of setting a broken bone (though not always perfectly) and treating the simpler manifestations of tropical F.U.O. (fever of unknown origin).

Of Kin and Kith

Schooling is always an anxiety for peripatetic Foreign Service parents. The burden is not so heavy financially as it was before establishment of the education allowance, but the quality and type of instruction remains a problem in many parts of the world—particularly with respect to meeting the standards of U.S. college entrance requirements.

In recent years, the Department of State has instituted the subsidizing, in degree proportionate to need, of American international schools overseas on somewhat the same basis as USIS binational centers; unlike the prewar British and French colonial schools and the postwar U.S. army schools, school board participation and school financing are a joint U.S.–host-country venture—although the Embassy or Consulate plays a prominent, and often unduly overworked, role in school board affairs. The attendance of local children is encouraged, the home representation sometimes outnumbering the American. As is the case with binational centers, the system is operative principally in Latin America, but it is spreading to other areas where there is no prohibition against instruction in a foreign language (basic instruction is in English, with study of the local language an important adjunct). The mix may vary according to cultures. At the new American school in Kuwait in 1965, for example, the student body was about equally divided between American and third-country children, the latter mostly the multinational offspring of the diplomatic corps—some learning English at the same time they were being taught in it.

The basic problem, however, is not so much one of language—many Foreign Service parents prefer their younger children to attend local schools, for greater exposure to the local tongue—but rather one of curriculum vis-à-vis eventual attendance at a U.S. college or university. If a good overseas school is not available (or not desired), the choice in primary schooling is usually between a local school and the Calvert system of parental home instruction; at the secondary level, one may leave the child in school in the States (with attendant logistical problems), send him to a good—and probably expensive—private institution abroad (e.g., in Switzerland), or take what the host country has to offer. The latter may range from A-1 to A-trocious, from the rigors of French parochial or British public schools to the confusion and overcrowding of the people's institutions in overpopulated, underdeveloped countries. Aside from the difficulties of adjustment and readjustment to one institution then another, there is an almost inevitable unevenness in progress—rapid at one post, slow at another—to add to the problem. And there is often a language barrier. One ten-year-old, very bright, was put in an African first grade because he did not know French, the language of instruction.

The problem of competitive preparation for higher learning in the United States exists even where there is a good overseas school available, especially from the ninth grade up, yet not many Foreign Service children fail to make college. In the old days, a good number completed their university training abroad; today few do, though some take a year or so before, during, or after U.S. college.

Schooling is one problem, periodically pulling up roots and

changing one's way of life is another. Foreign Service parents, presenting their brood to a visitor, may remark detachedly, "This is John—he's a German. This is Mary. She's Greek. And little Audrey here is our American, born in the U.S.A. during our Washington tour." With more homecomings and a more widespread American presence abroad, the problem of child "foreignness" has diminished to a considerable degree, but in pre-World War II days it was very real, and many an American youngster reached his 'teens speaking English with an unusual accent—or at least a quaint turn of phrase. Even today, there are problems of readjustment when a returning child is old enough to have to adapt on his own to the American way of life. Aside from differences between the reality and the images he has built up from afar, he may suffer from a lack of "in-ness" because for a time he cannot even understand much of what his home-grown contemporaries are talking about.

The child of a diplomat is, at least, spared the citizenship problems that may confront his private-enterprise schoolmate where local law insists on *jus soli* rather than *jus sanguinis* (citizenship by country of birth rather than by blood). That child obtains perfectly valid American citizenship through registration at a consulate, but certain countries still hold that he belongs to them—and, if male, must among other things do his military service at age eighteen if he stays in the country that long. (Some American business families do, but more often it is missionaries who have the problem.) One British brigadier, much decorated in World War II, was subject to arrest as a deserter if he ever set foot in Argentina. He had been born there of British parents, but left at age six.

The problems of child adjustment are, to be sure, only one part of the general picture of adjustment to Foreign Service life, with its periodic uprootings and, often, abrupt changes from posh to primitive and back. Moreover, since the Service is rather given to the peremptory ordering of an officer from one part of the world to another—and that on the double—

it is not infrequently the wife who gets what has been called the "p.p.f. (pay, pack, follow) card."*

If an officer or his wife cannot adjust to the life it is best that they cut their losses—and the U.S. Government's—earlier rather than later. One of the best young officers the writer ever had under him saw this, and regretfully but decisively severed his connection with the Service at the end of his first tour. He had taken the examinations and accepted appointment under his wife's protest, hoping that she would adapt to the life once she got into it. Despite sincere effort, she could not, so with hardly a backward glance he returned to academe and the small-town American atmosphere she loved. Fortunately this couple was an exception in not being able to take the life.

The problems of social relations and relationships are, of course, not unique to the Foreign Service and its overseas affiliates, but living abroad does tend to magnify such problems—sometimes for better, sometimes for worse. This is especially true in less-developed areas, where "Europeans" (as Caucasians are called) perforce lead something of a life apart and where smallish groups must live in each other's pockets. At a large post like Paris, a junior officer or clerk may, if he chooses, live his own life in a French setting and have almost as little out-of-hours contact with his fellow workers as he would in Washington (excepting, of course, when auxiliary representational duty calls). At a small or out-of-the-way post, even where there is considerable host-country contact, Americans are thrown together like it or not. This togetherness is fine as long as the apples are healthy, but when a sour one appears there can be trouble for all. Fortunately, as a senior officer has put it, one generally finds a better class of people at the hardship posts—that is, the same individuals tend to behave better toward each other when there is shared hardship or shared cultural apartness. There is nothing like making do

---

* A reference to "p.p.c. cards" (*"pour prendre congé"*—"to take leave"), which diplomatic usage requires be spread among local and diplomatic officialdom on leaving a post.

with scarce supplies or exposure to local hostility to stimulate intramural comity.

Hostility and danger may not always be taken lightly, as was brought home by the shockingly wanton political assassination of Ambassador John Gordon Mein by Guatemalan terrorists on August 28, 1968. Although he was the first American ambassador to be killed in the line of duty, Mein's name was the latest of an honored company to qualify for inscription on a marble plaque in the State Department lobby "Erected by members of the American Foreign Service Association in honor of diplomatic and consular officers of the United States who while on active duty lost their lives under heroic or tragic circumstances." The list is headed by the name of William Palfrey, former paymaster general of the Continental Army, who was the first American consul ever to be appointed; he was en route to France in 1780, but was lost at sea and never reached his post. Second was the poet-diplomat Joel Barlow who, while on a mission to Napoleon's winter headquarters in Poland, got caught up in the retreat from Moscow and died of exposure at Zarnowice on Christmas eve, 1812.

Hardship and danger apart, there are bound to be rivalries and cliquishness at any post, between groups as well as between individuals—especially where there is compound living or a comparable way of life. At one post, other-agency people maintain a separatist attitude, or at best an armed truce, toward "the Embassy." At another (probably one where the other agencies are not outsize) the various groups coexist like colleagues and compatriots. Sometimes physical and psychological barriers make full integration impossible, but an outgoing and hospitable attitude on the part of the chief of mission and his wife can go a long way toward bridging the "livability gap." The tone is set at the top. As noted in Chapter VI, other-agency elements which remained separatist under one principal officer may find themselves in full communion with the Foreign Service under another.

LE CORPS DIPLOMATIQUE

It was stupid of me not to have seen at once that
he was connected with the diplomatic service. He
had all the marks of the profession. He had the
supercilious courtesy that is so well calculated
to put up the backs of the general public and the
aloofness due to the consciousness the diplomat
has that he is not as other men are, joined with
the shyness occasioned by his uneasy feeling that
other men do not quite realise it.

W. SOMERSET MAUGHAM, in *The Human Element*

One cardinal reason for wariness of "embassy types" on the
part of other-agency people is that many of the latter, believing themselves plain citizens and good red-blooded Americans, arrive overseas prepared to find a Foreign Service still
patterned on Mr. Maugham's British diplomat of some fifty
years ago. The fact that today's Foreign Service officer seldom
fits that pattern does not always suffice to get out of their
heads the idea that he ought to. Embassy types are diplomats,
and diplomats by definition are cynical, devious, and tricky—
and cookie-pushers to boot.

For all the distrust that some other-agency colleagues—and
many Americans back home—may hold for the diplomatic
way of life, the Foreign Service officer finds his membership
in the diplomatic corps a useful thing. Although its principal
assigned functions are for purposes of ceremony and the protection of the rights and privileges of its members, this multinational community also serves as a sort of diplomatic clearing house. The corps reflects a pattern of living and working
that has grown out of centuries of experience as diplomats
have represented their governments abroad, evolved and prac-
ticed a set of international conventions, and shared the common problems that diplomats face regardless of nationality.
The postwar expansion of American representation abroad,
together with the growth of American world power, has not

unnaturally had its effect upon the usages of world diplomacy
—as has the concomitant growth of the Communist adversary.
Not only has the former preoccupation with calling cards,
precedence, and ceremonial relaxed considerably, but soft
understatement is often replaced by calculated rantings and
boorishness. Yet the accumulated skills, attitudes, and values
of the past have by no means been discarded, and the tradi-
tions and norms of diplomatic custom are still very much alive.
It would be wrong to pronounce the second "p" in "diplomatic
corps."

The Foreign Service officer has in effect three publics—the
host country, the American community, and what has been
called the "third culture" of the diplomatic corps. Assignment
to a new country entails boning up on its culture and mores,
but at least one does not have to start all over in dealing with
one's colleagues of the corps. From them, the Foreign Service
officer knows fairly well what to expect—and the more posts
he puts behind him, the more old friends and friends of friends
he is likely to meet at a new post.

Membership in such a cosmopolitan fraternity naturally
brings forth frequent accusations of internationalism, lack of
patriotic zeal, and the like. In virtually every national group,
the citizenry has tended to distrust its diplomats. (In May,
1968, Tokyo's intellectual *Asahi Journal* raked Japan's foreign
service over the coals with a long enumeration of its shortcomings, only a few of which were, in informal translation:
"conservative, secrecyism, politely impolite, only negotiations
and no policies, international feeling without national senti-
ments.") Yet, the diplomatic corps remains a device whereby
the representatives of nations may get along with their business, and with each other, to the benefit of all. Allies compare
notes and prepare approaches; adversaries maintain a cool
civility and even, at times when there is a relative thaw on at
the top, display some conviviality;* third-country representa-

* In 1956, the small diplomatic corps in Laos (which included the Indians, Canadians, and Poles of the International Control Commission)
underwent a shattering experience en masse when, on a provincial excursion,

tives talk to both sides and often make themselves useful as intermediaries. Nor is discreet contact between adversaries unknown.

The corps is not only useful as a professional operating medium; it can be helpful socially, as a clearing house for local lore and gossip. The established members fill in the newcomers, and the latter in turn move up to established status and do the same for later newcomers. Wives find the system handy —although it can work both ways. Rivalries within the corps, unconnected with national interests, can become sharp indeed.

The diplomatic corps is usually fairly homogeneous in that most of its members, political appointees excepted, are of the same profession. Not so the consular corps, which in developed countries tends to be made up largely of consuls *ad honorem*—private citizens of the host country who have made some contribution (not infrequently financial) for the luster of an honorary consulship. (In Germany, where titles mean much, a consul general of one of the smallest European states was approached by a burgher who averred that the honorary consul generalship at the seaport where he lived would be worth $20,000 to him.) Some honoraries are natives of the country they represent, already established in the host country; they presumably do not pay for the privilege.

As is the case with consular agents (with whom they should not be confused), honorary consuls' duties are largely notarial, plus taking care of visiting firemen of the accrediting country and hosting an annual national day affair. They are entitled to consular license plates and display the principal's coat of arms, but do not enjoy free-import privileges or personal immunities. The system seems to work fairly well, with

---

they were soaked to the skin by a cloudburst, then obliged to go through a long night of ceremony in dripping wet clothes. The Pole remained pokerfaced and silent throughout. Four months or so later, when a temporary thaw developed between Washington and Warsaw, he took the first opportunity to press fraternal vodka upon his American colleague and reminisce boisterously in fluent broken English: "Boy oh boy, vat a night! *Boj moi,* vas ve a bonch'a sed secks!"

both parties getting something out of it, but it is hard for the career newcomer to recall that a big, bullet-headed blond is "the Thai" while a small, dark Latin is "the Dane."

A lengthy discussion of "protocol," which might be defined as diplomacy's self-imposed code of rules and ethics whereby the representatives of sovereign nations are assured of the respect and consideration which is their due, is not within the province of the present chapter. To give it more than a passing mention could open up a Pandora's box of ruffled plumes and diplomatic sword play. Even the United States has not been immune to the latter, although the protagonists were not American; John C. Calhoun in 1848 harked back to a day when swords had been drawn in a White House antechamber during a dispute over precedence between the British and French ministers.

The Congress of Vienna in 1815 provided a basic solution to the problem of precedence (the diplomatic pecking order) when it established the principal of "first come, first served"— i.e., precedence based on seniority at a post regardless of a nation's size and power (with certain exceptions, such as the Papal representative in a Catholic country). For the rest, the body of today's protocolar usage, while considerably more formal than the etiquette of modern American suburbia, is in reality little more than a codification of long-established, upper-crust good manners—and permits of a good bit of latitude in common-sense interpretation and adaptation. Not long ago, the young wife of a first-post FSO paid her duty call on the principal officer's wife, and the latter, finding her new charge both interested and pervious, went on at some length about how things were done at the post—when hats were worn, on whom cards were dropped, and so forth. Finally, the newcomer exclaimed, "My, how did you ever learn all these things?" The answer: "My dear, I have not learned all these things. I have learned basic principles—which you must do, too—and from them I improvise as I go along."

X

The Winds of Change

The plain fact is that good policy demands both good men and good machinery. And although it may be true that good men can triumph over *poor* machinery, it is also true that they are more effective when they work with *good* machinery.

Senator Jackson's remarks, made in 1960,* are very relevant to the situation of the U.S. foreign affairs community today, both government-wide and within the Foreign Service itself. There has been growing concern in Service circles over the proliferation of the country's organization for the conduct of foreign affairs and the structural disorder that has developed as a result of it. Many Foreign Service people, moreover, fault their own system for what they consider a consistent misallocation of personnel resources, with resultant unsettling effects on Service morale—let alone efficiency—at all levels.

Near the end of 1967, the outgoing president of the American Foreign Service Association (AFSA) wrote:

I believe the time has come—as it seems to do every 20 years—when we must step back and take a critical look at the institutions with which we are familiar and confortable. I think we must ask ourselves whether they are as pertinent to the world of 1967 as they were to the world of 1946, or whether the passage of time and the distortions of *ad hoc* responses to emergent problems don't suggest that we should be considering new solutions. I think we should.

* Senator Henry M. Jackson, "Organizing for Survival" *Foreign Affairs,* April, 1960, p. 44.

A few months earlier, the same senior officer observed in a speech that the portents of change were many, and that actions and statements in Congress, and rumblings in various sectors of the executive branch, suggested unhappiness with the manner in which foreign affairs were conducted and the foreign affairs community organized. The Director General of the Foreign Service, during the same period, expressed the view that the question of a continued career system was not really one of whether, but rather what new concepts must be employed to meet new demands. Other Service sources were agreed that the climate was increasingly open to reform—and this feeling grew as the year 1968 took its course.

In May, 1968, Senator J. William Fulbright introduced a Senate joint resolution relating to the conduct of foreign relations in the 1970's—a project to establish a high-level commission on organizational reforms. He did not press the resolution at that time, saying he did not believe that the appointment of such a commission should be one of the last acts of a retiring Administration, but noted that he did consider it a matter of high priority for the Administration taking office on January 20, 1969.*

The Foreign Service, for its part, asserts its readiness to do everything in its power to "modernize" foreign affairs. It confesses that the professionals have not always been as hospitable to new ideas and new techniques as they might have been, but now recognizes that the success of the nation's future foreign policy depends substantially on three cardinal points: 1) organizing for executive leadership; 2) speaking with a single voice abroad; and 3) taking advantage of the best of the nation's science and technology.

As AFSA's outgoing president remarked, a time for reassessment of the U.S. Government's foreign affairs institutions seems to roll around every twenty years or so. The year 1906 marked the definitive establishment of the consular merit system, 1924 the Rogers Act, and 1946 the Foreign Ser-

* Congressional Record (GP), May 22, 1968, p. S 6128.

vice Act which, as amended from time to time, constitutes the organic law of the Service today. In 1968—a year in which it was early made known that regardless of Party there would be a new President—the professionals turned their eyes toward a new regime and the business of organizing for the conduct of foreign affairs in the 1970's.

The voice of the AFSA has been a prominent one in this respect. In mid-1967, certain officers—including one from USIA and one from AID—decided to run as a write-in ticket for election to all eighteen offices of the Association. These officers (dubbed, inevitably, the "Young Turks") won the October, 1967, election handily, and with it a mandate to lead the Association into taking a more activist role in Foreign Service affairs. As they set to work, they kept before them Alfred North Whitehead's admonition on the vitality of thought: "Ideas won't keep; something must be done with them!" Although the AFSA makes it clear that its views do not represent an official position of the Department of State, its activity has stimulated a running debate within Service circles—not only in the pages of the *Foreign Service Journal* but also in an open dialogue between junior and senior officers.

TOWARD A UNIFIED FOREIGN SERVICE

Secretary of State Dulles insisted that the Department concentrate on "policy" and divest itself of "operations." In so doing, he made later attempts toward foreign affairs unification more difficult, although several such efforts were initiated. The latest and strongest of these came in a bill sponsored in 1965 by Representative Wayne L. Hays for creation of a single, government-wide foreign affairs establishment. The Hays Bill passed the House, but was killed in Senate committee. Although most Foreign Service officers opposed the bill at the time it was under discussion, a great many now realize that some form of unification is desirable—to restore, in effect, a principal and basic aim of the Foreign Service Act of 1946, that the nation speak with one voice abroad. That Act still provides a solid organic base for unification: Not a few of the organizational reforms currently being suggested could be achieved in large part through reaffirmation of its principles.

With the present proliferation of American activity abroad, some 80 per cent of those representing U.S. Government interests in other countries are not under the direct supervision of the Department of State—and within the remaining 20 per cent, career Foreign Service officers are a smaller contingent still. Assuming that the principles of 1946 are to be upheld, can a select Foreign Service continue to serve as the instrument therefor?

Most Service commentators say yes. They see an elite group, distinct from the Civil Service, as still the best answer—rather than settling for less eliteness and more uniformity—but recognize that structure and procedures must be streamlined and updated. In any new set-up, many believe, the Foreign Service proper would serve as a bellwether to what the Herter Committee has called a family of compatible services (notably, a "Foreign Information Service" and a "Foreign Development Service") to be administered on parallel lines within the framework of a basically uniform personnel system. There would be reasonable, but not necessarily constraining, uniformity among groups—and a reasonable degree of personnel interchange among them, although not so much as to weaken their separate identities and self-administration.

Any such reorganization would, however, take time—and would probably entail lengthy study by a high-level group (such as that envisaged by Senator J. William Fulbright), followed by new legislation. Meantime, the AFSA has suggested, as an immediate step to meet the more pressing requirements of the situation, that the new President use his reorganization powers to restore an active guiding role to the Board of the Foreign Service. The Act of 1946 charged the Board, *inter alia,* with recommending to the Secretary policies and procedures to govern the administration and personnel management of the Service, but since 1965—when it was relegated to an advisory role by Presidential reorganization order—it has played no more than a passive role in Service affairs. The reconstituted Board would be made up of high-level representatives of all principal agencies of the foreign affairs community, possibly including public members, and headed by a prestigious public figure from outside government who would enjoy authority and status comparable to that of the chairman of the Civil Service Commission. The Director General of the Foreign Service would wear two hats: one as a regular member of the board (as he is now) participating in policy-making, the other as director of a picked executive staff charged with implementation of policy decisions and follow-through on other agencies' compliance.

A related proposal is for the establishment, as third-ranking position in the Department, of the office of "permanent under secretary of State," to ensure coordination of interagency relationships and the interlocking functioning of all foreign affairs machinery. Such a position was recommended by the Herter Committee in 1962 (to be called "executive under secretary"), but the recommendation was not acted on. The permanent under secretary's office would provide a strong, centralized management position, thus freeing the Secretary (and with him the under secretary) to exercise the authority and responsibility vested in him by the President for over-all leadership in the formulation of foreign policy and the conduct of foreign relations. The permanent under secretary, acting for the Secretary, would work across agency lines in carrying out forward planning and then ensuring that agreed-upon policies were translated into coordinated action programs—and that the financial and logistical resources therefor were made available. Something like this could be done within the present statutory framework, it is argued, by assigning the duties of permanent under secretary to the existing position of under secretary for political affairs, now Number Three in the State Department hierarchy. The term "permanent" would adhere to the position, not the individual chosen. The British and

French services have long had such a post, always staffed by a career officer—and in 1959, when Robert D. Murphy was installed as first incumbent under secretary of State for political affairs, he voiced the belief at his swearing-in that this Number Three position could and should be reserved for a career officer with permanent under secretary status.

Reaffirmation of the roles of an ambassador abroad (Kennedy letter, etc.) and of the Secretary himself has helped considerably toward re-establishing the primacy of State in foreign affairs, but, in practice, interagency organizational and personnel difficulties have by no means been overcome. Implicit in the proposal for an upgraded Board of the Foreign Service is the belief that at present no body, mechanism, or office within the Department of State commands the full confidence and cooperation of the other foreign affairs agencies. A problem of today's alignment is that these other foreign services do not trust the Department to safeguard their interests to the same degree that it does its own. Hence, they feel the need to seek independent solutions.

Nonetheless, imposition of a Service czar from outside, be he ever so able and prestigious, is understandably unacceptable to many career Foreign Service officers. At least one Service leader has suggested combining the two AFSA proposals by making the permanent (or executive) under secretary also chairman of the Board of the Foreign Service. Installation of a career officer of unquestioned integrity, and under him a reconstituted Board that would, in effect, be a high-level watchdog group looking out for the interests of all components of the foreign affairs community, could represent a long step toward unification *de facto*—and could, possibly, obviate the necessity for a reorganization *de jure*.*

* On May 7, 1969, Secretary of State William P. Rogers announced an important first step toward such unification, the upgrading of the Board of the Foreign Service. He named the under secretary of State (Number Two, not Number Three) to its chairmanship, and reconstituted the Board at a high interagency level, charging it with the study of what changes might be required to ensure the best possible use of "our unique personnel resources." The AFSA lauded the Secretary's move as a good beginning toward a program of reform.

THE BATTLE OF THE BULGE

Interagency coordination and unification constitute one problem; imbalance in the rank structure of the Service itself is another. For some years, graphic representations of Foreign Service strength (FSR and FSSO as well as FSO) have shown a considerable bulge in the middle and just above it, as may be seen from the FSO figures in the January, 1968, "summary of employment":

CA-CM—60
FSO-1—319
FSO-2—451
FSO-3—651
FSO-4—643
FSO-5—528
FSO-6—422
FSO-7—255
FSO-8—109

This bulge has long been a source of Service preoccupation, but the problem has become more acute in recent years. It is generally ascribed to (1) the introduction of too many people into the Service at the upper and middle levels, (2) a too sparing use of the selection-out process and of inducements toward early voluntary retirement at the upper levels, and (3) a promotion policy that has been based on advancing as many as funds permit rather than on inventoried needs for officers in each grade. These factors have had backup effects throughout the system.

In 1939, the Foreign Service officer corps numbered 833, including 114 commercial and agricultural officers absorbed during the amalgamation of that year. By early 1946, as a result of virtual suspension of career recruitment during World War II, the number had actually declined by some 10 per cent to 750. By 1954, as Wristonization began to get under way, there were approximately 1,300 FSO's, 200 FSR's, 1,600

FSSO's, and 2,400 FSS's. By the beginning of 1968, the FSO complement had almost tripled, the FSR's had multiplied manyfold, and the staff corps was half again as large despite the skimming off of FSSO's via the Wriston route. Such expansion was manifestly necessary, to keep pace with the nation's ever expanding role in world affairs, but the merger process inevitably brought tensions, which have diminished noticeably but have not disappeared.

There also has been a tendency in recent years to appoint people to middle-grade and senior levels through other than the established lateral entry channel—and without any clear provision for departures to match arrivals. In the early 1960's, the Reserve route was being used to supplement Civil Service appointments, and in 1965—in anticipation of passage of the Hays Bill—a number of domestically based Civil Service people were encouraged to convert to the FSR and FSS categories. When the Hays Bill missed fire, this "domestic" FSR-FSS group—not being subject to service abroad—became an anomaly, and, in early 1968, procedures were set up whereby its members might revert to Civil Service status as soon as feasible. In August, however, as mentioned in Chapter II, came the amendment to the USIA Act creating the Foreign Service Reserve with unlimited tenure (FSRU), which the officer corps could not help but view as one more camel's nose under the tent. There have been general feelings of unsettledness at all levels ever since.*

Also mentioned above was what some have seen as a too sparing use of the selection-out process and of inducements to early retirement. This tendency has, indeed, added somewhat to the problem of the bulge, but merely crying for riddance of

---

* At a general meeting of the Foreign Service Association in September, 1968, top management assured the corps that Reserve officers would be appointed to positions generally filled by FSO's *only* in the few instances where a qualified FSO was not available and the position had to be filled. It was expected that FSR appointments would be used for all specialized officer positions other than those specifically designated for either Foreign Service or Civil Service officers. FSRU's, it might be noted, participate in the Foreign Service retirement system but are also subject to selection-out.

"deadwood" oversimplifies things and solves nothing. Service standards are high, as anyone who has served on a selection board well knows, with the result that the large group described as "of average competence" in any middle or senior class still represents a high level of performance and ability—and experience to boot. There are those who would arbitrarily get rid of a given percentage of the officer corps from the middle up. Such a move would not only work unfair hardship on loyal and dedicated men but would also deprive the Service, for some time to come, of much needed expertise in that large portion of the work load that may not call for top brilliance but still needs doing by experienced and solid professionals. Periodic weeding out *is* needed at all levels, including the lower ranks, if the system is to work properly—but it should not be overdone.

It has long been recognized that a fully successful and coordinated personnel management system could not be achieved until a concerted effort had been made to identify and classify the totality of Foreign Service positions, so that personnel decisions—including those affecting promotion and selection-out—might be made with full consideration of all the implications of a given situation. Successive administrative chiefs of the Department (those brought in from the outside as well as those appointed from within) have deplored the lack of such an inventory and have made efforts to initiate one, but without success until the advent of the deputy under secretary for administration who took office in early 1967.

The inventory project, fortunately, is now well under way under the direction of the deputy assistant secretary for personnel—the Director General's deputy who, as noted in Chapter III, has been made personnel chief of the Foreign Service and of the Civil Service element within the Department. In the early fall of 1968, consultations began on the initial draft of a project to define manpower needs by category and look searchingly at every position and every skill in the Department and overseas—officer and nonofficer, lowest to highest—with a

view not only to determining type and level but also to desig-
nating which should eventually be filled by FSO's, FSR's,
FSS's, and Civil Service people. And, heartening to report, the
modus operandi has been thoroughly modernized to make
large-scale use of the computer. The machines can perform, in
twenty-four hours, many operations that would take a task
force six weeks.

THE NEW BREED

The Foreign Service, by tradition, has been conditioned to
play the "good soldier"—to go where it is sent and not make
heavy weather about such matters as promotion or placement.
Even officers who entered in the late 1950's refer to themselves as the "silent generation." Not so the new breed of FSO.

Principally, the junior officer of today wants a "piece of the
action." Relatively low pay and relatively slow promotion are
secondary considerations; the main thing is a job that can
"turn him on" and keep him "turned on." He has joined the
Service, often in the face of more lucrative counteroffers, in
the belief that it is the best avenue to major responsibility in
the conduct of the country's foreign relations—and, if he discovers that his assumption was erroneous and that his talents
are being underutilized, he may look elsewhere.

A principal *bête noire* in this connection appears to be consular work, at least that of the routine variety. Hand in hand
with consular duty goes administrative work, although junior
FSO assignments other than rotational ones are not usually
of this nature, since most of it is handled by staff corps specialists.

Generally speaking, the junior group approves of first-post
rotation through all phases of Service activity, including the
consular and administrative—and even, if at a consulate, rotation through all phases of consular activity. It does believe,
however, that no officer who enters with a qualified professional background—as many now do—should be required to
serve an outmoded apprenticeship such as two full years in the

routine of a "visa mill." That work, the officers maintain, is better left to staff specialists and locals.

Here, it may be said, management has been responsive of late to junior officer pressure and is trying to do away with visa-mill service for FSO's, at least as a standard practice. Wherever possible, first-post consular positions are being reduced to those of the "single officer" variety—for example, at an embassy in Africa where one officer handles all the consular work and, as *the* consular officer, has plenty of responsibility and plenty to do.* Current policy also looks to keeping open a "healthy proportion" of middle-level consular jobs for FSO's in order to give them an "excursion into supervisory experience"—running a section of a dozen or more—a type of experience becoming harder for officers at the FSO-4/0-5 level to get in today's Service.

The junior group further advocates the creation, by downgrading, of more junior substantive positions. This would ease its problem with respect to satisfying jobs, to be sure, but it would be robbing Peter to pay Paul, since there would be that many less such positions for the inhabitants of the middle-grade bulge.

There is, however, another source of substantive jobs at all levels, authorized by the Foreign Service Act of 1946—that of assigning or detailing FSO's for duty "in any Government agency, or in any international organization, international commission, or international body" for up to four years, subject to extension through another four years by the Secretary (Sec. 571). This outlet has been utilized more and more of late—especially since the balance-of-payments problem brought more officers back for home service, but even to some extent before that. As noted in Chapter II, "other-agency detail" accounted for some 10 per cent of officer strength in

---

* It might be noted, in this connection, that junior consular assignments have long been welcomed at Iron Curtain posts. These jobs are understood to give not only responsibility but also a continuing chance to meet the people and get a workout in the language.

1968. Until recently, many senior and middle-grade officers resisted assignment to an interchange program, considering it a form of exile and outside the main career stream. Since mid-1968, however, they have been provided with safeguards against being forgotten, chief among which is their inclusion in the regular Foreign Service inspection process. Given these safeguards, the young officer of today would presumably prefer a temporary but challenging job outside foreign affairs—with the Department of Housing and Urban Development, for example—to two years of "clerk work" at a post overseas. The new generation, unlike the old guard, does not necessarily look only to service abroad for meaningful Foreign Service employment.

There is no gainsaying that morale is not all it should be in the younger ranks. There have been too many voluntary resignations, over the past several years, because of dissatisfaction with what has been considered a lack of challenge and responsibility in the first stage of the career. This group apart, today's juniors saw and understood the total system early, and they realize that their problems are shared by the middle-grade and senior officers.

The lifeblood of a career service requires continuous renewal if that service is to remain healthy, and this can only be achieved through a continuous intake of young career officers. From what he has seen of the new talent, the writer believes the Service is attracting the caliber of youth it needs. According to a 1967 report, more than 1 per cent of America's college students try each year to enter the Foreign Service officer corps at the bottom, and, according to the testimony of some of those who have made it, they look to the Service for a chance to play a serious role in the conduct of foreign affairs. It is up to the Service to see to it that these young men and women—and those who come after them—get the training and guidance they need and are provided with a fitting framework in which to operate. Management, fortunately, appears to be well aware of this.

WHAT OF THE FUTURE?

This chapter has attempted, without suggesting solutions, to outline the major problems confronting today's Foreign Service—which, as will have been seen, does not lack self-critics. Yet even the severest of these—those within the AFSA leadership—have recognized that morale in the 1969 Service is surprisingly good and that, possibly because the winds of change are abroad, attitudes in general are surprisingly optimistic.

Optimist or pessimist, almost every Foreign Service officer has one basic question uppermost in his mind: Is traditionally conceived careerism in the field of foreign affairs outmoded, or are its basic concepts still valid and viable? Foreign Service leaders, while recognizing the already noted need for organizational reorientation, firmly believe that the elite concept is not outmoded; that, if ever the country needed a select, well-trained, highly motivated and disciplined career service, it does now; and that the changing demands of the future will, if anything, increase rather than diminish that need. They in no way dispute the collateral need for a variety of talent from government and other sources, to bring all possible experience to bear on our total foreign affairs problems. On the contrary, they consider the two concepts complementary: The greater the expertise at the center, for continuity, consistency, and guidance, the greater the possibilities for maximum utilization of the foreign affairs community as a whole.

Assuming the continuing need for a select career group to serve as keystone for the U.S. effort abroad, it should be recognized—without dishonor to those who have served so well in the past—that the Foreign Service of the future must maintain standards of intellect and expertise considerably beyond those once found acceptable. To attract and hold the people needed for great and difficult tasks, the Service must be so organized that its officers not only are trained to be part of a highly professional corps but are also consistently provided, at all levels, with highly professional work to do. There is also the matter of the companion career service of the Foreign Service Staff Corps—and of the Foreign Service Reserve and the departmental Civil Service, as well. These too will need to have their own clearly defined areas of specialization and their own built-in incentives.

In closing, the writer of this volume notes his belief that any career Foreign Service, present or future, will and must be completely compatible with our time-honored political institutions and will and must give its full loyalty to the nation's political leadership. Without vigorous and imaginative people, supported by a sound organizational framework responsive to Presidential direction and the advice of Congress, the conduct of our foreign affairs can never fully prosper.

In the golden age of American diplomacy, our pioneer diplomats were among the best the times had to offer; the cause of our struggling new nation could afford no less. The developing course of human events today demonstrates clearly, once again, that we cannot afford anything short of the best in the management of our foreign affairs—and that means not only good men but also good machinery, with strong, cohesive, centralized direction. The pace of events is too rapid; the problems, too complicated—and the stakes, far too high —to permit of anything else.

Appendix I

List of Principal Statutes and Executive Orders Relating to the Foreign Service

Act of July 27, 1789 (I Stat. 28)—establishing an executive department to be denominated the Department of Foreign Affairs, the principal officer to be called the Secretary for the Department of Foreign Affairs.

Act of September 15, 1789 (I Stat. 68)—changing the name of the above to Department of State, and of its principal officer to Secretary of State (among other provisions).

Act. of July 1, 1790 (I Stat. 128)—authorizing the sum of $40,000 annually for the expenses of foreign intercourse and fixing the salaries of diplomatic officers.

Act of April 14, 1792 (I Stat. 254)—defining the powers and functions of consular officers.

Act of March 1, 1855 (10 Stat. 619)—prescribing grades, posts, and salaries in the Diplomatic and Consular services. (Repealed by Act of August 18, 1856.)

Act of August 18, 1856 (11 Stat. 52)—establishing an organic framework for the Diplomatic and Consular services, with provisions fixing new salary rates for diplomatic officers, classifying consular posts according to method of compensation (that is, salary or fees), and establishing regulations to govern the exercise of consular duties.

Act of June 20, 1864 (13 Stat. 139)—authorizing the appointment of 13 consular clerks to have permanent tenure during good behavior.

Act of March 1, 1893 (27 Stat. 497)—providing for the appointment of ambassadors on a reciprocal basis. The first American ambassadors were appointed following this act.

Executive Order of September 20, 1895—providing for appointments on a merit basis to consular offices with annual compensation of from $1,000 to $2,500.

Executive Order No. 367 of November 10, 1905—extending the merit system of appointment to all consular offices with annual compensation of more than $1,000.

Executive Order No. 368 of November 10, 1905—providing for appointments of diplomatic secretaries on a merit basis.

Act of April 5, 1906 (34 Stat. 99)—providing for the reorganization of the Consular Service, including the reclassification of consular officers, periodic inspections of consular posts, and other administrative provisions.

Executive Order No. 469 of June 27, 1906—prescribing regulations governing appointments and promotions in the Consular Service in accordance with Civil Service provisions.

Executive Order No. 1143 of November 26, 1909—prescribing regulations governing appointments and promotions in the Diplomatic Service in accordance with Civil Service provisions.

Act of February 5, 1915 (38 Stat. 805)—establishing the merit system in the Diplomatic and Consular services on a statutory basis; providing for appointments to classes rather than to posts; and reclassifying diplomatic and consular officers.

Act of May 24, 1924 (43 Stat. 140)—the "Rogers Act," amalgamating the Diplomatic and Consular services into the Foreign Service of the United States and establishing the Service on a career basis with provision for a more adequate scale of salaries and allowances and a retirement system.

Act of February 23, 1931 (46 Stat. 1207)—providing for a more liberal system of allowances, ingrade salary increases, improved personnel administration, and the classification of Foreign Service clerks.

Executive order of July 1, 1939—transferring to the Foreign Service the foreign activities and personnel of the Departments of Commerce and Agriculture.

Act of July 3, 1946 (60 Stat. 426)—providing for the lateral appointment of up to 250 Foreign Service officers with special experience and qualifications.

Act of August 13, 1946 (60 Stat. 999)—the basic organic act of the present-day Foreign Service, replacing the Rogers Act of 1924. Provided for new personnel structure, increased salaries and allowances, new promotion and retirement systems, and establishment of the Foreign Service Institute for inservice training.

Act of May 26, 1949 (63 Stat. 111)—transferring to the Secretary of State the powers given under the Foreign Service Act of 1946 to the Assistant Secretary for Administration and the Director General of the Foreign Service.

Act of April 5, 1955 (69 Stat. 24)—the "Foreign Service Act Amendments of 1955," providing, among other things, for the payment of salary differentials not exceeding 25 per cent to all Foreign Service personnel assigned to hardship posts; for a system of educational allowances for Foreign Service personnel; and for various changes in the provisions governing selection-out and lateral entry of Foreign Service officers.

Act of July 28, 1956 (70 Stat. 704)—the "Foreign Service Act Amendments of 1956," providing for (1) increased salaries for chiefs of mission; (2) an increase in the number of classes of Foreign Service officers to 10 classes, including the classes of career minister and career ambassador; (3) authority to establish Government commissary and recreation facilities at posts abroad; and (4) various medical and hospital benefits for Foreign Service personnel and their dependents.

Act of September 8, 1960 (74 Stat. 831)—the "Foreign Service Act Amendments of 1960," adding a number of provisions liberalizing the Foreign Service Retirement and Disability System, setting forth a significant statement of policy regarding the language and area qualifications of chiefs of mission and Foreign Service officers, and providing for other changes of a technical, clarifying, or perfecting nature.

Act of December 23, 1967 (81 Stat. 671)—the "Vietnam Amendments," to improve certain provisions for employees who serve in high-risk areas, and for other purposes.

Appendix II

The Foreign Service as a Career

ENTRANCE AND ELIGIBILITY REQUIREMENTS

Foreign Service Officers

The usual procedure for entry into the Foreign Service officer corps is through competitive examination for appointment to one of the two entrance classes, FSO-8 or FSO-7. Application forms for such entry may be obtained by writing the *Board of Examiners, U.S. Department of State, Washington, D.C. 20520.* Candidates must complete the application form and send it to the Board of Examiners on or before the filing date, which is usually six weeks before the date set for the written examination. (This is generally given in the fall of the year, in several hundred cities in the United States and at Foreign Service posts abroad.)

To be eligible to take the written examination an applicant must have been a citizen of the United States for at least 7½ years on the date of the examination. As of that date, he or she must be at least 21 and under 31 years of age, except that a candidate 20 years of age may apply if he has successfully completed the junior year in college. After passing examination, no candidate may be certified for appointment as a Foreign Service officer unless he or she is at least 21 and has been a U.S. citizen for at least 10 years. A candidate whose spouse is an alien may take the written and oral examinations but may not be accepted as a Foreign Service officer unless the spouse has become a citizen by the time of appointment. Candidates must further understand and agree that they will be available for assignment anywhere in the world.

Candidates making application may at the same time request and obtain a booklet containing sample questions from previous written examinations, as well as a brochure on the Foreign Service career which explains entrance procedures and tells something of the conditions of service. Salaries at the entrance level are $7,639 per annum for an FSO-8, $8,916 for an FSO-7.* The class structure is based on 8 numbered classes, 8 to 1, plus two additional top grades designated "career minister" and "career ambassador." The present salary ceiling for class 1 is $33,495; for career minister, $36,000; for career ambassador, $38,000.

Although most FSO's enter at the Class 8-7 levels, the need for certain skills and abilities is so great, and requirements change so rapidly, that a very limited number of outstanding candidates are admitted through "lateral appointment" to classes 6 through 1. A candidate for lateral entry must have rendered at least four years' actual service prior to appointment in a position of responsibility in a government agency, or agencies, except that if he has reached the age of 31 years the requirement as to service may be reduced to three years. He must undergo an evaluation of training and experience and pass an oral examination. Most lateral-entry appointees are over 31 years of age.

Foreign Service Reserve Officers

Interested candidates may write to *Chief of Employment, Department of State, Washington, D.C. 20520.* With rare exceptions, a candidate for a Foreign Service Reserve appointment must have passed his 31st birthday and must have been an American citizen for not less than five years. In some instances, appointments require a longer period of citizenship.

Prior to selection, a candidate must appear before a panel of officers, including one who is a specialist in the field in which he is applying to work. Reserve officers have the same pay and allowance schedules as Foreign Service officers.

Foreign Service Staff Officers and Employees

There are 10 grades in the staff corps. The top 6, classes 6 through 1, are of officer rank (Foreign Service staff officers, or FSSO's) and equate roughly to FSO classes 8 through 3. Classes 10 through 7 represent the FSS group, or Foreign Service staff employees. FSSO salaries range from $8,536 to $25,617; FSS salaries from $5,522 to $9,950. Interested candidates may write to *Chief of Employment, Department of State, Washington, D.C. 20520.* Applicants must be at least 21 years of age and must have held U.S. citizenship for at least 5 years. If married, the spouse must also be a citizen.

Most Foreign Service staff officers are career specialists in the administrative and consular fields. In addition to the regular FSSO class structure (6 through 1) there is a "trainee" level—class 7, with

* All salaries quoted as of Federal pay raise of July, 1969.

occasional admission to class 6—for junior staff officers. Candidates are given the Federal Service Entrance Examination of the U.S. Civil Service Commission, plus an oral examination similar to that given candidates for appointment as FSO.

Most Foreign Service staff employees fill secretarial and clerical positions; well over half of them are women. Secretarial applicants must be high school graduates or the equivalent, single with no dependents* and competent at typing and shorthand. As with applicants for all categories they must be willing to accept assignment anywhere in the world.

Diplomatic Couriers

Male applicants meeting the following criteria will be considered: age 21 to 31; U.S. citizen for at least 5 years; minimum of 2 years' college (junior college degree, associate degree, or 60 semester hours' college work successfully completed); have satisfied military obligations and obtain written release from local draft board to leave the U.S. for at least 3 years; single without dependents and agree to remain so for at least 1 year after appointment; minimum tour of duty, 2 years worldwide; be able to pass a military-type pre-employment medical examination; drive a car; pass qualifying tests as noted below.

The required tests, given at any State Employment Service office in the U.S., are: typing, spelling (T-62 or T-63) and verbal ability (CBI-J or GATB-IV). The examining office should be asked to forward the *raw scores* to the *Recruitment Branch, Employment Division, Department of State, Washington, D.C. 20520.*

Couriers enter as FSS's and may advance to FSSO status. (A few become FSO's, but this is after their courier duty.) Starting salary is $6,865 per annum, plus allowances when stationed overseas and while traveling. As noted in Chapter III, vacancies are few. The requirements listed above are minimum, and the selection process is highly competitive.

General Requirements

Applicants for all categories of the Service—FSO, FSR, FSSO, and FSS—must qualify under established criteria for medical, background and security approval.

Foreign Service personnel are not exempt from military service, and those subject to Selective Service may not leave the country without permission of their draft boards. Officers with Reserve obligations may request military leave and serve their required period of active duty.

* Exceptions to this are possible but rare.

GENERAL BENEFITS

In addition to salary, employees in all categories receive certain other benefits. These include: government quarters where available, a quarters allowance where not; a cost-of-living allowance at posts where living costs are substantially higher than in Washington; a salary differential (extra pay) at posts where there are exceptionally difficult living or health problems; an education allowance to defray extraordinary expenses of elementary and secondary schooling for children, plus one round trip for dependents enrolled in U.S. colleges and universities.

"Home leave" is accumulated at the rate of three weeks for each year of duty abroad, and is generally granted after two or three years at a post, with round-trip travel for the employee and his dependents. The cost of shipping household and personal effects, on transfer, is paid within prescribed limits on weight and space.

Members of the Service are covered automatically by a term life-insurance program unless they elect otherwise. If an employee requires hospitalization while serving abroad, costs will be paid by the Department of State.

Congress has provided a generous retirement system for Foreign Service officers, with officers below the grade of career minister retired mandatorily at age sixty. Foreign Service Reserve and staff corps personnel are covered by the Civil Service retirement system rather than that of the FSO corps.

EQUAL EMPLOYMENT OPPORTUNITY PROGRAM

This program is auxiliary to the regular entrance procedures, and is designed to assist members of minority groups (Negroes, Orientals, Spanish-Americans, American Indians) to embark on a career in foreign affairs. Eligibility requirements: age twenty-one to thirty-one; U.S. citizen at least 10 years and spouse also a citizen; minimum educational requirement of bachelor's degree. Interested candidates may write to *The Director, Equal Employment Opportunity Program, Department of State, Washington, D.C. 20520.* Successful candidates are assigned to junior Foreign Service jobs in Washington and overseas. Initial appointment, via oral examination, is for a five-year FSR tenure, but incumbents are encouraged and expected to qualify for career appointments via lateral entry (or the regular FSO written-oral examination cycle) within 3 to 5 years.

COLLEGE RECRUITMENT

The State Department's college relations program is an active recruiting force. Foreign Service officers visit colleges throughout the country, speak to student groups, talk with professors in foreign affairs or international studies programs, and try to interest top students in a Foreign Service career.

Summer Intern Program

A major program of the college relations staff is to invite 100 or so students, nominated by their schools, to a summer internship in the Department or at a Foreign Service post abroad. In the summer of 1967, the program placed 17 students at overseas posts and another 95 in Washington—including 20 under the Equal Employment Opportunities program. The intern program is geared to those interested in a Foreign Service career and, particularly, to those who have passed the written examination but have 1 or more years of study to finish before they can enter the Service. While not binding, participation in the program is looked upon in the light of a prelude to a Foreign Service career.

Pay for the summer ranges from $450 to $500 a month. The intern must provide his own housing, and transportation to Washington or to the foreign post. This may be underwritten by the college or a foundation. Participants are chosen by their own colleges, *not* by the Foreign Service, which means that information on the program must be obtained from the student's own college or university. Colleges and universities are invited to take part in the program largely on the basis of their record of participation in the annual written Foreign Service examination.

"Senior Fellows"

Ancillary to the college relations program is the Foreign Service Institute's "senior fellows program," initiated in 1964. In the scholastic year 1967–68, nine high-ranking FSO's, recently back from tours abroad, were assigned to spend a year on college campuses under agreement with the schools' administrations. Their job: to explain United States policies and stimulate interest in a Foreign Service career through teaching, lecturing, TV appearances, individual consultations, and general "bull sessions."

CYCLE OF QUALIFICATION FOR APPOINTMENT AS A FOREIGN SERVICE OFFICER

There are five steps by which a candidate for appointment to one of the entrance classes of the Foreign Service officer corps establishes his eligibility and fitness for selection. These are (1) written examination, (2) oral examination, (3) medical examination, (4) background and security investigation, and (5) final evaluation. A brief description of the procedural cycle follows.

Written Examination

This requires a full day and is given on a Saturday in nearly 300 cities throughout the United States and at any Foreign Service post abroad at which a candidate may ask to take it. The examination tests ability to solve problems, general understanding of the ideas and events that produced the world of today and are shaping the future, and skill in writing. It is divided into 4 parts: (1) general ability; (2) English expression; (3) general background, and (4) a choice of one of three special optional tests in (a) history, government, social sciences, and public affairs; (b) administration; or (c) economics and commerce. As mentioned earlier, a booklet containing sample questions from previous written examinations may be obtained by writing to the Board of Examiners. During a 5-year period in the recent past, 24,335 persons completed the written examination. Of these, 23 per cent, or 5778, passed.

Oral Examination

Qualifying candidates who pass the written examination are invited to take the "oral" as soon as the "written" has been graded and all candidates have been informed of their scores. The "oral" will be scheduled during the 9-month period following the date of the "written." It may be postponed, however, if the candidate is outside the United States and thus unable to present himself within 9 months in any of a number of cities, including Washington, where panels of senior officers conduct oral examinations at various periods of the year. While the written examination is designed essentially to test a candidate's general intelligence and, especially, the range of his knowledge, the purpose of the "oral" is to measure the candidate's personal qualities: his resourcefulness and versatility, the breadth and depth of his interests, his ability to express and defend his views, his potential for development, and, in general, his suitability as a representative of his country abroad. The candidate may expect questions on a wide variety of subjects; he is judged primarily on his ability to "think on his feet" and express his thoughts clearly and concisely. The oral examination usually lasts between 1½ and 2 hours. During the 5-year period cited above, 27 per cent of those passing the written examination passed the oral examination.*

Medical Examination

Upon passing the oral examination, the candidate is subjected to a thorough medical check-up. This may be done at the Department of

---

* Note that only 68 per cent of those who passed the written examination went on to take the oral.

State in Washington or at an authorized U.S. Government health or medical establishment elsewhere. Should that not be possible the medical examination may be given by a private physician, in which case the candidate will be reimbursed. A Foreign Service officer's dependents must also pass a medical examination before they may accompany him overseas. Since an officer may be assigned to posts where health hazards are high and medical facilities limited, a candidate will generally be disqualified by a disability which necessitates special diet or prolonged treatment, requires special orthopedic appliances, threatens the function of a vital organ, causes marked disfigurement, or may bring about premature retirement.

Background and Security Investigation

After he has successfully completed the medical examination, the candidate will be given a thorough background investigation in order to establish his suitability for the career and to complete the information needed by the final review panel.

Final Review Panel

This panel, meeting in Washington, considers all the information developed during the first four stages of the examination cycle and determines what candidates are eligible for appointment. A candidate declared eligible by the panel will be inscribed in one of three rank-order registers (i.e., lists with the highest-scoring candidates at the top, and so on down) depending on which of the three optional tests he elected to take during the written examination. He will remain eligible for a period of 30 months after the date of the written examination— exclusive of time spent in civilian U.S. Government service abroad or *required* active military service *subsequent to establishing eligibility for appointment.*

Appointments are made from the rank-order registers from time to time, in accordance with the candidates' standing on the register and the number and types of officers required by the Service. A new officer normally receives two commissions from the President—one as a Foreign Service Officer of the United States and one as a consular officer and a secretary in the diplomatic service of the United States. Appointments must be confirmed by the Senate.

A candidate who is at least 23 years old, and who has a record of graduate training or employment demonstrating a high level of ability for which there is a Service need, may be orally examined for and appointed to class 7. Other successful candidates will be appointed to class 8. All FSO's initially appointed to classes 7 and 8 are in a probationary status that continues until they receive their first promotion and have passed the prescribed language examination. During the cited 5-year period, 19 per cent of those who passed the written examination were adjudged eligible for appointment.*

Repeating Examinations

A candidate who is unsuccessful in the written or the oral examination may reapply, without prejudice, to take the written again to establish a new candidacy—so long as he continues to meet the eligibility requirements of age and citizenship.

The Foreign Language Factor

While inability to speak a foreign language will not preclude the appointment of otherwise successful candidates, such officers may not receive more than one promotion until a useful level of competence is attained. Those who speak no foreign language receive intensive language training prior to their assignment to posts where English is not the primary tongue. However, since the importance of foreign-language skill to a successful Foreign Service career is recognized, higher salaries are paid to junior officers who enter with competence in certain difficult languages. To determine their eligibility for such salaries, recently appointed officers are tested in language soon after they enter on duty.

PATTERN OF A CAREER

A Foreign Service officer is in training from the day he enters on duty till the day he retires. Most training is obtained on the job—this is the most effective type—but at certain points an officer must take time out for schools and courses, to meet the increasingly specialized needs of the Service.

The career is a competitive one, with promotion strictly on the basis of relative merit. Selection boards made up of FSO's, public members, and representatives of other government agencies meet annually to weigh every officer vis-à-vis his class peers and promote a certain number. Selection boards for junior probationary officers meet twice a year. Officers who have served the maximum time in a class without being promoted,† or whose performance has been adjudged sub-

---

* Period ending in September, 1967. Figures for March, 1968, while comparable, were not complete enough to be usable: of the 856 who passed the December, 1967, written, 826 had not yet taken concrete steps regarding the oral. Of the 30 who did, 22 withdrew before the oral, 8 were orally examined, and 7 passed and were pending appointment.

† Criteria vary from time to time. As of mid–1968, the maximum years-in-class limits ranged from 4 years for junior officers to 12 for those in class 1.

standard, are subject to involuntary retirement ("selection-out"). Assuming this unhappy contingency does not arise, a successful Foreign Service career might develop along the following general lines:

1. Upon entry into the Service the new officer is given several months' orientation and basic training at the Foreign Service Institute in Arlington, Virginia, where special courses are also offered for Foreign Service wives.

2. A 2-year assignment to a post abroad, with rotation through a variety of jobs to give experience and identify those fields in which he may have special aptitudes. This will ordinarily be followed by a 2-year tour in a different part of the world, to broaden his overseas experience, then a further 2 years in the State Department—or perhaps in another of the other Washington foreign affairs agencies—to familiarize him with the operations of the U.S. Government at home.

3. By the end of the second phase, the officer should be ready for specialization, in which he will devote a major part of his time to a particular geographic area or functional field. He may enter "hard-language" training—up to two years of rigorous language and area studies at the FSI and elsewhere—or he may elect a functional speciality such as economics, with possibly a year's graduate training at a university.

4. Some six years abroad follow, during which he is "majoring" in his specialty. He may be shifted for a tour of duty with another agency overseas—AID or the U.S. Information Service, for example—to gain a different perspective.

5. Back to Washington on a country desk, for four years, which may include or be followed by a year at one of the armed services colleges—for example, the Army War College at Carlisle, Pennsylvania. By the end of this stage, the officer should be ready for senior leadership responsibility.

6. Assuming he has what it takes, overseas again for four years as a deputy chief of mission, or consul general at an important constituent post—or, possibly, one tour in each capacity.

7. Back to Washington in a high-level job such as member of the policy planning staff or deputy assistant secretary of State in a regional bureau. From this point on, the officer may be selected for top leadership and return to the field as an ambassador.

Every Foreign Service career is different, of course, but almost all tend to follow certain general patterns. The one given above sketches a career which peaks at the optimum. Other officers enjoy rewarding and interesting careers which culminate at lesser but still high levels of responsibility, such as deputy chief of mission, consul general, deputy assistant secretary of State. Still others opt early for the minimum full retirement (fifty years' age; twenty years' service) and embark on a second career in the academic or business world.

Appendix III

List of Foreign Service Posts

(As of July 1, 1968)

Afghanistan
EMBASSY: Kabul

Algeria
Embassy Algiers and Consulates Oran and Constantine closed until further notice. Protecting power: Switzerland. Limited U.S. staff remains.*

Argentina
EMBASSY: Buenos Aires

Australia
EMBASSY: Canberra
CONSULATES GENERAL: Melbourne, Sydney.

CONSULATES: Adelaide, Brisbane, Perth.

Austria
EMBASSY: Vienna
U.S. MISSION TO INTERNATIONAL ATOMIC ENERGY AGENCY (IAEA): Vienna

Barbados
EMBASSY: Bridgetown

Belgium
EMBASSY: Brussels
U.S. MISSION TO THE EUROPEAN COMMUNITIES (USEC): Brussels

* When two states break diplomatic relations a trilateral relationship customarily develops: the protection of the interests of state "X" by diplomatic and consular officers of state "Y" within the territory of state "Z." Modern political times being what they are, practical modifications of the straight X-Y-Z arrangement are permitted more and more when no state of belligerency exists. In this case, a ten-man U.S. staff ("X") remains as the U.S. interests section of the Swiss Embassy ("Y") but works in the former U.S. chancery building in Algiers ("Z").

Belgium (Continued)
U.S. MISSION TO THE
NORTH ATLANTIC
TREATY ORGANIZATION
(NATO): Brussels
CONSULATE GENERAL:
Antwerp

Bolivia
EMBASSY: La Paz
CONSULATE: Cochabamba

Botswana
EMBASSY: Gaberones

Brazil
EMBASSY: Rio de Janeiro
EMBASSY BRANCH: Brasilia
CONSULATES GENERAL:
Recife, São Paulo
CONSULATES: Belém, Belo
Horizonte, Pôrto Alegre,
Salvador (Bahia)
CONSULAR AGENCIES:
Manaus, São Luiz
(Maranhão)

Bulgaria
EMBASSY: Sofia

Burma
EMBASSY: Rangoon
CONSULATE: Mandalay

Burundi
EMBASSY: Bujumbura

Cameroon
EMBASSY: Yaoundé
CONSULATE: Douala

Canada
EMBASSY: Ottawa
U.S. MISSION TO THE
INTERNATIONAL CIVIL
AVIATION ORGANIZA-
TION (ICAO): Montreal
CONSULATES GENERAL:
Calgary, Halifax, Montreal,
Quebec, St. John's (New-
foundland), Toronto, Van-
couver, Winnipeg
CONSULATES: Saint John
(New Brunswick), Windsor

Central African Republic
EMBASSY: Bangui

Ceylon
EMBASSY: Colombo

Chad
EMBASSY: Fort Lamy

Chile
EMBASSY: Santiago
CONSULAR AGENCIES:
Concepción, Valparaíso

China
EMBASSY: Taipei (Taiwan)

Colombia
EMBASSY: Bogotá
CONSULATES: Barranquilla,
Cali, Medellín
CONSULAR AGENCIES:
Buenaventura, Leticia

Congo (*Brazzaville*)
Embassy Brazzaville closed until further notice. Protecting
power: Federal Republic of
Germany.

Congo (*Kinshasha*)
EMBASSY: Kinshasha
CONSULATE: Lubumbashi
Consulates Bukavu and Kisan-
gani closed until further notice.

Costa Rica
EMBASSY: San José
CONSULAR AGENCY:
Puntarenas

Cuba
Embassy Habana, Consulate
Santiago de Cuba, Consular
Agencies Camagüey, Sagua la
Grande and Antilla closed fol-
lowing severance of diplomatic
and consular relations. Protect-
ing power: Switzerland.

Cyprus
EMBASSY: Nicosia

Czechoslovakia
EMBASSY: Prague

Dahomey
EMBASSY: Cotonou

Denmark
EMBASSY: Copenhagen

Dominican Republic
EMBASSY: Santo Domingo
CONSULATE: Santiago de los
Caballeros

Ecuador
EMBASSY: Quito
CONSULATE GENERAL:
Guayaquil

El Salvador
EMBASSY: San Salvador

Ethiopia
EMBASSY: Addis Ababa
CONSULATE GENERAL:
Asmara

Finland
EMBASSY: Helsinki

France
EMBASSY: Paris
U.S. MISSION TO THE OR-
GANIZATION FOR ECO-
NOMIC COOPERATION
AND DEVELOPMENT
(OECD): Paris
OFFICE OF THE PERMA-
NENT U.S. REPRESENTA-
TIVE TO THE UNITED NA-
TIONS EDUCATIONAL,
SCIENTIFIC AND CUL-
TURAL ORGANIZATION
(UNESCO): Paris
CONSULATES GENERAL:
Bordeaux, Lyon, Marseille,
Strasbourg
CONSULATES: Nice, Mar-
tinique (French West Indies)

Gabon
EMBASSY: Libreville

Gambia, The
EMBASSY: Bathurst

Germany
EMBASSY: Bonn
MISSION: Berlin*
CONSULATES GENERAL:
Bremen, Düsseldorf, Frank-

* Fulfiils regular diplomatic and consular functions (which the special
missions to international organizations do not) but is called a mission because Berlin, technically speaking, is still under Allied military occupation.
The U.S. Commander, Berlin, is chief of the mission *de jure*, with a senior
FSO under him as principal officer *de facto*.

Germany (Continued)
    furt/Main, Hamburg, Munich, Stuttgart

Ghana
    EMBASSY: Accra

Greece
    EMBASSY: Athens
    CONSULATE GENERAL:
        Thessaloníki

Guatemala
    EMBASSY: Guatemala

Guinea
    EMBASSY: Conakry

Guyana
    EMBASSY: Georgetown

Haiti
    EMBASSY: Port-au-Prince
    CONSULAR AGENCY: Cap
        Haitien

Honduras
    EMBASSY: Tegucigalpa
    CONSULATE: San Pedro Sula

Hungary
    EMBASSY: Budapest

Iceland
    EMBASSY: Reykjavik

India
    EMBASSY: New Delhi
    CONSULATES GENERAL:
        Bombay, Calcutta, Madras

Indonesia
    EMBASSY: Djakarta
    CONSULATES: Medan, Surabaya

Iran
    EMBASSY: Tehran
    CONSULATES: Isfahan,
        Khorramshahr, Meshed, Tabriz

Iraq
    Embassy Baghdad and Consulate Basra closed until further notice. Protecting power: Belgium.

Ireland (Eire)
    EMBASSY: Dublin

Israel
    EMBASSY: Tel Aviv
    CONSULAR AGENCY: Haifa

Italy
    EMBASSY: Rome
    CONSULATES GENERAL:
        Genoa, Milan, Naples, Palermo
    CONSULATES: Florence,
        Trieste, Turin

Ivory Coast
    EMBASSY: Abidjan

Jamaica
    EMBASSY: Kingston

Japan
    EMBASSY: Tokyo
    CONSULATE GENERAL:
        Kobe-Osaka
    CONSULATES: Fukuoka, Nagoya, Sapporo
    CONSULAR UNIT: Naha
        (Okinawa)

Jerusalem
    CONSULATE GENERAL:
        Jerusalem

Jordan
EMBASSY: Amman

Kenya
EMBASSY: Nairobi

Korea
EMBASSY: Seoul

Kuwait
EMBASSY: Kuwait

Laos
EMBASSY: Vientiane

Lebanon
EMBASSY: Beirut

Lesotho
EMBASSY: Maseru

Liberia
EMBASSY: Monrovia

Libya
EMBASSY: Tripoli
EMBASSY BRANCHES:
Baida, Benghazi

Liechtenstein
CONSULATE GENERAL:
Vaduz. No office maintained; principal officer resident in Zürich, Switzerland.

Luxembourg
EMBASSY: Luxembourg

Malagasy Republic
EMBASSY: Tananarive

Malawi
EMBASSY: Zomba

Malaysia
EMBASSY: Kuala Lumpur

CONSULATE: Kuching

Maldive Islands
EMBASSY: Malé. No office maintained: Ambassador resident in Colombo, Ceylon.

Mali
EMBASSY: Bamako

Malta
EMBASSY: Valletta

Mauritania
Embassy Nouakchott closed until further notice. Protecting power: Spain.

Mauritius
EMBASSY: Port Louis

Mexico
EMBASSY: Mexico, D.F.
CONSULATES GENERAL:
Guadalajara, Hermosillo, Monterrey, Tijuana
CONSULATES: Chihuahua, Ciudad Juárez, Matamoros, Mazatlán, Mérida, Mexicali, Morelia, Nogales, Nuevo Laredo, Piedras Negras, San Luis Potosí, Tampico, Veracruz

Monaco
CONSULATE: Monaco. No office maintained: consular officer resident in Nice, France.

Morocco
EMBASSY: Rabat
CONSULATES GENERAL:
Tangier, Casablanca

Muscat and Oman, The Sultanate of
CONSULATE: Muscat. No office maintained: Principal officer resident in Aden, Southern Yemen.

Nepal
EMBASSY: Kathmandu

Netherlands
EMBASSY: The Hague
CONSULATES GENERAL: Amsterdam, Rotterdam, Curaçao (Netherlands Antilles), Paramaribo (Surinam)

New Zealand
EMBASSY: Wellington
CONSULATE: Auckland
CONSULAR AGENCY: Christchurch

Nicaragua
EMBASSY: Managua

Niger
EMBASSY: Niamey

Nigeria
EMBASSY: Lagos
CONSULATES: Ibadan, Kaduna. Consulate Enugu closed until further notice.

Norway
EMBASSY: Oslo

Pakistan
EMBASSY: Rawalpindi
EMBASSY BRANCH: Karachi
CONSULATES GENERAL: Dacca, Lahore

CONSULATE: Peshawar

Panamá
EMBASSY: Panamá
CONSULATE: David

Paraguay
EMBASSY: Asunción

Perú
EMBASSY: Lima
CONSULAR AGENCIES: Arequipa, Piura

Philippines
EMBASSY: Manila
CONSULATE: Cebú

Poland
EMBASSY: Warsaw
CONSULATE: Poznan

Portugal
EMBASSY: Lisbon
CONSULATES GENERAL: Lourenço Marques (Mozambique), Luanda (Angola)
CONSULATES: Oporto, Ponta Delgada (Azores)
CONSULAR AGENCY: Funchal (Madeira)

Romania
EMBASSY: Bucharest

Rwanda
EMBASSY: Kigali

San Marino
CONSULATE: San Marino. No office maintained: principal officer resident in Florence, Italy.

Saudi Arabia
EMBASSY: Jidda

Saudi Arabia (Continued)
CONSULATE GENERAL:
  Dhahran

Senegal
  EMBASSY: Dakar

Sierra Leone
  EMBASSY: Freetown

Singapore
  EMBASSY: Singapore

Somali Republic
  EMBASSY: Mogadiscio

South Africa, Republic of
  EMBASSY: Pretoria
  CONSULATES GENERAL:
    Cape Town, Durban, Johannesburg
  CONSULATE: Port Elizabeth

Southern Yemen
  EMBASSY: Aden

Spain
  EMBASSY: Madrid
  CONSULATES GENERAL:
    Barcelona, Sevilla
  CONSULATES: Bilbao, Valencia
  CONSULAR AGENCIES: Las Palmas (Canary Islands), Palma de Mallorca

Sudan
  Embassy Khartoum closed until further notice. Protecting power: The Netherlands. Limited U.S. staff remains.

Sweden
  EMBASSY: Stockholm

CONSULATE GENERAL:
  Göteborg

Switzerland
  EMBASSY: Bern
  U.S. MISSION TO THE EUROPEAN OFFICE OF THE U.N. AND OTHER INTERNATIONAL ORGANIZATIONS: Geneva
  CONSULATE GENERAL:
    Zürich

Syrian Arab Republic
  Embassy Damascus and Consulate General Aleppo closed until further notice. Protecting power: Italy.

Tanzania
  EMBASSY: Dar es Salaam
  CONSULATE: Zanzibar

Thailand
  EMBASSY: Bangkok
  CONSULATES: Chiang Mai, Udorn

Togo
  EMBASSY: Lomé

Trinidad and Tobago
  EMBASSY: Port-of-Spain

Tunisia
  EMBASSY: Tunis

Turkey
  EMBASSY: Ankara
  CONSULATES GENERAL:
    Istanbul, Izmir
  CONSULATE: Adana

Uganda
  EMBASSY: Kampala

Union of Soviet Socialist Republics

EMBASSY: Moscow

United Arab Republic

Embassy Cairo, Consulate General Alexandria and Consulate Port Said closed until further notice. Protecting power: Spain. Limited U.S. staff remains.

United Kingdom

EMBASSY: London
CONSULATES GENERAL:
Belfast, Edinburgh, Hong Kong, Liverpool, Salisbury (Southern Rhodesia), Hamilton (Bermuda), Nassau (Bahamas)
CONSULATES: Suva (Fiji Islands), Mbabane (Swaziland), Belize (British Honduras)

Upper Volta

EMBASSY: Ouagadougou

Uruguay

EMBASSY: Montevideo

Venezuela

EMBASSY: Caracas
CONSULATES: Maracaibo, Puerto La Cruz

Viet Nam

EMBASSY: Saigon

Yemen

Embassy San'a and embassy branch at Taiz closed until further notice. Protecting power: Italy.

Yugoslavia

EMBASSY: Belgrade
CONSULATE GENERAL: Zagreb

Zambia

EMBASSY: Lusaka

Closed indefinitely:

Estonia: Legation Tallinn
Latvia: Legation Riga
Lithuania: Legation Kaunas

Bibliography

BARNES, WILLIAM, and MORGAN, JOHN HEATH. *The Foreign Service of the United States: Origins, Development, and Functions.* Washington: Government Printing Office, 1961.

BARNETT, VINCENT M., JR. (ed.). *The Representation of the United States Abroad.* New York: Published for the American Assembly by Frederick A. Praeger, Inc., 1965.

BUSK, SIR DOUGLAS. *The Craft of Diplomacy.* New York: Frederick A. Praeger, Inc., 1967.

CHILDS, J. RIVES. *American Foreign Service.* New York: Henry Holt, 1948.

The Country Team: An Illustrated Profile of Our American Missions Abroad. Washington: Government Printing Office, 1967.

ELDER, ROBERT E. *Overseas Representation and Services for Federal Domestic Agencies.* Washington: The Carnegie Endowment for International Peace on behalf of the Committee on Foreign Affairs Personnel, 1965.

FISHER, GLEN H. "The Foreign Service Officer," *The Annals of the American Academy of Political and Social Sciences,* November, 1966, 71–82.

Foreign Service Journal, August, 1967, through October, 1968. Many articles in this professional journal of the American Foreign Service, published monthly by the American Foreign Service Association in Washington, have been drawn upon for factual data and Service opinions cited in the book.

HARR, JOHN E. *The Anatomy of the Foreign Service—A Statistical Profile.* Washington: The Carnegie Endowment for International Peace on behalf of the Committee on Foreign Affairs Personnel, 1965.

HERTER, CHRISTIAN A., and others. *Personnel for the New Diplomacy—Report of the Committee on Foreign Affairs Personnel.* Washington: The Carnegie Endowment for International Peace on behalf of the Committee on Foreign Affairs Personnel, 1962.

JACKSON, HENRY M. (ed.). *The Secretary of State and the Ambassador. (Jackson Subcommittee Papers on the Conduct of American Foreign Policy).* New York: Frederick A. Praeger, Inc., 1964.

MOORE, JOHN BASSETT. *American Diplomacy, its Spirit and Achievements.* New York: Harper & Brothers, 1905.

PLISCHKE, ELMER. *Conduct of American Diplomacy* (3rd ed.). Princeton, N.J.: Van Nostrand, 1967.

THAYER, CHARLES W. *Diplomat*. New York: Harper & Brothers, 1959.

"This Worked for Me . . . ": Mission Chiefs Pool Useful Ideas and Techniques. Washington: Government Printing Office, 1964.

Toward a Modern Diplomacy: A Report to the American Foreign Service Association. Washington: American Foreign Service Association, 1968.

WRISTON, HENRY M. *Diplomacy in a Democracy*. New York: Harper & Brothers, 1956.

Index